BLACK TEXAS WOMEN

A Sourcebook

BLACK TEXAS WOMEN

A SOURCEBOOK
Documents, Biographies, Timeline

Ruthe Winegarten

Janet G. Humphrey and Frieda Werden
Consulting Editors

University of Texas Press Austin

Uvalde Jr. High
School Library

Copyright © 1996 by the University of Texas Press

All rights reserved

Printed in the United States of America

First edition, 1996

Requests for permission to reproduce material from this work should be sent to Permissions, University of Texas Press, Box 7819, Austin, TX 78713-7819.

♾The paper used in this publication meets the minimum requirements of American National Standard for Information Sciences—Permanence of Paper for Printed Library Materials, ANSI Z39.48-1984.

ISBN 0-292-79092-9   ISBN 0-292-79100-3 pbk.

Library of Congress Cataloging-in-Publication Data

Winegarten, Ruthe.
    Black Texas women : a sourcebook : documents, biographies, timeline / Ruthe Winegarten ; Janet G. Humphrey and Frieda Werden, consulting editors .— 1st ed.
        p.   cm.
    ISBN 0-292-79092-9 (alk. paper). — ISBN 0-292-79100-3 (pbk. : alk. paper)
    1. Afro-American women—Texas—History—Sources.   2. Afro-American women—Texas—Biography.   3. Texas—History—1846–1950—Sources.
4. Texas—History—1951—Sources.   5. Texas—Biography.   I. Title.
E185.93.T4W56   1996
305.48'8960730764—dc20   95-41733

Cover photos: *top left,* Adeline Waldon, courtesy Center for American History, University of Texas at Austin; *top right,* Lucille Moore, photo by Elnora Teale, courtesy Mrs. Thelma Justice; *center left,* Carlette Guidry-White, photo © Susan Allen Sigmon, University of Texas at Austin; *center,* Ana Sisnett, photo © 1993 by Danna Byrom; *center right,* women making comforts, courtesy Permanent Collections—Archives/Special Collections Department, John B. Coleman Library, Prairie View A&M University, Prairie View; *bottom left,* Congresswoman Eddie Bernice Johnson; *bottom center,* Aaronetta Pierce, photo by Al Rendon, courtesy *Images* magazine (*San Antonio Express-News*); *bottom right,* Dr. Barbara W. White, photo by Deborah Cannon.

This book is dedicated to my close friends and colleagues Ada C. Anderson and Dorothea W. Brown of Austin. We have labored together in the vineyards of Texas women's history and other community endeavors for almost twenty years. Their insights, encouragement, and support have been not only inspirational but crucial in the success of many projects with which I have been involved. Many heartfelt thanks to them both for their contributions.

In memoriam Barbara Jordan, 1936–1996.

Saturday Afternoon, When Chores Are Done

I've cleaned house
and the kitchen smells like pine.
I can hear the kids yelling
through the back screen door.
While they play tug-of-war
with an old jumprope
and while these blackeyed peas
boil on the stove,
I'm gonna sit here at the table
and plait my hair.

I oil my hair and brush it soft.
Then, with the brush in my lap,
I gather the hair in my hands,
pull the strands smooth and tight,
and weave three sections into a fat shiny braid
that hangs straight down my back.

I remember mama teaching me to plait my hair
one Saturday afternoon when chores were done.
My fingers were stubby and short.
I could barely hold three strands at once,
and my braids would fray apart
no sooner than I'd finished them.
Mama said, "Just takes practice, is all."
Now my hands work swiftly, doing easy
what was once so hard to do.

Between time on the job,
keeping house, and raising two girls by myself,
there's never much time like this,
for thinking and being alone,
Time to gather life together
before it unravels like an old jumprope
and comes apart at the ends.

Suddenly I notice the silence.
The noisy tug-of-war has stopped.
I get up to check out back,
see what my girls are up to now.
I look out over the kitchen sink,
where the sweet potato plant
spreads green in the window.
They sit quietly on the back porch steps,
Melinda plaiting Carla's hair
into a crooked braid.

Older daughter,
you are learning what I am learning:
to gather the strands together
with strong fingers,
to keep what we do
from coming apart at the ends.

—Harryette Mullen, *Tree Tall Woman*
(Galveston: Energy Earth
Communications, Inc., 1981)

CONTENTS

Black Texas Women: A Sourcebook is designed to be a companion volume to *Black Texas Women: 150 Years of Trial and Triumph*, published by the University of Texas Press in 1995. It took fifteen years of trial and triumph to write that first volume, and most of the time was spent trying to compile enough source material to analyze. This book presents the tools and raw material (retaining original spelling and punctuation throughout) that served as the basis for the first volume, so that the next writers investigating black Texas women's history—and I hope there will be many—will not have to retrace my steps looking for sources. All research materials collected for this book will be deposited at the Center for American History, University of Texas at Austin.

I also want to be very open about the material that the first volume was based on. Sometimes the information was slim, and often anecdotal. Sometimes it came from clearly prejudiced sources. A historian has the obligation and challenge of reading between the lines to find "her story"— and not everyone will draw the same conclusions. Again, I hope there will be new and creative interpretations of the material. And I especially hope that black scholars will apply their lenses to these documents and tell the story in their own way.

My original impulse to study black Texas women's history came from my work with the Texas Women's History Project sponsored by the Foundation for Women's Resources. I was hired in 1978 to be its research director and curator of the resulting museum exhibit, *Texas Women—A Celebration of History*, which toured the state for two years and is now on permanent display at Texas Woman's University. As a preliminary to producing the exhibit, we had to develop a bibliography and an archive on women in Texas history, because those resources simply did not exist. Inspired by county commissioner Ann Richards, and captained by project director Mary Beth Rogers, hundreds of women (and men) around the state dug out artifacts, records, and papers on women who had been left out of history.

One of my aims as research director was to make sure that minority women were well represented in the research and that the product would be fully multicultural. The support of scholars and community activists like Willie Lee Gay, Ada Simond, Ada Anderson, Fannie Mae Lawless, Algerene Craig, Janie Harrison, Lenora Rolla, Dorothea Brown, Mamie McKnight, Helen Spencer, and many others gave us access to a fascinating wealth of stories, documents, and perspectives on black Texas women.

One of the methods used to analyze the mass of material for the women's history project was to construct a timeline—putting all the events we discovered in chronological order and looking for longitudinal patterns. We added to the timeline well-known facts about Texas history, as reference points, but soon realized that most of these well-known facts were focused on white men.

Associate curator Frieda Werden and I decided that the only way we could determine what was significant in black Texas women's history was to put that information in a separate timeline and add important dates from black history and black Texas history to flesh out the story. When the data were treated separately, we could immediately see some interesting themes that perhaps no one had ever written history about. One of the most striking facts was the role of laundering clothes as an economic base for black women—highlighted by the petitions to remain in the Republic by free women of color who were laundresses and by the Galveston laundresses' strike of 1877. Another fact that stands out from the timeline is the close relationship of the Civil Rights Act of 1964 to the massive shift of black women out of domestic labor and into other fields.

I began to save information especially for the timeline. Every tiny fact about a black Texas woman that appeared in a book or article on some other subject was inserted into the timeline. As themes and significant individuals emerged, I created file folders for them, filled with Xeroxes or notes of conversations. Sometimes I was fortunate enough to find a major treasure—a whole book by a black Texas woman, such as Josie Hall's *Moral and Mental Capsule for the Economic and Domestic Life of the Negro*. My Virgo soul became obsessed with collecting and organizing this rare information, and the collection continued long after the museum exhibit project was completed. After a while, there was enough to write a book. I continued to research, visiting many Texas libraries and archives and visiting Washington, D.C., to examine the Mary Church Terrell papers at the Library of Congress.

As it turned out, the book—even after editing—was over 400 pages long, and to make it that short I had to leave out far too much of my favorite information. I wanted to include biographies of many black women of significance as well as long quotations from the women themselves and full texts of rare documents. I also wanted to publish the timeline. To my delight, the executive editor of the University of Texas Press, Theresa J. May, agreed that I could do so—as long as it was in a second book. And here it is!

Many individuals and institutions made it possible for me to produce a book with over 250 documents, 50 biographical sketches, and a lengthy timeline. Such a work can be produced only with the assistance and support of dozens of dedicated professionals and colleagues to whom I am deeply grateful. Special thanks go to my consulting editors, Jan Humphrey and Frieda Werden, who helped select the documents used and make sense out of the enormous amount of information which we reviewed. Archivists and staff of many organizations and institutions, as well as friends and community leaders, enriched the work. May I acknowledge in particular the archives of the Austin History Center; the Center for American History, the University of Texas at Austin; the Dallas Public Library; the Houston Public Library; the Institute of Texan Cultures; the African American Museum, Dallas; the National Council of Negro Women; Prairie View A&M University; the Rosenberg Library; the Schomburg Center for Research in Black Culture, the New York Public Library; Texas A&M University; the Texas Collection at Baylor University; the Texas State Archives; and Texas Woman's University. And most especially, the wonderful staff of the University of Texas Press!

LIST OF DOCUMENTS

Chapter 1. Free Women of Color

Chapter 5. The Arts

Chapter 6. Churches, Clubs, and Community Building

Chapter 8. Politics and Protest

FREE WOMEN OF COLOR

When Mexico became independent of Spain in 1821, the government enacted laws and decrees prohibiting slavery.[1] Texas was part of Mexico before winning its own independence in 1836. Free people of color were legally unwelcome from the days of the Republic.

Although most black women in antebellum Texas were slaves, several hundred held an anomalous legal status as free women of color. They used petitions, the judicial process, and even defiance of the law to avoid being sold into slavery or banished from the Republic. Their relatively unknown but highly significant stories refute the notion that all African-Americans in antebellum Texas were slaves and challenge the stereotype of weak, submissive women.

Free women of color were either manumitted slaves or descendants of manumitted slaves. Most were emancipated after their immigration to Texas. Some purchased their own freedom; some had their freedom purchased by their free husbands; and some were manumitted by their owners.

Because the Constitutions of the Republic of Texas and later the state of Texas forbade free people of color from remaining, those who wished to stay had to petition for that right, go to court, or remain illegally.

Document 1
Texas Bans Free Black Residents
[Texas Constitution of 1836]

No free person of African descent, either in whole or in part, shall be permitted to reside permanently in the Republic [of Texas] without the consent of Congress.

Document 2
Celia Allen's Emancipation Document
[Original in possession of Robert Davis, Waco; copy in author's possession]

Celia Allen, a free woman of color living in San Felipe, Austin County, needed legal help to protect her status as a free woman. Her owner, John M. Allen, had emancipated her for "faithful service" along with her four children in 1832, but a prominent pioneer, William H. Jack, claimed her as a slave in 1833. With her attorney, William B. Travis, who used the emancipation document filed by Allen, she won the case and lived free until her death in 1841. Her estate at that time was valued at $214.65.[2]

In the town of San Felipe de Austin, on the Twenty second day of March, in the year one thousand eight hundred and thirty two, appeared before me, Horatio Chreisman, first Alcalde of the Municipality of Austin . . . the citizen John M. Allen, a resident settler of this colony whom I certify I know, and declared: that for the faithfull services of his negro slave Celia, and her longtried fidelity, and assiduous and tender care of his person and interests, moved by his spontaneous will, . . . quits, renounces and abdicates totally all right, property, and dominion whatsoever which he has had and has in the person, labor and services of the above-named Celia and the issue of her body: to wit her son Henry, aged about six years; her daughter Dollyann, aged about four years, her son Rankin aged about three years; and her son Yarboro aged about one year and a half: in consequence of which, he confers upon her, and them the most ample, efficacious and irrevocable power, by and for themselves, and for their own proper use, utility, profit and advantage, to employ themselves in labor, commerce, trade, or whatever thing may seem most fit to them; to contract, to appear in judgment, administer by herself, or agents, the property she may acquire; to use it, and dispose of it according to her pleasure, by contract or testament, freely according to the laws of this Republic; . . . to form all necessary instruments of writing; to demand judicially what may belong to her; and generally to do whatever a freeman might lawfully do. For which end he, the said Celia and her children the issue of her body, does by the present henceforward forever, emancipate, manumit and set free: and does desist quit, renounce and separate himself absolutely from all right, which as master and owner he had or might have over their persons and to their labor and services; and he grants concedes and transfers it to the said Celia and her issue; and being necessary he makes them, a pure, perfect and irrevocable donation of the same . . . and in token of true and perpetual emancipation, he took the abovenamed Celia and her children by the hand, and separated them from him, and emancipated them in my presence. . . .

J. M. Allen   Celia's Mark X

Document 3
Estate Inventory of Celia Allen
[Robert B. Davis., ed., *The Diary of William B. Travis* (Waco: Texian Press, 1966), pp. 95–96]

(1) one bay mare about 10 years old
(2) one grey spanish filley 3 years old
(3) seven head of cattle, 2 cows, 2 calves, 2 yearlins, 1 heifer
(4) one sow and 5 pigs—2 barrows
(5) ¼ of town lot where Celia lived immediately proceeding her death
(6) one feather bed—good, one blanket ½ worn
    two bed quilts worn (2 pillows and one case)
(7) one feather bed, one pillow
(8) one broken pot, 3 skillets, 1 without lid and one oven kettle, handle missing
(9) old spoons (3), knives eating 2, forks 2
(10) Grid iron tongs and pot hooks
(11) 3 pans one gallon crock one wooden bucket 1 looking glass
(12) 3 trunks worn
(13) 1 doz plates, 6 tumblers, 1 soup turion [tureen?] large, 3 deep dishes, 1 stake dish, 2 pitchers, 1 cracked
(14) 1 wash pan, 5 old chairs, 1 table (old)
(15) 5 midlings of bacon about 45 pounds value .12 cents per lb. The foregoing inventory amounting to $214.65.

Document 4
Dr. John F. and Puss Webber, an Interracial Couple
[Noah Smithwick, *Evolution of a State* (Austin: University of Texas Press, 1983), pp. 163–166]

In the 1830s, Dr. John Webber bought his wife, Puss (or Silvia), and their children out of slavery, and the family established a home in a settlement near Austin, which came to be known as Webberville. Their friend and neighbor, Noah Smithwick, recalled their history.

The Webber family of course could not mingle with the white people, and, owing to the strong prejudice against free negroes, they were not allowed to mix with the slaves, even had they so desired; so they were constrained to keep to themselves. Still there wasn't a white woman in the vicinity but knew and liked Puss, . . . for, if there was need of help, Puss was every ready to render assistance, without money and without price. . . . One notable instance was that of a poor orphan girl who had gone astray and had been turned out of doors by her kindred. Having nowhere to lay her head, she sought refuge with the Webbers. Too true a woman to turn the despairing sinner away, Puss took her in, comforting her and caring for her in her time of sorest trial. . . . Webber and his wife merited and enjoyed the good will, and, to a certain extent the respect, of the early settlers. The ladies visited Puss sometimes, not as an equal, but because they appreciated her kindness. At such times she flew around and set out the best meal which her larder afforded; but neither herself nor her children offered to sit down and eat with her guests, and when she returned the visit she was set down in the kitchen to eat alone. After the Indians had been driven back, . . . a new lot of people came . . . and they at once set to work to drive Webber out. His children could not attend school, so he hired an Englishman to come to his house and teach them, upon which his persecutors raised a hue and cry about the effect it would have on the slave negroes, and even went so far as to threaten to mob the tutor. . . .

The bitter prejudice, coupled with a desire to get Webber's land and improvements, became so threatening that I at length counseled him to sell out and take his family to Mexico, where there was no distinction of color [1851?]. He took my advice, and I never afterward saw or heard of him.

Document 5
The Webber Family in 1850
["1850 Census Travis County, Texas, #42," *The State of Texas General Population Schedules, Seventh Census of the United States, 1850*, vol. 4, transcribed by Mrs. V. K. Carpenter (Huntsville, Ark.: Century Enterprises, 1969); typescript at the Austin History Center, Austin Public Library]

John and Puss (Silvia) Webber and their eight children were living in Travis County as late as 1850, according to the census of that year. They were among the wealthier families in the area, with property valued at $5,000. The identities of the other adults in the household, John McDivit and Robert G. McAdoo, are not known. It is possible that one or both were tutors of the Webber children.

#42 Farmer ($5000)

| John F. WEBBER | 64 m | Vt |
| Silvia = (Black) | 43 f | Fla |

Elcy	(Mulatto)	22 f	Tex
Henry	"	18 m	"
Leonard	"	14 m	"
Sarah	"	12 f	"
James	"	10 m	"
Willson	"	8 m	"
Sabrina	"	7 f	"
Andrew	"	4 m	"
John McDIVIT		48 m	Pa
Robert G. McAdoo	(tech)	37 m	NC

Document 6
Petition for Patsey
[House Journal, 5th Congress, 504; Memorials and Petitions, Mem. No. 144, File 74, December 31, 1840, 2-1/128, OFB 74-144, Archives Division, Texas State Library, Austin]

Five citizens of Rutersville, "well acquainted with the old Free Black Wooman Patsey," joined John Robb, with whom she lived, in supporting her petition.

She is honest, and mindes her own bisaisn [business]. She is about fifty-five or sixty years of Age and we believe She will do no harm by being purmitted to remain in the Republic.

Document 7
Betsy's Petition
[Memorials and Petitions, Archives Division, Texas State Library]

Mrs. E. I. Hardin and twenty-eight other whites signed a petition on behalf of Betsy. She was emancipated in 1856 by her Galveston owner, David Webster, who bequeathed her his entire estate, including horses, household goods, and twenty-one town lots.[3]

The petition of the undersigned citizens of Galveston County, respectfully prays for the passage of a law allowing Betsy a free Negro woman to remain in this State. Betsy is over 65 years of age, is quiet, orderly and respectful, and has ample means for her support during her life, having been set free and provided for by the last will of her late owner David Webster deceased.
    July 1st, 1856.

Document 8
Emeline Hires a Law Firm
[Cited in Andrew Forest Muir, "The Free Negro in Harris County, Texas," *Southwestern Historical Quarterly* 46, no. 3 (January 1943), 230–233, reprinted with permission of the Texas State Historical Association, Austin]

In 1847, Emeline hired the law firm of Peter W. Gray and Abner Cooke, Jr., to file a petition on her behalf in Harris County claiming that she was a free woman of color who had been sold as a slave in a case of mistaken identity and that her mother, Rhoda, was free at the time of Emeline's birth and was still free.

[O]n or about December 20, 1846, in Houston, Jesse P. Bowles "with force and arms assaulted your petition[er] and then and there took, imposed and restrained her and her children of their liberty, and held her & them in servitude from said day to the commencement of this suit against the laws of the land and the will of petitioner."

She amended the petition five weeks later:

"And your petitioner further shows that living under the charge & custody of the said Bolls she is very much restricted in her movements and has not had an opportunity to consult with her Lawyers & take their advice as to the means necessary to protect her rights and has therefore left that matter to her Sister Lucy Thompson [of New Orleans] who is aiding her to establish her freedom and came to Texas for that purpose."

After a year and a half of collecting evidence and depositions by both sides, the case finally went to court. Emeline and her children were freed by the jury, composed almost entirely of slaveholders, who ruled on November 24, 1848, that "Emeline . . . and her children are free as claimed by her" and assessed her damages of one dollar. The judge told Emeline and her children to "go hence free from the service of defendant & all others."

Document 9
Sylvia Routh Receives Her Freedom and 320 Acres
[Cited in Andrew Forest Muir, "The Free Negro in Harris County, Texas," *Southwestern Historical Quarterly* 46, no. 3 (January 1943), 225–226, reprinted with permission of the Texas State Historical Association, Austin]

On January 25, 1837, James Routh of Galveston Bay made his will emancipating Sylvia Routh and leaving considerable property to her and her children, possibly because he was their father.

I hereby will and bequeath full freedom to my negro woman, Sylvia & her six children and her further increase . . . upon the following conditions:

Sally Ann and Mary Jane to be bound to live, as servants with Ophelia [Mrs. James] Morgan until they arrive at the age of twenty one years— the balance of the children to live with their Mother, Sylvia, to be supported and protected by her, untill their Guardian may think proper to bind them out, which is to be done, untill they shall arrive at the age of twenty one years, to have their freedom . . . as far forth as the laws of the country will allow.

To Sylvia, I will her full freedom at my death, provided she takes care of & protects her children as heretofore stated . . . and I wish my executors to endevor to have Sylvias children before named, educated, so far as to read and write, & to pay for the same out of my Estate and hereby authorize them to appropriate three hundred Dollars for that purpose. . . .

And I hereby constitute & appoint my friends Dr. George M. Patrick and Col. James Morgan my only executors . . . and testament and constitute them Guardians to Sylvia & her six children, before named as well as to Jim, whom I have set free by these presents.

Routh died seven months later, on July 19, 1837. On April 14, 1838, Colonel Morgan applied to the chief justice of the County, Andrew Briscoe, "for commitment of negro slave Silvie belonging to the estate of said Routh, who he alleged has become unruly and refused to submit to his authority." Briscoe, a slaveholder, committed Sylvia to the county jail. The length of her imprisonment is not known. On November 27, 1843, Sylvia petitioned the probate court for letters of guardianship of Sally Ann, Mary Jane, Emily, Jackson, Isabella, and Margaret. Her request was granted, and title to the 320 acres passed to her and her children.

Document 10
"The Yellow Rose of Texas" Applies for a Passport
[Passport application of Emily D. West (Morgan), 1837, Archives Division, Texas State Library, Austin]

Emily D. West [Morgan], better known as the Yellow Rose of Texas, was probably a free mulatto from New York state. She came to Texas with Mrs. Lorenzo de Zavala in 1835 and may have been captured by General Antonio López de Santa Anna on his way to meet Sam Houston's forces in 1836. A famous Texas myth holds that she "distracted" Santa Anna during the Battle of San Jacinto, thus allowing Houston to win the battle quickly. Another part of the myth holds that she sent Sam Houston information on the whereabouts of Santa Anna's army. In 1837, Emily West applied for a passport back to New York, stating that she had lost her freedom papers on the San Jacinto battlefield.[4]

To the Hon. Dr. [Robert] Irion [secretary of state]
Capitol, Thursday Morning
    The bearer of this—Emily D. West has been, since my first acquaintance with her, in April of —36 a free woman—she emigrated to this Country with Col. Jas. Morgan from the State of New York in September of '35 and is now anxious to return and wishes a passport. I believe, myself, that she is entitled to one and has requested me to give her this note to you.

Your obedient servant,

I. [Isaac] N. Moreland

Her free papers were lost at San Jacinto as I am informed and believe in April of —36.

Moreland
7-37 [July 1837?]

Document 11
Will of Peggy Jervais
[Will Books, Probate Records of Matagorda County]

In 1838, Judge Sinclair D. Gervais's will freeing his slave Peggy "on account of her faithful behavior" took effect. She lived in Matagorda for many years and executed her will in 1855, two years before her death. Unfortunately her will, probated in 1856, was not carried out because her executor, John Culver, failed to file it. Another man claimed that the estate owed him money for wood, medical bills, and Peggy's funeral bills. Her house was sold at public auction for less than his claims.[5]

I, Peggy Jervais, a free woman of color, of the State of Texas, Town and County of Matagorda, being weak in body but sound of mind and memory, do make this my last will and testament, hereby revoking and making void all former wills by me at any time heretofore made. First—I will and bequeath unto Laura Cyrena and Clara Mary Culver, minor children of John Culver of the town of Matagorda, my homestead place in the town of Matagorda, consisting of Lot No. 4, Block No. 7—Tier No. 4. . . .
    This bequest is made on the following conditions, To wit, first that the said John Culver shall pay all the debts due by me at my death—Second that the said John Culver shall on my death take charge of and support for his natural life, my aged friend Samuel Robinson:—If the said John Culver shall faithfully perform the above conditions, then it is my wish that his said two children shall inherit all of my said above described property, otherwise it is not my intention to give them anything by this my last will.
    I desire that the County Clerk shall have nothing to do with this will

Adeline Waldon was one of hundreds of former slaves whose stories were preserved in interviews by federal Works Progress Administration workers during the 1930s. (Center for American History, University of Texas at Austin)

excepting admitting it to probate—This is to avoid expense. I desire that John Culver of the town of Matagorda, act as my sole executor. . . .

In witness whereof I Peggy Jervais, the testator, have to this my last will, set my mark for my signature and my scroll and after having the same read over to me, in the town of Matagorda this eleventh day of June A.D. One thousand eight hundred and fifty five.

Peggy her + mark Jervais

Document 12
Fanny McFarland Petitions to Remain Free
[Memorials and Petitions, October 30, 1840, Archives Division, Texas State Library, Austin]

Fanny McFarland was one of several Houston laundresses who petitioned the Texas Congress in 1840. Many influential whites, including Harris County Chief Justice Isaac N. Moreland, cabinet members, and army officers, supported these efforts. Fanny McFarland's petition was signed by seventy-nine Houstonians. She had been brought to Texas in 1827 at the age of thirteen and freed in 1835 by William McFarland in consideration of her long and faithful services, but her four children were still slaves. Fanny McFarland was apparently one of Houston's first real estate developers. She engaged in a number of property transfers, making a profit on her investments. She lived in Houston at least from 1834 to her death in 1866, although she was in Brownsville at the time of the 1850 census. Despite the refusal of the Congress to grant her permission to remain, she stayed anyway, apparently unmolested.[6]

To the honorable the Senate and House of Representatives of the Republic of Texas in Congress assembled.

The petition of Fanny McFarland humbly represents. That in the year 1827 being thirteen years ago she was brought to this country by William McFarland Esq who in consideration of her long and faithful services to himself and his family gave unto her her freedom in the year 1835. That at the time of the Mexican invasion your petitioner was a resident of the town of San Felipe de Austin from which place she was driven by said invasion loosing all that she possessed in the world. Your petitioner further represents that in the year 1834 she took up her abode in this city [Houston] and by her industry prudence and economy she has been enabled to gather together a little property, she would further represent that she has four children held as slaves in this Republic so that all her hopes and prospects in this life lie here. And your petition would beg leave to urge upon your Honors the hardship of being obliged in her old age to leave her children to sacrifice her hard earned property to be obliged to part from friends of years standing to be obliged to leave her only home and be turned loose upon the wide world. And your petitioner begs that when your Honors take all these things into consideration your Honors will in your wisdom grant her your gracious permission to spend the few remaining days of her life as a resident and citizen of this republic. . . .

We the undersigned citizens of Houston and Republic of Texas would respectfully second the petition of Fanny McFarland a free woman of Colour to remain as a citizen of this Republic. And hereby recommend her as a good and useful citizen.

Houston October 30, 1840

Document 13
Zelia (Zylpha) Husk, A Houston "Washerwoman"
[Petition of Zelia Husk, December 14, 1840, Memorials and Petitions, Archives Division, Texas State Library, Austin]

In 1835 or 1836, Zelia Husk emigrated from Georgia to Texas with her daughter. A Houston washerwoman, she petitioned Congress at least twice for permission to remain in Texas. Husk's petitions were denied, but, like McFarland, she stayed anyway.[7]

A Petition of Zelia Husk and Daughter Free Colored People Ask That They May Remain in the Republic
 Dated December 14, 1840
 To the Honble the Senate of the house of Representatives of the Republic of Texas in Congress assembled. The petition of the undersigned citizens of Harris County respectfully represents that Zelia Husk a free woman of color and her daughter Emily have resided in this county during the last four years having come into the Republic in the year 1835 [may have been 1836] previous to the declaration of the Independence of the Republic, and for the last two years lived in the City of Houston exercising the industry of a Washerwoman. That she is a good and industrious woman peaceably earning her own livelihood, and that she has not the means of removing with her child beyond the limits of the Republic. In consideration of all which your petitions pray that you will be pleased to pass an act for her relief, permitting her to service so long she shall behave herself peaceably and your petitions will ever pray,

[Signed by 56 or 57]

Document 14
Zelia [Zylpha] Husk's Second Petition
[Memorials and Petitions, December 16, 1841, Archives Division, Texas State Library, Austin]

Houston, Dec. 16, 1841
We the undersigned do hereby certify that we have known Zylph[a] Husk for the last two or three years as a free woman of color; that so far as our knowledge extends, she has conducted herself well and earned her living by honest industry in the capacity of a washerwoman and would respectfully recommend the annexed petition for relief to the consideration of the Hon.l Congress of the Republic.

[Signed by 50]

Republic of Texas
County of Harris

To the Honorable senate and house of representatives of the Republic of Texas

The petition of Zylpha Husk a free woman of color. A native of Richmond County state of Georgia, about 27 years of age, would respectfully represent that she emigrated to this country about five years since . . . that the law requiring all of her condition to leave the country on or before the first of January [1842] next would bear heavily upon herself and her daughter Emily Husk about thirteen years of age, inasmuch as she would know not where to go if driven hence, having always been obedient and respectful of the laws for evidence of which she refers to the annexed certificate of the citizens of Houston and pledging herself to continue so in future she humbly prays your Honorable body to grant her permission to reside in the Republic as heretofore with her daughter Emily above named and to grant her all such other and further relief as your Honorable body may deem just and proper.

Houston, Dec. 16, 1841.
Zylpha Husk
mark

Document 15
Rachel Grumbles Enslaves Herself
[Slave Stories of Travis County, Center for American History, University of Texas at Austin]

As the Civil War drew near, the Texas legislature passed a law permitting free blacks to choose masters. The newly enslaved persons would become free of debt and all liens and be allowed to remain in the state. Some sad cases of voluntary enslavement occurred. Rachel Grumbles's story was recalled by her son, James Grumbles, who was interviewed during the 1930s as part of a massive Works Progress Administration oral history project. The interviewers transcribed these narratives in dialect. Rachel's original owner, Andrew J. (Jack) Hamilton, later became the state's provisional governor (1865–1866).

De white folks said dat de free niggers was ruinin' de other slaves. Mammy was called a free woman by her mater. Mawster Jack Hamilton brought her to Texas f'om Randolph County, Alabama. Dey come to Texas in 1847. Little befo' de beginnin' ob de Civil War mammy left de Hamilton place, and hired out to other white folks. Mawster Jack said dat he wouldn't hold no claim gainst her 'cause he didn't believe in slavery. But befo' mammy left Mawster Jack's place I was bawn in a box cabin near de big house.

Mammy was free so when dey passed dat law against free niggers she was put in jail at Austin [1858] until she would choose a guardeen. . . . I didn't have to stay wid her 'cause I was only about four years old. . . . A pusson could name anybody dat he chose, and dat pusson had to come and git him. But dat didn't cost de guardeen nothin', cept to feed and care fo' him.

De same day dat she was put in jail mammy chose Aaron Burleson as her guardeen. He had a large cotton plantation at which is now de new State Feeble-Minded School. . . .

Mawster Burleson had about twenty-five slaves, I think. He thought mo' ob his slaves dan most anyone I ever saw. He wouldn't allow no patrols on his place and dey had better not whoop any of his slaves without consultin' him either. His slaves didn't have passes to go anywhere, he jus' give orders fo' people not to bother his niggers. He was a mighty fine man.

Mammy was most ob all a nuss [nurse]. Mammy's job . . . was to take care ob Maggie [Burleson's daughter]. . . . Mammy now had her guardeen and I was wid her; but uncle Henry Perry didn't choose nobody and he was allowed to leave de state, jus' got up and left.

SLAVERY

Slavery in Texas was a cruel institution which had a particularly devastating impact on women. Sales resulted in the separation of mothers from their children, wives from their husbands, and sisters from their brothers. Women labored under the double burden of racial and sexual oppression, being exploited for both their labor and their reproductive ability. Yet thousands resisted the institution by just surviving. They stole food, feigned illness, practiced birth control and abortion, ran away, committed suicide, and, in desperation, sometimes murdered their masters and mistresses. They married, had families, and helped create a rich culture.

Document 16
The Value of Slaves
[Julien Sidney Devereaux Collection, Record Book, 1832–1856, Appraisal by William Reagan Enoch Spivy and Silvanus Everett, April 23, 1848, Center for American History, University of Texas at Austin]

Scott, an old man	$ 300
Tabby, an old woman	200
Henry negro man (diseased)	300
Mary and 3 children Ham, Anthony & Phoebe	1200
Amy & 3 children—Charles Mahala & Sara	1200
Polly and 4 children Cyrus Lucy Ossion & little Scott	1350
Flora and child Collin	800
Cynthia and child Betty	700
Daniel	650

Louisa	500
Matilda	500
Randal	500
Diana & 2 children Jesse & Harrison	750
Total	$8950

Document 17
Sale of Slaves

[*Galveston Civilian and Gazette*, August 17, 1848]

A LIKELY MULATTO WOMAN AGED about 23 or 24 years with her two children—a girl aged 4½ and a boy aged 11 years—is offered for sale, and a female field hand will be taken in part payment—title indisputable. She is a good cook, washer, ironer, sewer and nurse.

—H. A. Cobb

Document 18
"Price of Negroes"

[*Texas State Gazette*, June 13, 1857]

We attended the sale of the property belonging to the estate of Smith Bradly, deceased, on Tuesday last. The negroes were sold at an average of $730, negro women and boys brought as high as $900. Of the number sold there was one child two years old and one five years old.

Document 19
"A large Emigration of negroes from Missi."

[Archie P. McDonald, *Hurrah for Texas: The Diary of Adolphus Sterne, 1838–1851* (Austin: Eakin Press, 1986), p. 27]

Monday [February] the 8th [1841] [Nacogdoches] nothing of consequence transpired to day—except a large Emigration of negroes from Missi. passed trough, glad of the late Law exempting negroes from Execution for debt contracted in the U.S.

Document 20
"Public Notice"

[*Texas Almanac Extra* (Austin), December 27, 1862, Newspaper Collection, Center for American History, Austin]

NEGROES FOR SALE.—I will offer for sale, in the City of Austin, before Stringer's Hotel, on the 1st day of January next, to the highest bidder, in Confederate or State Treasury Notes, the following lot of likely Negroes, to wit. Three Negro Girls and two Boys, ages ranging from 15 to 16 years. The title to said Negroes is indisputable.

dec 25−2t* [1862] SQUIRE S. CONNETT

Document 21
"Lincoln and the Southland"
[Bernice Love Wiggins, *Tuneful Tales* (El Paso: privately printed, 1925), p. 122 (excerpt)]

What if a mother be torn from her loved ones,
  She gave them birth, but dare claim them her own,
Nay, they are slaves and belong to her master,
  Ah, cruel master, his will must be done.
What if a sister be torn from a brother,
  What if a husband be torn from a wife,
Why should he grieve, can he not find another,
  Why cling to one woman all of one's life.

Document 22
Painful Separations
[George P. Rawick, ed., *The American Slave: A Composite Autobiography*, Suppl., ser. 2, X, pt. 9, Lulu Wilson (1938), p. 4194, reprinted with permission of Greenwood Publishing Group, Inc., Westport, Conn., copyright © 1979]

I gets to thinkin' how Wash Hodges sold off Maw's chillen. He'd . . . have the folks come for 'em when my maw was in the fields. When she'd come back, she'd raise a ruckus. Then many the time I seed her plop down to a settin' and cry about it. But she allowed there weren't nothing could be done, cause it's the slavery law. She said, "Oh, Lord, let me see the end of it before I die!"

Document 23
"My name is Clara Anderson"
[Slave Stories of Travis County, Austin History Center, Austin]

Clara Anderson's firsthand recollections in 1937 of her life as a slave provide a heartbreaking picture of one woman's experiences.

My name is Clara Anderson, and I was bawn on Christmas day, 93 years ago. I was bawn at Eastern Shore, Maryland.

  My mother was Cassie . . . don't know her other name. My father was

Jim Wark. I remember one brother, Tom, and one sister, Caroline. I don't know whether they is livin'.

Mother worked as a cook; my father worked on a boat. I still remember how we could see the boat comin' in.

One day I was playin' in de sand wid another cullud girl, and a white fellow in a spring-wagon drove up. He said:

"Don't you-all want to ride?"

We tol' him, yas, sah! We thought he was jes' goin' fo' a ride. . . .

The man carried us to his brother's house, where we got our meals. It was night when we got to his brother's house. I wasn't scared, 'cause I thought he would take us back.

This man took us to a boat and he said, "If your mothers is not here to see you off, you will never see them again!"

Then I let out a holler. He then led us on to de boat.

The man said, "I'm goin' to take you-all out to west Texas, where money grows on trees." That didn't interest me none, 'cause I was jes' thinkin' of my folks. . . .

The ship landed at Mobile, Alabama, and other points, but I don' remember where we landed in Texas.

This man's name was Richard Chisum. Was he mean to us? Lawd, child, don't talk! See this scar above my eye? That's where he almost knocked out my eyeball. A Dr. Taylor bound the eye and helped it. I suffered a long time with it.

This all happened in Austin, Texas. The folks would give me a little to eat, and half of the time I was almost starved to death. There was some little Jewish chillun who lived nearby, and every day when they would come from school, they'd leave me some food. They'd hide this food in a tree-stump, where I'd go and git it. Those chillum would bring me buttered bread, cakes and other things. I never did git much chance to talk with 'em, but I know one's name was Kate, and the other Nellie.

My first boss beat me so much that a neighbor—Martin Townsend— come over one day and asked how much he would take fo' me. Marster Townsend paid $1,100 fo' me. I was so happy to git away from my mean boss, that I grabbed my new Marster's coat-tail and followed him like a dog.

The Townsends treated me fine, and I got only one slap in twelb years . . . and that's *one* time that I needed a good whoopin'. When I got the slap, Mrs. Townsend went into her room and cried about it. She's the one who slapped me, but she was as good as a mother to me.

The kind of work I had to do fo' the Chisums and the Townsends was to scrub the floors, wash the dishes, and sich as that. When I was growin' up and got smarter, I helped to do big things. I had to run errands and sich.

After twelb years, the Townsends sold me. They went away from here.

I still remember how I was then put on the hoss with another man, and we went to the Haines' place on Gilliland Creek, which is east of Austin. Mr. Haines had a 'still-house' . . . he made likker. The Haines' family treated me all right. My boss was mighty good to me . . . and I stayed with 'em until I was free.

My work fo' the Haines' family was a little of everything. I done house-work and field-work. I turned over about thirty acres of land with two yokes of oxen; and at times I'd go five miles from home, chop down little postoak trees, and haul the wood home with the oxen.

My marster's folks would know I was comin', when I would pop the whip. . . . and then I would sing:

> If you want to hear me holler
> Come and buckle up my collar—
> Charlie Mirango-ho!
> I want another dram, and a cool drink of water,
> Charlie Mirango-ho!

and then I'd pop my whip again. . . .

At times I'd bring butter to town, with two, long tin buckets danglin' from each side of my saddle. I milked fifteen cows, twice a day, and did all the churnin'. I would have to go to the pasture and git the cows . . . and a big coachwhip snake was usually out there, rarin' its head above the weeds! . . .

The white folks never helped me to read or write. I always had to work, and to this day, I barely know my A-B-C's. . . .

My first job after slavery was as a field-worker fo' some cullud folks. Later, I went back to the Haines' and worked. I got paid fo' it this time.

I married "Doc" Anderson, and was married on the Haines' place. Mrs. Haines' daughter give me two dresses fo' my weddin'. We had a big supper and a big dance.

We had three chillun—Zack, Ausmond, and 'Liza, but everybody calls her Elizabeth. My two boys is dead. 'Liza lives here with me. She's been married, but her husband's dead. 'Liza works fo' the Wroes, here in Austin. I had four grandchillun, and two is dead. They ain't here in Austin. Clara-belle is in California; and I don't know where Lois is.

Document 24
Sold Twice in One Day

[George P. Rawick, ed., *The American Slave: A Composite Autobiography*, Suppl., ser. 2, VII, pt. 6, Mintie Maria Miller (1938), pp. 2687–2688, reprinted with permission of Greenwood Publishing Group, Inc., Westport, Conn., copyright © 1979]

When I was still pretty little, my brother, uncle, aunt an' mother was sold an' I went with 'em. My father wasn' sold so he couldn' go. . . . My sister got on de wagon to go, too, and de marster said, "Adeline, you can' come. You got to stay here with Mistress." Dat's de last I ever seen my sister. She was four years old den. . . .

After we come to Texas we live on a big place. It was somewhere 'round Lynchburg. Dr. Massie own it. He had two girls an' I use' to sleep on de foot of dere bed. Dey was nice to me, dey spoil me in fack. Dey use to have picnics an' de girls would take me. . . .

Den dey said dey was going to sell me. Miss Nancy's father-in-law died an' dey got rid of some of us. Young Miss Nancy didn't want to give me up an' she tol' me to be sassy an' no one would buy me. De next day dey took me to Houston. . . .

Dey stood me up on a block of wood an' a man bid me in. I felt mad. You see I was young den, too young to know better. I don't know how much dey sold me for. I know dat de man dat bought me made me open my mouth while he look at my teeth. Dey did all de slaves dat way. Sold dem jus' like you sell a horse.

Den my old marster tol' me goodbye an' tried to give me a dog. But I 'membered what Miss Nancy had tol' me an' I sassed him an' slapped de dog out of his hand. Den de new man who had bought me said, "When one o'clock come you got to sell 'er again for she's sassy. If she did me dat way I'd kill 'er." So dey sold me twice in de same day.

Document 25
"I never knowed no mamma or no papa"

[George P. Rawick, ed., *The American Slave: A Composite Autobiography*, Suppl., ser. 2, VII, pt. 6, Adeline Marshall, pp. 2576–2578, reprinted with permission of Greenwood Publishing Group, Inc., Westport, Conn., copyright © 1979]

When interviewed in 1938, Adeline Marshall was living in Houston. This is an interesting all-round narrative dealing with early separation from parents, life as a slave, work, punishment, and concubinage.

Lord, Lord, dat sure was bad times. Black folks jes' raised up like cattle in a stable, yes suh, only Cap'n Brevard, he what owned me, treat de hosses and cattle better 'n he do de niggers. . . . He says I'm a South Ca'lina nigger what he bought back dere and brung me with him here to Texas when I was jes' a baby. I reckon it's de truth 'cause I never knowed no mamma or no papa neither one. . . .

We works every day 'cept Sundays, and we has to do our washing den. Does anyone get sick during week days and can't work for mebbe two days, dey has to work two Sundays to make it up. And when we comes in at night we has to go right to bed. Dey don't 'low us to have no light in de quarters, and you better be in bed and not sitting 'round after work if you don't want to get a whipping.

All we gets to wear is jes' a plain cotton slip with a string 'round de neck, jes' de same kind of stuff what dey make de picking sacks of. Don't make no diff'rence if it winter or summer, dat's all we get to wear.

Old Cap'n has a big house, but I jes' see it from de quarters, 'cause we wasn't 'lowed to go up in de yard. I hear 'em say he don't have no wife, but has a black woman what stays at de house. Dat's de reason why dere is so many "No Nation" niggers 'round now. Some call 'em "Bright" niggers, but I calls 'em "No Nation" niggers, 'cause dat's what dey is,—dey ain't all Black and dey ain't white, but dey is mixed.

Document 26

A "Kind" Master

[George P. Rawick, ed., *The American Slave: A Composite Autobiography*, Suppl., ser. 2, VII, pt. 6, Hannah Mullins, pp. 2874–2876, reprinted with permission of Greenwood Publishing Group, Inc., Westport, Conn., copyright © 1979]

Hannah Mullins was interviewed in 1937 in Fort Worth. Her mother had been the farm midwife and children's nurse.

Ise sho bo'n slave and 'wisht Ise nevah freed 'cause 'twas de bestest life a nigger lived 'cause him don't have to worry 'bout nothin' long's he's a slave. Ise bo'n on Col. M. T. Johnson's plantation at Johnson Station, Tex. a little ovah 81 years ago an' Ise been told 'twas on June 19th. . . . Each fam'ly have a double log house. Dat is dere am two rooms sep'tated by a hall 'twixt dem an' de houses am in rows lak a city. Den Marster have de shoe shop, where de hide tannin' am done an' de blacksmith shop, de gin mill, dere am de spinnin' room where de cotton an' wool am spun into thread an' de looms where de thread am ran into cloth so's de seamstresses make de clothes. Marster Johnson's plantation am self supportin' far's Ise knows an' raises de cotton to make de money crop. . . .

Ise raised in de nursery 'til Ise 'bout five yeahs old. De nursery am where de mammies brings deys babies 'til dey can git 'em back aftah workin' hours. Dis nursery am wo'k aplenty fo' de womens dat runs it 'cause dey am s'posed to keep de kids outer fights. 'Twas a big job 'cause de kids will fight evah time de womens have dey backs turned. De real trouble comes off when meal time come around. 'Twas sev'al long wood troughs put on de table an' each kid am give a wood spoon. Usual de troughs have milk wid co'n bread crumblin's in it an' de kids am lined up an' down de table. De nurse gives de word when to eat an' de kids all tries to git mo' dan de rest of dem. Dat starts de a'guments an' de fights all ovah. De nursery also has slides fo' to play on an sev'al sand boxes. Marster Johnson am so good to all de little kids.

Mammy am de mid-wife fo' de whole place. She am sorts hunchback an' not able to work good but am good at mid-wifin' so de Marster gets her at dat an' carin' fo' de little piccaninnies 'til deys able to be in de nursery wid de rest of de kids. Mammy mid-wifed fo' ol' Mistez too.

Miztez have four-five chillun an' after Ise five yeahs ol' Ise took out to stay wid dem as de nurse[maid]. 'Twarnt any nursin' to be done but Ise jus' to do what dey wants me to do lak gwine aftah wautah, he'pin' dress and so on. De Johnson kids could have made it hard gwine fo' me but deys good to me an' we all plays togedder lak Ise white as dey is. Ise fed de same victuals an' wears de same clothes as dey does.

Document 27
Hard Work
[Norman Yetman, ed., *Voices from Slavery* (New York: Holt, Rinehart, 1970), Katie Darling (ca. 1937), p. 69]

Katie Darling was interviewed at age eighty-eight near Marshall.

You is talkin' now to a nigger what nursed seven white chillen in them bullwhip days. Miss Stella, my young missy, got all our ages down in the Bible, and it say I'se born in 1849. . . .

Massa have six chillen . . . and I nursed all of 'em. I stays in the house with 'em and slept on a pallet on the floor, and soon I'sed big 'nough to tote the milk pail they puts me to milkin', too. Massa have more 'n one hundred cows and most of the time me and Violet do all the milkin'. We better be in that cow pen by five o'clock. . . . At night the men had to shuck corn and the women card and spin. . . . We had to work Saturday all day and if that grass was in the field we didn't get no Sunday, either.

Document 28
A Plantation Journal
[Max S. Lale and Randolph B. Campbell, eds., "The Plantation Journal of John B. Webster," *Southwestern Historical Quarterly* 84, no. 1 (July 1980): 58–77, reprinted with permission of the Texas State Historical Association, Austin]

This plantation journal of John B. Webster reveals that women often did the same tasks as men—some of them back-breaking.

1858

> Feb 18 —Charles and Emaline hauling cotton
> Feb 19 —Sarah and Sophia covering with harrows, Patsey and three chaps dropping corn
> Feb 22 —Charles and Emaline hauling manure and cotton seed
> Mar 3   —Amos, Peggy and Caroline covering corn in new ground with harrows
> Mar 10—Emaline nursing the sick
> June 2 —Patsey and Jane working potato patch . . . Rachel carrying to the plow hands
> June 7 —Alsey spinning at the house
> June 8 —Patsey and Jane working in overseer's garden
> Aug 6   —Emaline and Malinda sewing

1859

> Jan 1   —Lewis and two women hauling rails [for Southern Pacific] . . . Patsey spinning fine thread
> Jan 5   —Three women attending to the lard
> Mar 8   —Charles and Elsa hauling rails
> June 1 —Harriett . . . nursing Mrs. Webster's baby
> June 4 —Synthia and Patsey working potatoes
> Aug 1   —Patsey cooking . . . Emaline peeling peaches

Document 29
Slavery in East Texas
[Susan Merritt, Slave Stories, Box 4H-357 (Marshall, Texas), Center for American History, University of Texas at Austin]

Susan Merritt was an expert spinner who was born near Henderson. Her parents belonged to different owners. Her father had been brought from North Carolina and her mother from Mississippi. She was interviewed in 1938 in Marshall.

I was a good size girl spinning all the thread for the white fo'ks clothes and helping Mistress with the looms when they let us loose after surrender. . . .

The hands was woke up in the morning with a big bell. When Master pulled that bell rope the Negroes fell out of them bunks like rain falling. They was in the fiel' 'fore day and stay until dusk dark. They worked slap up till Saturday night, then they all had to wash their clothes. Some time on Saturday night there was parties where we played ring plays. . . .

Mary Kincheon Edwards, who was brought to Texas from Louisiana before the Civil War, claimed to be 127 years old when she was interviewed in the late 1930s. She recalled that she "picked two and three hunnert pounds ob cotton a day, and one day I picked about four hunnert pounds. Sometimes a prize was given by the owner . . . to de slave whut could pick the most. . . . One time I won a fine dress and another time a pair ob shoes fo' pickin de most. . . . I'd be so fast I could take two rows at a time." (Photo courtesy Library of Congress; quotation from George P. Rawick, ed., *The American Slave: A Composite Autobiography,* Supplement, Series 2, vol. 4, pt. 3, date of interview August 14, 1937 [Westport, Conn.: Greenwood Press, 1972, 1977, 1979], pp. 1278–1280)

When the hands come in from the fiel' at night, they had to tote water from the spring, cook and eat supper and be in bed by the time that bell rang at nine o'clock. . . .

Master Watt didn't have no overseer, but he had a "Nigger driver" that was just as bad. He carried a long whip 'round his neck and beat the other Negroes just like he was a white man. I'se seen slaves tied to a tree and cow-hided till the blood run down off them onto the ground. Some of the women would get slothful and not able to do their part but they made them do it. They dug a hole, 'bout body deep, and would make the women lie face down in it and beat them nearly to death. . . .

Document 30

Hired Out Slaves

[Judith Trask to her father Israel Trask, July 5, 1835, Trask Papers, Texas Collection, Baylor University, Waco]

Some slaves were hired out by their owners for wages.

I gave $11.00 per month for a negro girl that at the north would not be worth 50 cts a week. . . . Labor is so high that it is almost impossible to hire at any price. . . . The white people if ever so poor, consider it degrading to work, and would rather stay at home in their dirt, and rags, than do the first days work for another. . . . This is one of the evils of slavery.

Document 31
Ann Almost Burns Down the House
[Mary Brown to "Dear Sister Hannah," February 13(?), 1855, John Henry Brown Papers, Center for American History, University of Texas at Austin]

Mary Brown wrote her sister expressing her frustrations with Ann, a teenaged Galveston slave whom she had hired from another woman.

Last night we went to a lecture on theatres. We came home a little after nine (having taken with us Julius and Samuel and left Pierre[?] Clara and Lizzie in the care of Ann a colored girl of about 16 years). The children were asleep—L in her cradle in the parlor all alone, a piece of candle placed on a pine box (without candle stick) in the dining room had burned down and as Samuel and J came home a little bit before us they found the blazing wick just in the act of falling over. . . . She [Ann] did not come home in less than an hour after we did. This morning Mr. B. gave her or rather undertook to give her a switching and the switch broke. As soon as he left for the office she started off to her Mistress to make complaint. I did not expect her to come back indeed I almost hoped she would not for I shall always be afraid to leave her and she is terrible aggravating. . . . There is nothing in the world more worthless than a free negro.—Well, she has come back and gone about her work. Yesterday morning she took occasion while I was dressing for church to make a neighborly visit, having her morning work waiting until her visit was out, and Lizzie to cry around me while I was dressing. And yet I am afraid that were I to send her off I might fare worse. It is of no use to fret though and I will try to make the best of it. We pay her mistress $12 a week for her and consider that in comparison cheap. A woman gets at least $15.

Document 32
Going to Church
[Susan Merritt, Slave Stories, Box 4H-357 (Marshall, Texas), Center for American History, University of Texas at Austin]

There warn't no chu'ch on the place for the Negroes. The white fo'ks had a big white chu'ch off the place. We'd hook up oxen to the wagon and go to church over there. They had a place for us in the back of the church. At night the slaves would gather round the fire place on their knees and pray, and sing, and cry, but they darsn't let the white fo'ks know anything about it. . . . Thank the Lord we can now worship when we wants to. I 'member one favorite song was:

"I heard the voice of Jesus saying
    'come unto me and live.'
Lie down, lie down weeping one
And rest they head on my breast
I come to Jesus as I was
Weary, lone, tired and sad
I found in him a resting place
And he has made me glad."

Document 33
"We all went to church once and awhile"
[George P. Rawick, ed., *The American Slave: A Composite Autobiography*, Suppl., ser. 2, VII, pt. 6, Calvin Moye (1938), p. 2838, reprinted with permission of Greenwood Publishing Group, Inc., Westport, Conn., copyright © 1979]

De church was about a mile from de plantation, but my mother went every chance she had. She and some of de other women folks and a few men belongs to de church, and Uncle Zeke belongs too, he went to church lots when de others didn't go. My father never did go unless my mother got after him too hot, and he would go once or twice to ease her off.

Document 34
Weekends and Holidays
[George P. Rawick, ed., *The American Slave: A Composite Autobiography*, Suppl., ser. 2, VII, pt. 6, Cassie Middleton (1935), p. 2652, reprinted with permission of Greenwood Publishing Group, Inc., Westport, Conn., copyright © 1979]

De slaves went to chu'ch. Dey read de Bible at home, an' sometime' de w'ite folks read de Bible to dem w'at couldn't read. Dey baptise' in holes dat dey clean' out in de creek. Dey sung all kinds of ol' timey chu'ch hymn. . . .

We didn't wuk Sattiday afternoon, we wash' and i'on us clo's for Sunday. We hab candy pullin's on Sattiday night, an' we hab hol'days on Crissmus an' New Year', an' June 19th. Offen we hab dances Sattiday night or hol'days. W'en we was li'l we play' "jump de rope" wid muscadine vines for ropes.

Document 35
A Christmas Party
[Lucadia Pease to "Dear Sister Maria," December 31, 1856, R. Niles Graham–
Pease Papers, Austin History Center, Austin Public Library, Austin]

Our servants gave a Christmas party and had a handsome supper—a
turkey, pair of ducks and chickens, roast beef, and two large loaves of
cakes. . . . Some of the niggers were church members, and consequently
their amusement was singing hymns. . . . They went to several parties
which were almost as genteel, Emily told us, as white folks parties.

Document 36
"I was a right smart dancing gal"
[Ronnie C. Tyler and Lawrence Murphy, eds., *The Slave Narratives of Texas* (Austin:
Encino Press, 1974), Lucy Lewis (ca. 1938), p. 71]

We used to cut all kinds of steps, the cotillion, and the waltz, and the shotty
[schottische]. . . . My preacher used to whip me if he heard I went to
dances, but I was a right smart dancing gal. I was little and sprite, and all
them young bucks wanted to dance with me.

Cinto [her husband] didn't know how to do any steps, but he did fiddle.
There was an old song which came back to me, "High heels and calico
stockings."

Fare you well, Miss Nancy Hawkins,
High heel shoes and calico stockings.

Document 37
Christmas
[Ronnie C. Tyler and Lawrence Murphy, eds., *The Slave Narratives of Texas* (Austin:
Encino Press, 1974), Eda Rains (1937 or 1938), pp. 73–74]

Our biggest time was Christmas. Massa'd give us maybe four-bits to spend
as we wanted, and maybe we'd give a string of beads or some such notion. On Christmas Eve we played games like "Young Gal Loves Candy,"
or "Hide and Whoop." . . . On Christmas morning . . . Massa always called
us together and gave us new clothes, shoes, too. . . . We got one pair of
shoes a year, at Christmas. Most times they were red, and I'd always paint
mine black.

Document 38
Ring Dances and Shoestring Roots
[Norman Yetman, ed., *Voices from Slavery* (New York: Holt, Rinehart, 1970), Silvia
King (ca. 1937), pp. 200–201]

Silvia King was born in Morocco, was married, and was the mother of three when she was kidnapped into bondage. She came to Texas by way of France and New Orleans.

De black folks gets off down in de bottom and shouts and sings and prays. Dey gets in de ring dance. It am just a kind of shuffle, den it get faster and faster and dey gets warmed up and moans and shouts and claps and dances. Some gets exhausted and drops out and de ring gets closer. Sometimes dey sings and shouts all night, but come break of day de nigger got to get to he cabin. Old Marse got to tell dem de tasks of de day. . . .

White folks just go through de woods and don't know nothin'. [If] you digs out splinters from de north side a old pine tree what been struck by lightnin', and gets dem hot in a iron skillet and burns dem to ashes; den you puts dem in a brown paper sack. Iffen de officers gets you and you goin' have it before de judge, you gets de sack and goes outdoors at midnight and hold de bag of ashes in you hand and look up at de moon—but don't you open you mouth. Next mornin' get up early and go to de courthouse and sprinkle dem ashes in de doorway and dat law trouble, it goin' get tore up just like de lightnin' done tore up dat tree.

De shoestring root am powerful strong. Iffen you chews on it and spits a ring round de person what you wants somethin' from, you goin' get it. You can get more money or a job or most anythin' dat way. I had a black cat bone, too, but it got away from me.

Document 39
Learning to Read
[Jakie L. Pruett and Everett B. Cole, *As We Lived: Stories by Black Story Tellers* (Austin: Eakin Press, 1982), Hattie Rooney (ca. 1970s), p. 11]

Many slaves learned to read and write because they wanted to read the Bible.

Some of them colored slaves could read and write a little. . . . They'd learn it from the white man's children. . . . Then, they'd show their mamas and daddies what they was learning. . . . Some of the older slaves would be . . . watching and listening, when the white children was reciting their lessons, and learned some more thataway. . . . So that's how they was some that could read the Bible a little at the church services.

Document 40
"I learned the alphabet"
[Susan Merritt, Slave Stories, Box 4H-357 (Marshall, Texas), Center for American History, University of Texas at Austin]

My young Mistress Bessie liked me and tried to learn me to read and write. She would slip to my room, and had me doin' right good. I learned the alphabet. One day Mistress Jane catch her 'schoolin' me, and lammed me over the head with the butt of a cowhide whip and tell Miss Bessie that she would cowhide her if she caught her learnin' me anything. "Niggers don't need to know anythin," she said.

Document 41
Slave Marriages

[George P. Rawick, ed., *The American Slave: A Composite Autobiography*, Suppl., ser. 2, v. 7, pt. 6, Calvin Moye, p. 2849, reprinted with permission of Greenwood Publishing Group, Inc., Westport, Conn., copyright © 1979]

Although slave marriages had no legal standing, slaves still had to receive permission from their owners to marry.

All de slaves married young, dat is most of dem did. . . . Maser Ingram . . . he makes dem all gets married by de preacher. . . . Most of de slave owners would have a sham weddin and lets dem go at dat, when dey wasn't legally married, but nothin like dat happened at Master Ingram's place even if one of de slaves was from another plantation.

Document 42
"Married to his own mother"

[George P. Rawick, ed., *The American Slave: A Composite Autobiography*, Suppl., ser. 2, III, pt. 2, Wesley Burrell (1937), p. 537, reprinted with permission of Greenwood Publishing Group, Inc., Westport, Conn., copyright © 1979]

The evils of slavery are demonstrated in this tragic story.

One boy was traded off from his mother when he was young an' after he was grown he was sold back to de same master an' married to his own mother. How she found out dis was her son, she had struck him in de head axcidental like when he was young with a hot poker iron, an' after dey was married, she looked in his head an' saw de scar an' asked him why it was dere. He began to tell her, an' she fainted 'cause it was her own son.

Document 43
Uncertain Paternity

[George P. Rawick, ed., *The American Slave: A Composite Autobiography*, Suppl., ser. 1, v. 4, William Byrd (1937), p. 182, reprinted with permission of Greenwood Publishing Group, Inc., Westport, Conn., copyright © 1979]

The labor of female slaves was essential to the development of the Texas agricultural industry. Most African American women in antebellum Texas spent their entire lives planting, chopping, and picking cotton. (Photo by Russell Lee; courtesy Photographs and Prints Division, Schomburg Center for Research in Black Culture, The New York Public Library, Astor, Lenox and Tilden Foundations)

I has a bill of sale what say I's born in 1840, so I knows I's ninety-seven years old. And I's owned by marse Sam Byrd. My mother's name was Fannie and I dunno pappy's name, 'cause my mother allus say she found me a stray in the woods. I'se always believed my master was also my father, but I never did know, cause my mother, she would never tell who my father was.

Document 44
Sexual Exploitation
[George P. Rawick, ed., *The American Slave: A Composite Autobiography*, Suppl., ser. 2, VII, pt. 6, Sam Meredith Mason (1937), p. 2599, reprinted with permission of Greenwood Publishing Group, Inc., Westport, Conn., copyright © 1979]

Why some of them slaves was bred lak hosses. A good, well-built man was hired out among a bunch of wimmen, so as to produce good, healthy chillun.

Document 45
"Accidental Killing"
[*Texas State Times*, March 15, 1856]

A little son of John C. Hampton of this city [Austin], accidentally killed a little negro girl belonging to Judge Sneed, by shooting her in the head with a pistol. The sad affair happened on Thursday evening.

Document 46
"Burned to Death"
[*Texas State Gazette*, January 6, 1855]

One day last week, the clothes of a little negro girl, eight or ten years of age belonging to the Hall House, in this city, caught fire, by which she was so severely burned that she died that night.

Document 47
Rape of a Teenager
[Ruthe Winegarten, *I Am Annie Mae: The Personal Story of a Black Texas Woman* (Austin: Rosegarden Press, 1983), p. 9]

Many teenagers were raped, like Matilda (Tildy) Boozie Randon of Washington County, whose story was recalled by her granddaughter, Annie Mae Hunt, in 1977. After the Civil War, Matilda's owners gave her 1,500 acres of land "on account of this illegitimate baby" she had "by this young mawster."

Grandma say that she were near 13 years old, behind the barn tee-'teein when Young Mawster come up behind her. . . . He put his hand up under her dress, and said, "Lay down, Tildy." . . . And so this thing happened, and her stomach began to get big. One day, Grandma and Old Mistress, they was puttin up the clean clothes. Old Mistress had a pair of socks . . . in her hand. She said, "Tildy, who been messin with you down there?" Grandma say, "Young Mawster." Old Mistress ran to her, and crammed these socks in her mouth and say, "Don't you never tell nobody. If you do, I'll skin you alive."

Document 48
Resisting Forced Breeding
[Ronnie C. Tyler and Lawrence Murphy, eds., *The Slave Narratives of Texas* (Austin: Encino Press, 1974), Rose Williams (1937), pp. 20–22]

There's one thing Massa Hawkins did to me that I can't shut from my mind. I know he didn't do it for meanness, but I always held it against him. What he did was force me to live with that nigger, Rufus, against my wants.

After I had been at his place about a year, the massa came to me and said, "You're going to live with Rufus in that cabin over yonder. Go fix it for living." I was about sixteen years old and had no learning. And I was just an ignorant child. I thought that meant for me to tend the cabin for Rufus and some other niggers. Well, that was the start of pestigation for me.

I took charge of the cabin after work was done and fixed supper. Now, I didn't like that Rufus, cause he was a bully. He was big and cause of that he thought everybody should do what he said. We had supper, then I went here and there talking till I was ready for sleep, and then I got in the bunk. After I was in, that nigger came and crawled in the bunk with me before I knew it. I said, "What do you mean, you fool nigger." He said for me to hush the mouth. "This is my bunk, too," he said.

"You're touched in the head. Get out." I told him, and I put the feet against him and gave him a shove, and out he went on the floor before he knew what I was doing. That nigger jumped up, and he was mad. He looked like a wild boar. He started for the bunk, and I jumped quickly for the poker. It was about three feet long, and when he came at me I let him have it over the head. Did that nigger stop in his tracks? I'll say he did. . . . Then he went and sat on the bench and said, "Just wait. You think you is smart, but you are foolish in the head. They're going to learn you something." . . .

The next day I went to see the missy and told her what Rufus wanted, and missy said that was the massa's wishes. She said, "You are the portly gal, and Rufus is the portly man. The massa wants you to bring forth portly children."

I was thinking about what the missy said, but said to myself, "I'm not going to live with that Rufus." That night when he came in the cabin I grabbed the poker and sat on the bench and said, "Get away from me, nigger, before I bust your brains out and stomp on them." He said nothing and got out.

The next day the massa called me and told me, "Woman, I've paid big money for you, and I've done that for the cause I want you to raise me children. I've put you to live with Rufus for that purpose. Now, if you don't want a whipping at the stake, you do what I want."

I thought about massa buying me off the block and saving me from being separated from my folks and about whipping at the stake. There I was. What was I to do? So I decided to do as massa wished, and so I yielded.

Document 49
Infant Mortality
[George P. Rawick, ed., *The American Slave: A Composite Autobiography*, Suppl., ser. 2, VII, pt. 6, Cassie Middleton (1937), p. 2650, reprinted with permission of Greenwood Publishing Group, Inc., Westport, Conn., copyright © 1979]

I hab five sisters w'at died w'en dey was babies, 'cause [of what] dey put my mudder through, an' mek her wuk so hard, an' didn't give her much care w'en she was sick.

Document 50
Midwifery
[George P. Rawick, ed., *The American Slave: A Composite Autobiography*, Suppl., ser. 2, VII, pt. 6, Maggie Whitehead Matthews (1937), pp. 2622–2623, reprinted with permission of Greenwood Publishing Group, Inc., Westport, Conn., copyright © 1979]

Mummy's name was Tempe Whitehead. She had thutteen chillun. . . . She was a midwife de biggest paht of de time. Whenever de neighbors wanted her, she was sent over to wait on 'em. I don't know whether she got paid or not. . . . She was a good midwife. Sometimes she had to help in de fields, though.

Document 51
Folk Medicine
[George P. Rawick, ed., *The American Slave: A Composite Autobiography*, Suppl., ser. 2, v. 3, Vinnie Brunson (1937), p. 513, reprinted with permission of Greenwood Publishing Group, Inc., Westport, Conn., copyright © 1979]

We did not have any Doctors hardly at all in dem days, but we had de remedies dat wuz handed down to us from de folks way back befo' we wuz born. . . . Hot sassafras tea cools de blood in de spring, redpepper tea cures heavy colds dat make de bones ache, red-oak bark tea drives out inward fevers an helps bad appetites an' night sweats, healing leaves seal up deep cuts, tea from violent leaves or Yacca [yucca?] heals foot sores, an hot cooked turnips cure chilblains, wet collard leaf tied on an aching head or skin sore will run de pain off, an two buck eyes carried in de pockets will cure de misery in old jints, Snake root tea cures de belly-ache, an de linin' from a chickens gizzard cures indigestion, put two lightning bugs in a bottle dat has held whiskey dat is de bes pain killer of all, an hickery switch roasted in hot ashes is good medicine fer young hides dat need to be loosed.

Document 52
Pregnancy and Fieldwork
[Ronnie C. Tyler and Lawrence R. Murphy, eds., *The Slave Narratives of Texas* (Austin: Encino Press, 1974), Van Moore (1938), p. 17]

I heard my mammy say she knew a slave woman owned by Massa Rickets . . . was working in the field, and she was heavy with child which was not yet born, and she had to sit down in the row to rest. She was having the misery and couldn't work good, and the boss man had a nigger dig a pit where her stomach fitted in, and flogged her till she lost her mind. Yes sir, that's de truth; my mammy said she knew that woman a long time after that, and she was never right in the head again.

Document 53
Motherhood and Abortions
[George P. Rawick, ed., *The American Slave: A Composite Autobiography*, Suppl., ser. 2, VI, pt. 5, Lu Lee (1938), pp. 2298, 2299, reprinted with permission of Greenwood Publishing Group, Inc., Westport, Conn., copyright © 1979]

When women had babies they had old granny women on the place to look after them. They stayed in bed three days and got up on the fourth. But if they had a bad time they let them stay in bed four days. The women who had nursing babies did work around the house or in the spinning rooms so they be where they can suckle the babies. . . .

I have known too of women that got pregnant and didn't want the baby and they unfixed themselves by taking calomel and turpentine. In them days the turpentine was strong and ten or twelve drops would miscarry you. But the makers found what it was used for and they changed the way of making turpentine.

Document 54
Contraception
[George P. Rawick, ed., *The American Slave: A Composite Autobiography*, Suppl., ser. 2, VI, pt. 5, Dave L. Byrd (1937), p. 568, reprinted with permission of Greenwood Publishing Group, Inc., Westport, Conn., copyright © 1979]

All the negro womens they had become wise to this here cotton root. They would chew that and they would not give birth to a baby. All of their Masers sho' did have to watch them, but sometimes they would slip out at night and get them a lot of cotton roots and bury them under their quarters.

Document 55
Beatings on Washdays
[Norman Yetman, ed., *Voices from Slavery* (New York: Holt, Rinehart, 1970), Jacob Branch (1937), p. 39]

The right of masters to punish slaves was guaranteed by the legal code and the Texas Constitution.[1]

My poor mama! Every washday old Missy give her de beatin'. She couldn't keep de flies from speckin' de clothes overnight. Old Missy get up soon in de mornin', before Mama have time get dem specks off. She snort and say, "Renee, I'se gwine to teach you how to wash." Den she beat Mama with de cowhide. Look like she cut my mama in two. Many's de time I edges up and tries take some dem licks off my mama.

Document 56
William Moore Defends His Mother
[George P. Rawick, ed., *The American Slave: A Composite Autobiography*, Suppl., ser. 2, VII. pt. 6, William Moore (1938), pp. 2767–2769, reprinted with permission of Greenwood Publishing Group, Inc., Westport, Conn., copyright © 1979]

My mammy had a back that was turrible bad once. . . . It is raw and bloody and she says Marse Tom done beat her with a hand saw with the teeth to her back. She died with the marks on her, with the teeth-holes going cross-wise on her back. . . . Nuther day . . . I see Marse Tom got my mammy tied to a tree with her clothes pulled down and he is laying it on her with the bull whip and the blood is running down her eyes and off her back. I goes crazy. I say, "Stop Marse Tom," and he swings the whip and don' reach me good but it cuts just the same. . . . I run around crazy like and I see a big rock and I take it and I throw it and it ketches Marse Tom in the skull and he goes down like a poled ox.

Document 57
Inhumanity
[J. Mason Brewer, ed., *An Historical Outline of the Negro in Travis County* (Austin: Negro History Class of Samuel Huston College, Summer 1940), interview with a former Travis County slave, p. 14]

I remember seeing my mother beat all over the head and back one day as she was sweeping the floor, because she asked her mistress to let her go see my little sick brother who was in our little cabin near the big house. She swept on as the blows fell hard and fast, and my little brother lay there in the cabin all day long deathly sick until he died.

Document 58
"Overseer Beats a Negro Woman to Death"
[*Texas State Gazette*, October 7, 1854]

Brutal—An inquest was held on yesterday, over the body of a negro woman belonging to Mr. Duval, a few miles from the city [Austin], at the plantation of Dr. Dawson. It appears that the overseer of Dr. Dawson, J. W. Morris, tied the woman up, on Thursday morning last, and whipped her until she fell dead. After a careful examination by Dr. Lane and Harrington, the Jury rendered a verdict of—died from violence. Morris, we understand, made his escape.

Document 59
"An Ordinance Relating to Slaves and Mexicans"
[*Austin City Gazette*, February 12, 1840]

Any negro, slave or slaves caught at night after 10 without a pass shall receive 10 lashes on the bare back. . . . Any white man or Mexican found in company with a negro shall pay a fine of not less than $50.

Document 60
Eliza Runs Away
[*Houston Telegraph and Texas Register*, February 12, 1845]

RAN AWAY from the subscriber, a little negro girl, about 8 or 9 years old, light black complexion, named Eliza. She had on a black calico dress when she ran away. A reward of twenty dollars will be given to any person who will deliver this runaway to the subscriber. A. EWING.

Document 61
"$25 REWARD—RANAWAY"
[*Galveston Civilian and Gazette*, June 26, 1847]

From the subscriber, in Galveston, about a month since, JANE, a girl about ten years of age—copper complexion, rather low stature, a scar on one cheek, near the temple—had on a plaid dress and plaid handkerchief on her head—wears her hair long. THOS BLACKWELL

Document 62
"Runaway Negro"
[*Houston Telegraph and Texas Register*, January 4, 1845]

A Negro woman named Emily. About 25 yrs. of age, dark complexion, medium height, and rather fleshy. Her hair is cut quite short, and the only article carried off which I can describe is a dark colored, coarse blanket. C. W. Buckley.

Document 63
Suicide
[John R. Lyons to William W. Renwick, April 4, 1854, William W. Renwick Papers, Special Collections Library, Duke University, Durham, North Carolina]

I had a negro girl to hang herself on last Saturday April 2nd under circumstances rather peculiar. She had run away twice and I had her confined in my smoke house for the purpose of punishing her, and on Saturday went in to turn her out to work. Found her hanging whether done wilfully or accidentally I don't know. But so it is. I had been offered $900 for her not two months ago, but damn her I would not have had it happened for twice her value. The fates pursue me.

Document 64
"Another Suicide"
[*Texas State Times*, July 21, 1855]

Within the last week it has been our painful duty to chronicle the committal of three suicides—that of Mrs. Ewing's negro woman, who drowned herself on the 28th ult— . . . [Other two not noted as being black.] Houston *Telegraph*

Document 65
Resistance
[*Journal and Advertiser* (San Augustine), February 21, 1841; copy at Austin History Center, Austin Public Library, Austin]

A number of slave women, driven to desperation, resorted to murder. Possibly the first woman legally hanged in Texas was Jane Elkins, a Dallas slave, executed for having murdered a Mr. Wisdom, on May 17, 1853. Elkins, hired to care for Wisdom's motherless child, was charged with splitting his head while he was asleep. A few years later, in Fannin County, "there was a negro woman that killed her mistress with an axe, and her two little ones. The people just flocked together, and hung her right up on the spot." ²

$200.00 Reward

Notice.—Is hereby given for the apprehension and delivery of two negro women, Nancy and Isabella, who broke from my custody in Sabine County, on the night of the 16th inst., where they were confined for the alledged murder of their master, Richard Bartelow. They are mother and daughter, both black and the youngest about eighteen years of age. The above reward will be paid for the delivery of the negroes to me in Sabine County.

Feb. 21, 1841   Wm. Earl, Sheriff
San Augustine   Sabine County

Document 66
"MURDER IN LIBERTY COUNTY"
[*Galveston Weekly News*, January 19, 1858]

Margaret, the accused in this case, appears to have avoided paying a legal penalty. Two court-appointed attorneys represented her at a hearing, and three witnesses, including a physician, testified on her behalf. The one-week hearing resulted in a hung jury, ten to convict, two for acquittal. The heirs solved the problem by selling her to someone who had not heard of the crime.[3]

Margaret, a bright mulatto woman, about twenty-one years of age, was arrested on Monday, on the charge of poisoning her master, Solomon Barrow, who resides near Cedar Bayou, by administering arsenic to him in bread and coffee. She mixed the batter for the bread and placed it away in the kitchen, telling the cook at the same time "not to touch it, for she wanted it for the old man when he returned home." The bread was baked on the arrival of Barrow and given to him. After he had eaten of it he was taken ill and died two or three days after. The negress was committed for further trial.

She had been for a long time the mistress of the deceased, who had his wife living in the same house, but had not spoken to her for eight years! Barrow had made a will giving Margaret her freedom after his death, and $500 dollars to carry her to a free State. He had resided at the place of death for thirty-five years, was extensively engaged in stock raising, and was one of the wealthiest men in the county.

Document 67
"HORRIBLE MURDER BY A SLAVE WOMAN"
[*Galveston Weekly News*, January 5, 1858]

Following the disappearance of her mistress, Mrs. Joseph Dougherty, Lucy was jailed on suspicion. When Mrs. Dougherty's body was found, Lucy confessed to the murder, saying, "Yes, and I would do it again."[4]

On Sunday morning last a cold-blooded murder was committed at the Columbia House [Hotel—corner of Strand and 24th] in this city, upon the body of Mrs. Dougherty, a young woman some twenty three years of age, wife of Joseph Dougherty, proprietor of the hotel above named, by her slave, Lucy, a negress of about fifty years. It appears that this servant was bought by Mr. Dougherty four or five weeks ago, and since that time has repeatedly run off and secreted herself for several days together, and while at work has been very impudent towards her master and mistress and showed a determination to act as rebellious as possible.—A week before the murder she suddenly disappeared, but was at last found under the house, and when ordered out by her master, refused to come until he went in after her, when she darted out before him, and catching up a billet of wood, struck at him a severe blow, which he fortunately warded off. The punishment which followed was too mild for the offense, but served to develop the fiendish disposition within her. She attempted to fire the house, and very nearly succeeded in burning it down. It was impossible to control her while she had the use of her limbs, and she was consequently put into the stocks every night during the last week.—On Sunday morning at ten o'clock she was at work in the kitchen with two young German girls preparing dinner, when Mrs. Dougherty entered and sent one of the girls (Ann Kreise) up stairs to make the beds, and the other (Mary Krise) into the dining room to attend the baby. As the latter went out, Lucy, the black woman, told her to shut the door, which she did, leaving Mrs. Dougherty and the servant alone in the kitchen. Soon after, Mary heard a noise, as though something had fallen in the kitchen. Then in a few minutes, Lucy opened the door and called Mary back. She went, and found Mrs. Dougherty gone. Mr. Dougherty missing his wife from the house, supposed at first that she had gone round to the Palmetto House, to visit her aunt, Mrs. McDonald. He went to that house and learned she had not been there. A general search was then instituted, and about 2 p.m. the dead body of Mrs. Dougherty was found in the cistern. It appears that as soon as Lucy was left alone with her mistress an altercation arose between them, probably by design of the negress, who seized a hatchet and struck two or three terrible blows upon the head of Mrs. Dougherty, causing, doubtless, her instant death. The black fiend then dragged the body into the pump room and thrust it into the cistern. As soon as Mrs. D. was missed, her husband asked Lucy where she was, and Lucy replied with perfect indifference that she did not know. Suspicion at once rested upon the servant, and she was lodged in jail immediately. When the body was found, Coroner Hanpay was notified, and a jury empannelled.—The inquest elicited the facts mainly as we have stated them. The jury examined the premises and found blood at different places leading from the kitchen to the cistern. Two cuts were found on the head of the deceased—one over the left temple and the other on the skull just above the centre of the forehead, and either sufficient to cause death. On one side of the neck was a spot having the appearance of a hard pressure of the thumb or fingers, as though she had been choked. The clothes of Lucy were examined on her and several spots of blood found on them. The verdict of the Jury was, "That the deceased came to her death by wounds inflicted on her head, and by other violence at the hands of Lucy, the slave woman, property of Joseph Dougherty."

Document 68
Daughter Buys Mother Out of Slavery

[Rev. H. Mattison, *Louisa Picquet, the Octoroon: A Tale of Southern Slave Life* (1861; reprint: *Collected Black Women's Narratives*, Schomburg Library of Nineteenth-Century Black Women Writers [New York: Oxford University Press, 1988]), pp. 30–36, reprinted with permission of Manuscripts, Archives and Rare Books Division, Schomburg Center for Research in Black Culture, The New York Public Library, Astor, Lenox and Tilden Foundations]

Elizabeth Ramsey was sold away from her daughter, Louisa Picquet, in Georgia in 1839 and taken to Texas by her new owner. After a twenty-year separation, Picquet, who had attained her freedom and moved to Ohio, located her mother on a Matagorda, Texas, plantation. She negotiated successfully for her purchase and raised the necessary funds. After their reunion in Cincinnati, Picquet took out a notice in the Cincinnati Daily Gazette *of October 15, 1860, "expressing her thanks to those ladies and gentlemen . . . that having accomplished through their kind aid the freedom of her mother, Elizabeth Ramsey, from slavery, by paying to her owner, Mr. A. C. Horton, of Texas, cash in hand, the sum of $900, collected by myself in small sums from different individuals, residing in this city and States of Ohio and New York. . . . My mother also desires to say that she is most grateful to you all, and that if any of those friends who have assisted her to her freedom, feel disposed to call on her at my residence on Third Street, near Race (No. 135), she will be happy to see them and thank them personally."*

Wharton [Texas], March 8, 1859

MY DEAR DAUGHTER

I a gane take my pen in hand to drop you a few lines.

I have written to you twice, but I hav not yet received an answer from you. . . . I sent to my little grand children a ring also a button in my first letter. . . . I said in my letter to you that Col. [A. C.] Horton would let you have me for $1000 dol. or a woman that could fill my place; I think you could get one cheaper where you are [Cincinnati] . . . than to pay him the money; I am anxios to hav you to make this trade. you have no Idea what my feelings are. I hav not spent one happy moment since I received your kind letter. it is true I was more than rejoyest to hear from you my Dear child; but my feelings on this subject are in Expressible. no one but a mother can tell my feelings. . . . I think that 1000 dollars is too much for me you must writ very kind to Col. Horton and try to Get me for less money. . . .

you Brother John sends his love to you and 100 kisses to your little son; Kiss my Dear little children 100 times for me particuler Elizabeth say to her that she must writ to her grand mar often; I want you to hav your ambrotipe taken also your children and send them to me I would giv this world to see you and my sweet little children; may God bless you my Dear child and protect you is my prayer.

Your affectionate mother,
ELIZABETH RAMSEY

W[ha]rton, W[h]arton County, March 13, '59
MY DEAR DAUGHTER,

I know of nothing on this earth that would gratify me so much as to meet with My Dear and only daughter, I fear that I should not be able to retain my senses on account of the great Joy it would create in me, But time alone will develup whether this meeting will tak plase on earth or not Hope keeps the soul alive. . . . Direct your letter to Goven [Governor] A. C. Horton, Matagorda, Texas. May God guide and protect you through Life, & Finally save You in Heaven is the prayer of your affectionate mother.

ELIZABETH RAMSEY

Matagorda, April 21, 1860.
DEAR DAUGHTER,

[M]y master . . . says he is willing to take a woman in exchange for me, of my age and capasity or he will . . . take nine hundred dollars in *cash* for me. . . . he always says that money cannot buy either Arthur [her husband] or John [her son] he is a training John to take charge of one of his Plantations he has unlimited confidence in him and will not part with him untel death parts them. . . . Farewell My Dear Daughter . . .

ELIZABETH RAMSEY

Document 69
White Woman Opposes Slavery
[C. A. Clausen, ed., *Lady with the Pen: Elise Waerenskjold in Texas* (Clifton, Tex.: Bosque Memorial Museum, 1976), pp. vii, 17, 19–20]

A few white women were brave enough to speak out against slavery.[5] *Norwegian Elise Waerenskjold lived in Four Mile Prairie, a small town east of Dallas. She taught school, wrote articles for Norwegian newspapers, started a reading club, and spoke out in favor of temperance. Her opinions against slavery were expressed in her "Confessions of Faith," written for her sons in 1858.*

I believe that slavery is absolutely contrary to the law of God, because the law commands us to love God and our neighbors as ourselves, and, further, that whatsoever we want others to do unto us, that we should do toward them. These rules are as . . . easily understood as they are true. . . . Let us now ask ourselves if we would be satisfied with being slaves, with being sold like animals, with being separated from our mates and our children whenever it might suit our masters, with seeing our children brought up in thralldom and ignorance without the slightest possibility of rising above the miserable state into which we were born, despite the fact that we might have the highest abilities and the greatest eagerness to learn. To all this we must without qualification answer "No!"—answer that it would make us immeasurably unhappy. Consequently slavery must be contrary to the will of God, must be an abomination. . . .

People have asked me if I would tolerate having a Negro woman as a daughter-in-law. I must admit that it would not please me very much, but I would rather have it thus than to have grandchildren who are slaves. . . .

I am convinced that in time slavery will be abolished either by gentle means or by force, because I believe that institutions founded on injustice cannot survive, but are doomed to fail.

Document 70
Reluctant Warriors
[Norman Yetman, ed., *Voices from Slavery* (New York: Holt, Rinehart, 1970), Katie Darling, p. 69]

"When the soldiers went to the war, every man took a slave to wait on him and take care of his camp and cook."[6]

Pappy run away while he and Massa Bill on their way to the battle of Mansfield. Massa say when he come back from the war, "That triflin' nigger run away and joins up with them damn Yankees."

Document 71
Sewing for Soldiers
[Harriet Person Perry to Theophilus Perry, September 24, 1862, Presley Carter Person Papers, Special Collections Library, Duke University, Durham, North Carolina]

A Marshall woman, Harriet Person Perry, wrote about slaves sewing for the Confederacy.

Mrs. Murrah is so busy, she makes her negroes spin until 10 or 12 o'clock at night. Your mother is making 90 yards of cloth a week—two looms going all the time.

Document 72
Fannie Perry Writes to Her Husband

[Fannie Perry to Norfleet Perry, December 28, 1862, Person Family Papers, Special Collections Library, Duke University, Durham, North Carolina]

Harriet Person Perry's husband, Theophilus Perry, like so many Civil War officers, took along his slave Norfleet Perry as his body servant and aide. This letter from Norfleet's wife Fannie is one of the few such documents to survive. A few months after the letter was written (and presumably received), Norfleet disappeared from camp and made his way home from the battlefield.[7]

Dec. 28th, 1862.

My dear Husband,

   I would be mighty glad to see you and I wish you would write back here and let me know how you're getting on. I am doing tolerable well and have enjoyed very good health since you left. I haven't forgot you nor, I never will forget you as long as the world stands even if you forget me. My love is just as great as the first night I married you and I hope it will be so with you. My heart and love is pinned to your breast, and I hope yours is to mine. If I never see you again, I hope to meet you in heaven. There is no time night or day but what I am studying about you.

   I haven't had a letter from you in some time. I am very anxious to hear from you. I heard once that you were sick but I heard afterwards that you had got well. I hope your health will be good hereafter. Mistress gave us 3 days Christmas. I wish you could have been here to enjoy it with me. I did not enjoy myself much because you were not there. I went up to Miss Ock's to a candy stew last Friday night. I wish you could have been here to have gone with me. I know I would have enjoyed myself so much better. Mother, Father, Grandmama, brothers and sisters say Howdy and they hope you will do well. Be sure to answer this soon, for I am always glad to hear from you. I hope it will not be long before you can come home.

Your loving wife, Fannie

   If you love me like I love you no knife
   Can cut our love into.

Document 73
Displaced Hostility
[Davis McAuley, "Slave Life and Work in Bastrop County, *Sayersville Centennial Historical Journal* 7 (Winter 1986): 23]

[Miss Julia] beat us so terrible. "Your master's out fighting and losing blood trying to save you from them Yankees, so you can get yourn here." Miss Julia would take me by the ears and butt my head against the wall.

Document 74
One Ambition: Freedom
[George P. Rawick, ed., *The American Slave: A Composite Autobiography*, Suppl., ser. 2, IX, pt. 8, Maria Tilden Thompson (ca. 1938), p. 3859, reprinted with permission of Greenwood Publishing Group, Inc., Westport, Conn., copyright © 1979]

De scared slaves would git together and talk about dere freedom. . . . Dey would git together, polish up dere huntin' guns and be ready to start something. [They had one ambition], to git dere freedom, but de mawsters had better not hear about it.

Document 75
Slaves Learn They Are Free
[Ronnie C. Tyler and Lawrence R. Murphy, eds., *The Slave Narratives of Texas* (Austin: Encino Press, 1974), Isabella Boyd, p. 125]

When emancipation came to Texas in 1865, most slaveholders found it hard to believe. Many tried to keep their chattel enslaved.

When we all got free, they were a long time letting us know. They wanted to get through with [harvesting] the corn and cotton before they let the hands loose. . . . We were working one day when somebody from Master Grissom's place came by and told us we were free, and we stopped working. They told us to go on working, and the boss man he came up, and he said he was going to knock us off the fence if we didn't go back to work. Mistress came out and said, "Aren't you going to make them niggers go to work?" He sent her back in the house, and he called for the carriage, and said he was going to town to see what the government was going to do. Next day he came back and said, "Well, you're just as free as I am."

RECONSTRUCTION AND BEYOND

Texas slaves greeted emancipation in a variety of ways. Millie Williams recalled, "They hug one another and almost tear their clothes off shouting." [1] *Yet wrenching adjustments were ahead; most were turned out with nothing: no housing, food, or jobs.*

Congress created the Bureau of Refugees, Freedmen, and Abandoned Lands in March 1865 to help the newly freed slaves adapt to the changes in their lives. Its responsibilities included supervising labor contracts. Although many women preferred to stay at home and care for their families, economic necessity soon drove them back to the labor market. Women took jobs as domestics, laundresses, cooks, part-time midwives, and vendors of farm produce, but the overwhelming majority continued to be agricultural workers. For rural families, a sharecropping agreement often provided the only practicable means for their support.

Memories of the days of slavery were still clear and fresh when freed people responded to injustices. Women protested in speeches, by strikes, and by acts of civil disobedience.

Document 76
Juneteenth
[Archives, Texas State Library, Austin]

On June 19, 1865, Union Major-General Gordon Granger landed at Galveston and informed the citizenry of Abraham Lincoln's Emancipation Proclamation, which had taken effect on January 1, 1863. June 19 came to be known as Juneteenth.

The people are informed that, in accordance with a proclamation from the Executive of the United States, all slaves are free. This involves an absolute equality of personal rights and rights of property, between former masters and slaves, and the connection heretofore existing between them, becomes that between employer and hired labor.—The Freedmen are advised to remain at their present homes, and work for wages. They are informed that they will not be allowed to collect at military posts; and that they will not be supported in idleness either there or elsewhere.

Document 77
"Mammy was the head runner"
[George P. Rawick, ed., *The American Slave: A Composite Autobiography*, Suppl., ser. 2, VII, pt. 6, William Moore (1938), pp. 2771–2772, reprinted with permission of Greenwood Publishing Group, Inc., Westport, Conn., copyright © 1979]

One day I'm in a simmon tree in the middle of a little pond . . . when my sister Mandy comes running. . . . She calls me to come down out'n the tree. "What for?" says I. She says, "The niggers is free." I didn't b'lieve nor think nothing much about it. She say, "Mammy free, you free, all us niggers free. Dont have to work for Marse Tom no more." I looked over to the house and I seen the niggers piling their little bunch of clothes and things outside they cabins and then fixing them in bundles and setting them on top of they heads.

Mammy and some other niggers came running down there and mammy was the head runner. . . . She told me that Marse Tom done told her that he going to keep me for a shepherd boy and he is going to pay her for it. She is ascared that I will stay if I want to or not and so she runs to beg me not to stay.

We get up to the house and all the niggers are standing there with they little bundles on they head and they all say, "Where we going?" Mammy said, "I don't know where you going, but me, myself is going to Miss Mary." So all the niggers get in with mammy and we start to Miss Mary's. She sees us coming in a drove and meets us outside the back door. She said to mammy, "Come in Jane and all your chilluns and all the restes of you. You kin see my door is open and the smokehouse door is open to you and I'll bed you down 'til we figurates a way for you niggers to make your way."

. . . We all cried and sang and prayed and we was so 'cited that we didn't eat no supper though mammy stirred up some vittles.

Twarnt long 'til Mr. McLendon found places to work for the niggers. He found us a place with a fine white man and told him we had had a rough time but we was honest and good. We worked there on sharance and we drifted round to some other place. We lived in Corsicana for a while and we bought mammy a house and she died there.

Document 78
"Harriet, you are free"
[Amelia E. Barr, *All the Days of My Life: An Autobiography* (New York: D. Appleton and Co., 1913), pp. 251–252]

June 24th The sheriff read the Emancipation Proclamation. . . . I went into the kitchen to tell Harriet. . . . Her child, a girl about a year old, was sitting on the floor playing with some empty spools. . . . "Harriet," I said, and she turned her eyes upon me but did not speak, "you are free, Harriet! From this hour as free as I am. You can stay here, or go; you can work or sleep; you are your own mistress, now, and forever." She stepped forward as I spoke, and was looking at me intently, "Say dem words again, Miss Milly!" she cried, "say dem again." I repeated what I had told her, making the fact still more emphatic; and as I did so, her sullen black face brightened, she darted to her child, and throwing it shoulder high, shrieked hysterically, *"Tamar, you'se free! You'se free, Tamar!"* She did not at that supreme moment think of herself. Freedom was for her child; she looked in its face, at its hands, at its feet. It was a new baby to her—a free baby. Actually the mother love in her face had humanized its dull, brutish expression. I said again, "You are also free, Harriet. You are your own mistress now. Will you hire yourself to me?" I asked. . . .

"I will give you six dollars a month."

"Six dollars too little, Miss Milly."

"It is what I paid your master."

"Thank de Lord, I's got no master now. I 'long to myself now. I want eight dollars now. When a nigger free, they worth more."

Document 79
Freedom Delayed Six Years
[Katie Darling, Marshall, Slave Stories of Texas, Center for American History, University of Texas at Austin]

When Massa come home from the War he wants let us loose, but Missy wouldn't do it. I stays on and works for them six years after the war. . . . Missy whip me after the War just like she did before. She has a hundred lashes laid up for me now, and this how it am. My brudders done left Massa after the War and move next door to the Ware place, and one Saturday some niggers come and tell me my brudder Peter am comin' to get me away from old Missy Sunday night. That night the cows and calves got together and Missy say it my fault. She say, "I' gwine give you 100 hun'erd lashes in the mornin', now go pen them calves."

I don't know whether them calves was ever penned or not 'cause Peter was waitin' for me at the lot and takes me to live with him on the Ware place. I'se so happy to get away from that old devil Missy, I don't know what to do, and I stays there several years and works out here and there for money. Then I marries and moves here and me and my man farms and nothin' exciting done happened.

Document 80
"I's free, I's free"

[Ronnie C. Tyler and Lawrence R. Murphy, eds., *The Slave Narratives of Texas* (Austin: Encino Press, 1974), Tempie Cummins (1937 or 1938), p. 125]

Mother was working in the house, and she cooked, too. She said she used to hide in the chimney corner and listen to what the white folks said. When freedom was declared, master wouldn't tell them, but mother, she heard him telling mistress that the slaves were free, but they didn't know it, and he was not going to tell 'em till he had made another crop or two. When mother heard that, she said she slipped out of the chimney corner and cracked her heels together four times and shouted, "I's free, I's free." Then she ran to the field, against master's will, and told all the other slaves, and they quit work. Then she ran away, and in the night she slipped into the big ravine near the house and had them bring me to her. Master, he came out with his gun and shot at mother, but she ran down the ravine and got away with me.

Document 81
Gold Dollar

[*Gold Dollar* (Austin), August 1876; Center for American History, University of Texas at Austin]

Reverend Jacob Fontaine started a newspaper with a gift from his sister.

The gold dollar is the name of this little Paper. Its name taken from a gold dollar which was presented to me by my sister nelly miller on a viset to Mississippi in 1872 as we had been sepperated by the evel of Slavery for twenty years this gold dollar I have traded with since that time and made sixty dollars of it with which I have bought this little Office and started this little paper.

Rev. Jacob Fontaine

Document 82
Blue Bonnet Flag

[George P. Rawick, ed., *The American Slave*, Suppl., ser. 2, VII, pt. 6, Maggie Whitehead Matthews(1937), p. 2625, reprinted with permission of Greenwood Publishing Group, Inc., Westport, Conn., copyright © 1979]

Maggie Whitehead recalled this song a year after freedom. The phrase "Yes I'm a radical girl" is intriguing. Was she referring to women's support of the Radical Republicans?

I remembah den how our first Nineteenth was celebrated on June 19, 1866, and de song we sang was

'DE BLUE BONNET FLAG

Hurrah fo' de Blue Bonnet Flag,
Hurrah fo' de home spun dresses
Dat de colored wimmen wear;
Yes I'm a radical girl
And glory in de name—
Hurrah fo' de home-spun dresses
Dat de colored women wear.

Document 83
Legal Marriage at Last
[Reprinted in Dorothy Sterling, ed., *The Trouble They Seen: Black People Tell the Story of Reconstruction* (Garden City: N.Y.: Doubleday, 1976; reprinted by Da Capo Press), pp. 218–220]

Official, legal marriage was one of the great benefits of freedom. After his first wife's death, Jesse McElroy continued to correspond with her sister. He modeled his second marriage after the traditional patriarchal white family of the day.

Henderson, Texas, March 29, 1867

Dear Sister [in-law]:
    . . . Since you heard from me last I have married again, and, what you will think stranger, a young and pretty girl about sixteen. She was from Alabama. . . . I found her a girl of good character, well-behaved and sensible . . . So far I am very much pleased with her. She does as I direct. What is my pleasure seems to be hers. . . .
    My children were, like all children, opposed to the marriage but she is so respectful to me and to them that I think it will wear off. Her name is Mariah. We had the first license that was issued to colored people. She is industrious as far as she knows and I think will learn very readily.
    You and many others no doubt will say I could, the few days I have to remain on earth, remained unmarried. It may be, but I was lonely wanted some kind hand to smooth my pillow, and a soft sweet voice to cheer my gloom. . . .
    I wish we all lived near each other. It would be so pleasant to converse,

sing, pray with each other, but Fate has otherwise decreed. Mariah sends her love to you and so do the children. Write soon.

Document 84
Home Wedding
[George P. Rawick, ed. *The American Slave: A Composite Autobiography*, Suppl., ser. 2, VII, pt. 6, Cassie Middleton, p. 2651, reprinted with permission of Greenwood Publishing Group, Inc., Westport, Conn., copyright © 1979]

I was marry at home atter freedom come. My dress was a dotted w'ite Swiss. My folks give me a feas' to one hunnerd head of people. Ol' man Alfred McFarlane, a Baptis' preacher, he marry us.

Document 85
"A change in husbands"
[*Flake's Bulletin* (Galveston), September 8, 1865, p. 2]

Mary Hall used emancipation to sever a bad marriage and change husbands. Her first husband sued her for adultery, but the judge dismissed the case.

Local Intelligence.

BEFORE JUSTICE J. SEWELL. James Hall, vs. Mary Hall and Clayborne Dyer. This case was brought before his honor by James Hall, who charged his wife Mary Hall with committing adultery with Dyer, all being free persons of color. It seems that James Hall married his Mary, some six or seven years ago, according to the plantation custom; that is by obtaining the written consent of the masters of both. For some cause or other, Mary since she has been made a free woman, desired to have a change in husbands, believing that it only came within the limits of what is meant by freedom. So the "false one" took Clayborne and they were married by the Provost Marshall in "ship shape." Jim don't believe in new funnybust notions and is fond of old associations, as well as believing in "first and only love," and determined to show to the world, how constant true love is, he brought suit against Dyer for stealing Mary's affections away from her; the loss of which he "deeply felt." Although his honor, and all those who were present sympathized with Jim, still under existing circumstances, the statute in such cases made and provided is not exactly the same thing. The statute in the case of whites makes such a case punishable by a fine of not less than $400, or more than $1000; but the penalty for negroes is whipping, branding or death, and free colored persons to have the same punishment as negroes. The proclamation of the President making all alike, the Judge dismissed the case, until the statute is so amended, that they can come under the same laws as the whites.

Document 86
"Good Hope women provided . . . support for one another"
[Cheryll Ann Cody, "Kin and Community among the Good Hope People after Emancipation," *Ethnohistory* 41, no. 1 (Winter 1994): 46–48, Copyright American Society for Ethnohistory, 1994; reprinted with permission]

By using plantation and census records and local documents, as well as acute de-tecting skills, historian Cheryll Ann Cody reconstructed movements of families, sep-arations, reunions, and kinship and friendship patterns. She found that the tightly knit community provided mutual support in helping its members purchase land and gain an education. Gatsey, along with several family members, moved from Arkansas to Falls County, Texas, and back again, at times residing with her friend Emma.

Charles [along with all the slaves of Good Hope plantation in South Caro-lina] was sold in 1859 to Augustus Smith. For the purpose of the sale, his owner had grouped his slaves by household, and Charles's included his young wife, Gatsey [Jane], her five-year-old daughter, Betty, and his uncle, Prince. . . . Charles's new owner moved the Good Hope people to Arkansas. . . . But when the Union army came, Smith tried to drive his slaves into Texas. Charles and Gatsey, along with their parents, were moved to Falls County, Texas. In 1864 their son, Tucker, was born. He was the first Good Hope child to be born in Texas. Two years later, Charles died. Gatsey was to lose her mother in the same year, leaving her a young widow with a small child.

Despite the loss of her husband and mother, Gatsey was not without family and friends in Falls County and up on the Arkansas River. Her Good Hope connections were to provide vital support. Her stepfather, Jake, re-married, and they continued to remain close. But she found herself relying more and more on her childhood friend, Emma. Gatsey and Emma shared many common experiences. Emma had also lost a husband when Cyrus "ran off" during the war. In February of 1870 Gatsey bore another child by a man whose identity was not recorded. And that spring she joined Emma, Emma's new husband, Smith Brown, and her stepfather Jake's new family in returning to Arkansas. Gatsey lived in Emma's house and worked in the fields as a farm laborer. Her stepfather lived next door. Good Hope women provided both economic and emotional support for one another.

Document 87
"The whites take all we make"
[U.S. Congress, *Report and Testimony of the Select Committee of the U.S. Senate to Inves-tigate the Causes of the Removal of the Negroes from the Southern States*, 46th Congress, 2nd Sess., S. Rept. 693, Washington, D.C., 1880]

Caleb and Susie Redus are pictured with two of their children, George Redus and Dorothy Redus (Robinson), 1910. The Reduses were South Texas sharecroppers who sacrificed so that their six children could obtain an education. Five were college graduates. Dorothy Robinson recalls that her mother wore one pair of dress shoes for five years, and when she went into town to get a new pair of shoes, she went in her stocking feet (telephone interview, June 6, 1995). (Courtesy Dorothy Redus Robinson; print copied from Dorothy Redus Robinson, *The Bell Rings at Four: A Black Teacher's Chronicle of Change* [Austin: Madrona Press, 1978])

In 1880, Henry Adams, a Louisiana freedman, began traveling around rural Texas, Louisiana, and Arkansas, keeping written records of the deplorable conditions of the sharecroppers. His lengthy testimony to a Senate investigating committee provides a chilling firsthand account.

I have seen colored children barefooted, half naked and even starved on their way to school. . . . The white people rob the colored people out of two-thirds of what they make. . . . From the mouth of Red River to Jefferson, Texas, no difference can be seen. Even in Arkansas and Texas where I traveled . . . I have seen along the banks of Red River colored people who were afraid to talk to me at landings. I asked several of them, "Do you not live well?" They told me, "No, the whites take all we make and if we say anything about our rights they beat us." . . . We have been working hard since the surrender, and have not got anything.

Document 88
Sharecropping
[Billingsley Papers, Land Papers, 1865–1893, Center for American History, University of Texas at Austin]

In the early years following emancipation, the Freedmen's Bureau helped negotiate written sharecropping contracts. Women contractors, like Dolly Lang, as well as the men, were charged exorbitant expenses.

Sharecropping contract between Dolly Lang and Mrs. V. C. Billingsley
State of Texas
Falls County
    I, Dolly Lang of said State and County, widow of Ellis Lang, hereby agree to the cancellation of a trade for Ellis Lang's tract of land, with J. B. Billingsley during his lifetime, and I hereby agree to lease from Mrs. V. C. Billingsley the said land, being the place on which I now live, containing about 48-⅔ acres, paying therefore yearly 3 bales of cotton, each weighing 500 pounds, and being the first three bales raised on said place; this lease to expire on December 31, 1889, unless otherwise agreed to by Mrs. V. C. Billingsley; said cotton to be delivered at Marlin at B. C. Clark's place of business.
    Witness my hand this Jany 9, 1889

Her
Dolly X Lang
Mark

Document 89
Women's Wage Labor
[Camilla Davis Trammell, *Seven Pines, Its Occupants and Their Letters, 1825–1872* (Houston: privately published, 1986), pp. 270–271 (revised edition, Southern Methodist University Press, 1987)]

The domestic service contract of Louisa Nash shows that she lacked both liberty and security.

Domestic Service Contract of Louisa Nash
    Memorandum of Contract Entered into this 18th day of March, 1867 between W. F. Hardin as Employer and the Freedwoman Louisa Nash:
The State of Texas
County of Liberty
Witnesseth—

That the said employer hath this day hired the said Freedwoman as a house servant from this date until the 23rd day of December next. The said employer obligates himself to furnish the said Freedwoman and her child, about three years old, with good quarters and sufficient rations, and medicines, but in no case to pay physician's bills. Time lost to sickness to be deducted from wages.

And the said Freedwoman obligates and binds herself to work diligently at all necessary work such as cooking, ironing, and milking and all such work as servants are required to do about a house and yard. Also not to leave the premises without the permission of the employer. . . . The said employer obligates and binds himself to pay to the said Freedman for the present month, March, five dollars in money or clothing. For the residue of the time, five dollars per month paid at the end of the year.

—W. F. Hardin
Louisa (X) Nash
(her mark)

Document 90
Laundresses Demand a Raise
[*Galveston Daily News*, August 1, 1877]

Some urban black women working together in commercial laundries developed solidarity and started to call for better pay. When striking women in Galveston demanded $1.50 a day, the local newspaper reported the women's actions satirically.

Another Raid
Monday night colored women, emboldened by the liberties allowed their fathers, husbands, and brothers, during Monday, and being of a jealous nature, determined to have a public hurrah yesterday of their own, and as the men had demanded two dollars for a day's labor they would ask $1.50 or $9 per week. As women are generally considered cleaners of dirty linen, their first move was against the steam laundry, corner of Avenue A and Tenth street, owned by Mr. J. N. Harding, who has in his employ several women, as it happened yesterday, all white.

About 6:30 a.m. colored women began collecting about his house, until they numbered about twenty-five, several men being with them. The laundry women were soon seen coming to work. When met and told that they should not work for less than $1.00 per day, four turned back; but one, a Miss Murphy, went into the house and began working. Seeing this, the women rushed in, caught her and carried her into the street, and by threats forced her to leave. As no other laborers were found, a council of war was being held, when a colored woman passed by and entered the home to collect money for Monday's labor. The cry was raised that Alice had gone back on them, and Alice, being generally obnoxious to one or two colored women, passed by and entered the home to collect money for Monday's labor. . . . A rush was made for her, but Alice is not slow in her motions; therefore the first who got in reach went to grass from a well directed blow, but they were too many for Alice, who was literally covered with women, clawing and pulling, until Alice's clothes were torn from her body and they could get no hold, then the poor woman was let up and driven off.

This success again emboldened the women to further demonstrations. The cry was raised, "Let's lock them out for good; here's nails I brought especially." An axe lying in the wood pile was grasped, and the laundry house doors and windows secured. Then off they started for the heathen Chinee, who "washes Melican man clothes so cheapee allee vile," but before leaving Mr. Harding was warned that this visit would be repeated at one o'clock and again today. "Now for the Chinee, we'll drive them away." So down Market Street they went, led by a portly colored lady, whose avoirdupois is not less than 250.

On the way many expressions as to their intentions were heard, such as "We will starve no longer," "Chinese got no business coming here taking our work from us." Each California laundry was visited in turn, according to its location, beginning at Slam Sling's on Twentieth street, between Market and Postoffice, and ending at Wau Loong's, corner of Bath avenue and Postoffice street. At these laundries all the women talked at once, telling Sam Lee, Slam Sling, Wau Loong and the rest that "they must close up and leave this city within fifteen days, or they would be driven away," each Chinaman responding, "Yees, yees," "Alee rightee," "Me go, yes," and closed their shops.

The women proceeded through Market street to Eighteenth where they scattered after vowing they would meet again at 4 o'clock on the corner of Market and Eleventh streets and visit each place where women are hired, and if they receive less than $1.50 per day or $9.00 per week they would force them to quit.

Document 91
"Dearest Friend"
[Norwood Papers, Correspondence, 1873–1903, Center for American History, University of Texas at Austin]

Dallas, Texas
July 15, 1893

Mrs. Norwood,

Dearest friend,—

How often I think of you. You can not imagine. It was a great pleasure for me to visit you, because you always made it very pleasant for me. I would have been at your house more often than I was there, should I had less work to do, but you know how busy I was untill the close of school.

Have you called on Mrs. Trice since I left? You ought to run over and see her some time, because she was always speaking of how well she likes you and enjoys being in your presence so much. . . .

Sincerely your friend,
Eliza Eubank
411 Flora St.
Dallas

Document 92

"A Brilliant Wedding"

[*Austin Daily Statesman*, January 23, 1896]

Last evening at 8 o'clock the Wesley Chapel on East Ninth Street was crowded with representative colored people, augmented by quite a number of white friends of the contract parties to witness the marriage of Mr. Lewis D. Lyons and Miss Eva A. Carrington, two prominent young people in Austin colored society. The wedding party arrived promptly on the hour and to the steps of the lively wedding march as played by Rubirth's Orchestra. . . . The bride was attired in a white figured silk, en train, with bridal veil, while the bridesmaid wore a costume of white also. The groom and attendants all wore dress suits. Upon the conclusion of the wedding, the bridal party and friends repaired to the home of the bride, where a reception was enjoyed until 11 o'clock.

Document 93

Men Protest Miscegenation Law

[Herbert Aptheker, ed., *A Documentary History of the Negro People of the United States* (New York: Citadel Press, 1951), pp. 687–688]

The Committee on Grievances of the 1883 Texas State Convention of Negroes protested a state law which forbade interracial sexual relations, pointing out that the authorities generally enforced it only with regard to marriage and winked at extramarital relationships. This approach, the delegates said, victimized colored females.

Loomis S. Rucker and Bertha V. Collins were married at the Pilot Knob Methodist Church near Austin in 1914. They moved to Los Angeles in 1920. (Courtesy Marie E. Bradley)

MISCEGENATION LAW

We find that the denial to the colored people of the free exercise of many of the rights of citizenship, is due to the fact of there being such great prejudice against them as a race. . . .

Prominent among the enactments in furtherance of this social disregard is a law of this State punishing as felons all persons who intermarry when one is a descendant of the Negro race and the other is not. The same series of laws impose an insignificant fine only for the same persons to live together in unlawful wedlock, or have carnal intercourse with each other without being married. In most cases, say ninety-nine cases in one hundred, parties of the two races thus unlawfully cohabiting are not even reported, or if reported not punished. . . . The result of this series of crimes . . . is to increase immorality in the lower classes of both races to an alarming extent. . . . Colored females, victims of this well-laid plan, called a law to protect public morals, and common decency and chastity, are severely censured, and our whole race indiscriminately described as a race without morals. . . . The law was intended to gratify the basest passions of certain classes of men who do not seek such gratification by means of lawful wedlock.

Document 94
Record of Criminal Offenses Committed (1866–1867)

["Criminal Offences Committed in State of Texas," Assistant Commissioner, Austin, vols. 11–13, Records of the Bureau of Refugees, Freedmen, and Abandoned Lands, Texas, Record Group 105, National Archives]

Excerpts from the records of the Freedmen's Bureau reveal the kinds of crimes committed against black women by whites. The criminals listed below are white, and all the injured parties are black women.

No.	Name of Criminal	County	Injured Party and Nature of Offence
79	James Gathing	Bosque	Whipping Susan
107	James Wise	Houston	Whipping and gouging eye of Emily Graves
108	Margaret Jones	Houston	Whipping and pounding with stock wood & shovel, Eliza Elders
838	John Fogarty (no action taken) [Agent noted, "Inhuman monster."]	Limestone	Cutting off the ears and burning arms to a crisp of Minerva Maid.
1227	? Jones Fined $25	Parker	Assault with intent to rape Jenny Goodfellow whom he had met coming from a wedding. Assault not successful.

Document 95
"I were a prisoner at the female farm"

[Lula Sanders to Governor T. M. Campbell, October 2, 1907, Letters Received, Thomas M. Campbell Papers, Archives Division, Texas State Library, Box 301-243, Folder October 2, 1907, to October 7, 1907]

For decades after emancipation, black prisoners, both men and women, were abused by the state's criminal justice system. An investigation in 1908–1909 finally resulted in legislation reorganizing the penitentiary system and providing for an end to the convict lease system. Testimony by black female prisoners confirmed stories of backbreaking farm labor, sexual misconduct by male guards, and chilling brutality. In 1909, of the seventy women in state prison, sixty-six (94 percent) were black, although blacks constituted only 18 percent of the state's population. The following letter was written to the governor by Lula Sanders following the completion of her three-year prison term for assault to murder. Within two weeks, the women were moved to another farm. In 1912, Ennis Carlisle and six other women were punished for "mutiny." [2]

Fort Worth Tex 10-2-07

To the Governor T. M. Campbell

Dear Sir

I were a prisoner at the female farm at Johnson farm seven miles from Hunsville Texas and I worked 2 years 8 mths and 12 day and there were never a more inhumane place in the world than there. women have to work from sun to sun rain or shine I speake from what I know[,] not from what I heard. Women that are in a delicate condition have to work in the field just as same as the others and if there times comes to give birth they have to lay down there hoes and lay down in the field and give birth and probably lay there 2 or three hours before there are cared for. and they have to cut and split rail build fences cut down trees cut cord wood and stack it and have to lift logs 8 and 10 feet long and dig ditches 5 feet deep and one mile long build dam and we have had to work in mud and water up to our kneese and when we were unable to work we were put in a dark sell six feet long and 4 feet wide there is 5 and 6 in one little sell together. and we had to cut Johnson grass so high that we couldnt see the guards on horses. one woman by the name of Louise Marshall carried potatoes in a croker sack when she were in labor and she went to the guard and told him about her being unable to work and he drove her out of the building and made her go to the field and work just the same. Alice Climons had the consumption and were put out on the galery one cold evening and chiled to death. Nellie Johnson were given some kind of medicine and from the effect died and they have worked so hard during the hot months untill they would get over heat and would fall out and they were dragged out under a tree and throwed water on like a dog, and the guards would curse and beat and choked and called all kinds of dirty names and if they see any woman in any squad that they want to use for there convenience they will take her out and then they will make the rest of the woman look up to her. The guards are very mean to the prisoners They pay but a very little attention to our comfort.

Dear Governer the Commissioners have been down there and they tell you all that they treat the convicts nice but it is a sad mistake. we were afraid to mention it to you for if we had it would have been hard for us one woman by the name Charity Williams whipped a woman by the name of Bess Baily over the head with a wash board because the guard told her she were two pretty to work. The guards women work if they want to and if they dont want to the guards make the rest of the women work for her. that is shure a tough place for poor female prisoners for they are treated like brutes. and when they whip poor women they tie there clothes up over their heads and expose their nackedness to all the guards and in some cases I have seen some of the women during their monthly period have been whipped so bad untill they have had to scrubbed the floor after them. the abuse from the guards is what caused that woman to run away in August. women have gotten on there kneese and begged me to make this apeal to you for there sake Oh Governer you shure ought to go down there and see the condition of those poor women. and concerning the women that get over heat I have seen as many as 8 at a time. after we work hard all day at night we are all urshed [ushered?] in an old building and it is all open and we sleep in shucks and have but two quilts and the fleas and bed bugs nearly eat us up. and some times we get enough something to eat and some time we dont and what we do get it isnt fit to eat for the bread is two or three days old. and we have had to work on the county road just as same as men. we have had to cut down trees and build roads like we were men. two thirds of the children that have been borned down there is the guards

Dear Govorner I hope you will read this letter very careful and study over the matter and go down there right away and take action just as soon as you can for those poor women are certainly abused and would be very glad for you to come to their rescue.

Oblige

Lula Sanders

Document 96
"Mrs. Henry (Mary) Miller Sued for Damages"
[*Galveston Daily News*, February 29, 1876]

In 1875, Congress passed a civil rights act designed to prevent discrimination in public places. Black women tested the law by purchasing theater tickets and occupying first-class railroad cars. After being forcibly ejected from her seat in the "white ladies' circle" of the Tremont Opera House in Galveston, Mrs. Henry (Mary) Miller sued for damages in federal court. The judge ruled that the owner *was guilty of depriving her of her civil rights and fined him $500, but later dismissed the fine. An outraged black community denounced the judge at a mass meeting.*

MEETING OF COLORED CITIZENS
They Denounce the Action of Judge Morrill
in the Civil Rights Case
N. W. Cuney Appeals to his Race
to Maintain their Rights

Last night the colored Methodist Church on Broadway, near Center street, was crowded with colored citizens, to take into consideration the action of Judge Morrill in the Greenwall civil rights case. The audience embraced the most prominent colored citizens of Galveston, besides a large number of women, who were doubtless drawn out from sympathy with one of their sex, Mrs. Henry Miller, the plaintiff in the case under consideration. The proceedings of the meeting were orderly throughout, any allusion to the glorious civil rights bill was greeted with enthusiastic applause. . . . N. W. Cuney then addressed the meeting. . . . "We come together to denounce as an unprecedented outrage on judicial proceedings [the act of Judge Amos Morrill]. . . . We must speak out when the occasion demands it, for by silence we invite oppression."

Document 97
Milly Anderson Tests the U.S. Civil Rights Act of 1875
[Case No. 14,976. *United States v. Dodge et al.*, (1 Tex. Law J. 47) District Court, W. D. Texas, October 3, 1877, University of Texas at Austin Law Library, Circuit and District Cases, 1789–1880]

Milly Anderson won a suit in U.S. District Court, Western District of Texas, in 1877 against the Houston and Texas Central Railroad for denying her admission to a railroad car. In his instructions to the jury, the judge indicated that a railway employee who denies a female passenger a right to ride in the only car for ladies alone, solely because she is a person of African descent, is guilty under the 1875 Civil Rights Act. Further, he noted that a female passenger who had a first-class ticket could not be denied access to the ladies' car solely because she was of African descent. In a foreshadowing of Plessy v. Ferguson, *however, he said that if there are two equally fit cars for the use of white females and colored females, then there is no offense.*

Civil Rights—Railway Passengers—Master and Servant
    [1. A railway employe who denies to a female passenger having a first class ticket a right to ride in the only car in the train appropriated for the

accommodation of ladies alone, solely because she is a person of African descent, is guilty, under the civil rights law of March 1, 1875 (18 Stat. 335), whether he acts under the instructions of his employer or not. If he acts under the instructions of superior officers of the railway company, they also are guilty under the law.]

[2. If there are two cars, equally fit and appropriate, in all respects, for the use of white female passengers as well as colored female passengers, then there is no offence, under the law in denying a colored female passenger entrance to one, and requiring her to ride in the other.]

DUVAL, District Judge (charging jury). The information filed in this case charges that W. E. Dodge, as president, W. R. Baker, as vice president, and J. Durand, as superintendent, of the Houston & Texas Central Railway Company, together with John Burdisch, an employe of said company, being in control and managing the cars of said road, did on the 26th of April, 1876, with an unlawful intent and purpose, deny to one Milly Anderson admission into a car intended and provided for the transportation of female passengers, for the sole reason that she was a person of African descent, contrary to the act of congress of March 1, 1875, entitled "An act to protect all citizens in their civil and legal rights." The act in question, so far as it bears upon the present case, provides "that all persons within the jurisdiction of the United States shall be entitled to the full and equal enjoyment of the accommodations, advantages, facilities and privileges of public conveyances on land or water," etc., "subject only to the conditions and limitations established by law, and applicable alike to citizens of every race and color, regardless of any previous condition of servitude." The act then goes on to denounce a penalty upon any person who shall violate this provision. Although the passage of this act, including the provision just read, was no doubt suggested by the condition of the late slave race of the Southern states, who had afterwards been made citizens of the United States, yet it is not confined in its operations to them alone. It extends to the white race, also, and embraces every person who is a citizen of the United States. One of the most valuable rights which every citizen of the United States enjoys is the right of passing from one place in the Union to the other, either for purposes of business or pleasure. To enable him to enjoy this liberty of locomotion, the incidental right exists, both by common and statute law, that he or she shall be conveyed on and over the great public lines of transportation which traverse the country by land or water. These lines of transportation, whether they consist of railroads, steamboats, or stages, are known to the law as common carriers. They owe to the public at large a general duty, independent of any contract in the particular case. The law imposes upon them the duty of transporting every citizen who pays the fare demanded to some designated point, and of giving him or her full and equal accommodation, convenience, and comfort, as is accorded to other passengers, male and female, who pay a like fare. This right of the citizen, and this duty of the common carrier, is recognized and exists by the common law of the land, and it is only to protect this right, and enforce this duty, that congress passed the provision of law which I read to you. Persons who refuse to conform to reasonable regulations on the part of the carrier, or who, for good reason, are not fit associates for other passengers, as, for instance, those who are drunk, disorderly, indecent, or offensive in their conduct, or who have contagious diseases, and the like, may properly be refused passage. But, with these and perhaps other like exceptions, every citizen of the United States, male or female, native born or naturalized, white or black, who pays to the carrier the fare demanded for the best accommodations, is entitled to the best provided for the different sexes; and no discrimination, as against the one, in favor of the other, can be legally made, provided they are decent in person and inoffensive in conduct. Mere race or color will not justify any such discrimination. The officers or employes of an incorporated railroad company are presumed, in the absence of proof to the contrary, to do their duty,—to act according to the instructions given them by their principal. But where an officer or employe of such company denies to a citizen of the United States admission into and passage upon a railroad car, to which such citizen is legally entitled (there being room for him or her to sit therein), then such officer or employe would be liable to a prosecution like the present, whether he acted under the instructions of his principal or not.

If the jury believe, from all the evidence in this case, that Milly Anderson, on the occasion referred to in the information, had purchased a first-class ticket, entitled her to a seat in a car of the Houston & Texas Central Railway Company, destined and appropriated for the accommodation of ladies alone, and there was but one such car, and, on presenting such ticket to the defendant Burdisch, she was by him denied admittance therein, solely because she was a person of African descent, then he would be guilty under the law, whether he acted under the instructions of his principal or not; and, furthermore, if the jury believe from the evidence that Burdisch, under such circumstances, acted under the authority and instructions of the other defendants, Dodge, Baker, and Durand, then the said defendants would be guilty; otherwise, they would not. But if the jury believe from the evidence that there were two cars on this occasion, and that they were equally used and appropriated for the carriage of ladies and gentlemen who had first-class tickets, without distinction of race or color, and that they afforded the same advantages, comforts, conveniences, and enjoyments; and if they further believe that under such circumstances the defendant Burdisch, while denying Milly Anderson entrance into one, gave her passage to the other, then he would not be liable to this prosecution, and the jury should return a verdict of not guilty, generally, as to the defendants. But in such case the jury should be fully satisfied from the evidence that the car in which passage was offered was in fact, in all respects, equal to the other, and was as fit and appropriate at that time for white female citizens as for colored female citizens. If there exists on the part of the jury, or any of them, any prejudice for or against the Houston & Texas Central Railroad Company, or for or against colored citizens, I beg that it will be discarded on this occasion, and that under the law as I have given it, and the evidence before them, this jury will determine the guilt or innocence of the defendants just as they would if the denial of rights charged in the information had been in reference to a white female citizen, instead of a colored one.

Document 98
Isabella Mabson Files Suit
[*Galveston News*, November 19, 1898]

The disposition of this case is not known.

EJECTED FROM A PALACE CAR
COLORED WOMAN WHO BOUGHT A TICKET IN KANSAS CITY
SUES FOR DAMAGES

Isabella E. Mabson, a femme sole, residing in Galveston, yesterday filed suit in the district court against the Mo, K and Tx railway company of Tx and the Wagner palace car company for damages in the sum of $1800. She avers that on Aug 25, 1898 she bought at Kansas City of the Missouri, Kansas and Texas railway company two first-class tickets for the transportation for herself and her three small children from Kansas City to Galveston, and that she purchased tickets and engaged passage of the Wagner company for herself and children in one of their palace cars, paying $11 for the berths, by reason of which the Wagner company obligated itself to carry her and her children in said palace car from Kansas City to Denison, Tex., and that upon reaching said last named place she and her children were ejected from the palace car by the authorized agents of the defendant companies, because, they said, plaintiff and her children were negroes,

and they were offered seats in a dirty, common coach provided for negroes, and which was filled with filth of person and language. She was sick
and in need of the comforts of the palace car, but upon being compelled to
enter the common coach aforesaid she left the train and purchased tickets
for the Houston and Texas Central railway. She claims that she was ejected
from the palace car in the presence of the passengers who had ridden in
that car with her all the way from Kansas City and that she was greatly
humiliated.

Document 99
Adelina Cuney Rides First Class
[Maud Cuney Hare, *Norris Wright Cuney: A Tribune of the Black People* (1913;
reprint, Austin: Steck-Vaughn, 1968), pp. 67–68]

*Maud Cuney Hare recalled how her mother, Adelina Dowdie Cuney, defied segre-
gation by climbing through a window into the first class coach of a railroad car
headed from Galveston to Houston in 1886. Many blacks were forced to ride in a
second-class coach even after purchasing first-class tickets.*

My uncle Joseph had gone to the depot with mother to see her off to Houston, where she was to join father, who was there attending a matter of
business. The conductor of the first-class coach saw them coming, and,
knowing them to be colored, he quickly locked the door of the coach, as
he knew from experience that no argument or force could compel mother
to enter a second-class car. After locking the door he disappeared. It was
then nearly train time and the coach was nearly filled with passengers. For
a second, disconcerted, mother looked around and then innocently turning to Uncle Joseph, said: "Well, Joe, there are people in the coach and I
see but one means of entrance and that is the window, so give me your
hand as a mount." And then, as if mounting a horse, she got in the window and took her seat demurely. It was now time for the train to leave, so
the conductor hastened forward, glanced hastily around, saw only Uncle
Joseph and surmising that his strategy had worked, unlocked the door and
cried with great satisfaction, "All aboard." Entering his coach to collect
tickets he was greatly chagrined and bewildered to see mother sitting there
quite contented and with perfect ease and indifference.

Document 100
Isabelle Smith Addresses Farm Delegates
[Unidentified news clipping, October 8, 1900(?), "Negro Scrapbook," Center for
American History, University of Texas at Austin]

Pictured with the original sewing class of St. Philip's College (later St. Philip's Academy) in San Antonio, 1898, are the new teacher, Alice Cowan; Rev. Marshall, the first minister of St. Philip's Church; and some small boys who attended and did small pieces of art work, along with the female students. (University of Texas Institute of Texan Cultures)

As president of the Farmers Improvement Society's Ladies' Auxiliary, Isabelle Smith addressed the organization's 500 male and female delegates in Hempstead around 1900.

Dr. Logan . . . was followed by Mrs. R. L. Smith, who declared that the farmer's wife had much to do with the success or failure of his crop, and she declared that the negro woman had much to do with fixing the status of the negro in this country, "and it is to you men," she said, "I appeal for the protection of our women. Look at what we have to pass through. Men of every nationality and race on the face of the globe feel that they have a right to insult us. In order to pass through this world with our womanhood we must fight unprincipled white men, and black men. For honest labor our girls are paid starvation wages, but for debauchery they are given almost any amount of money. Just to think of it, an honest girl for honest labor can only get from $5 to $12 a month, and out of this she must meet her expenses, pay her debts and buy her clothes. She likes to look nice like

Viola Cornelia Scull Fedford (seated, far right), was a prominent Galveston educator and club leader. She is pictured with her family, ca. 1900. Top, left to right, her father, Ralph Albert Scull, her brother, Ralph Horace Scull, and her mother, Florence Ella Scull. Bottom, her brother, Ira L. Scull and in the photograph, her sister, Florence Scull, who died at age eighteen months. (Courtesy of the Rosenberg Library, Galveston)

other women. This is one of the evils which must be met. What can we do for our girls?

"We are trying to establish and build up for our boys and girls a practical school [at Ladonia]. Already our farmers have shown an interest in this work. They are giving of their money and we have some farmers who are in good circumstances, and who will contribute liberally for the establishment of our school as soon as we prove ourselves worthy, and this we must do. I am aware of the fact that the state has provided for our boys and girls good schools, missionary societies of the north, and the negro has looked after himself, and still there is a class that these schools are not reaching and we must reach them ourselves. The farmers must do our part. We want a school in Texas that will not be second, even to Tuskegee [Institute, Booker T. Washington's school, in Alabama], and in order to do this we men and women must do our duty. The negro farmer has it in his power to do great work, if he will."

Document 101
Exodusters
[*Denison Daily News*, September 27, 1879]

In the late 1870s, the subject of migrating to Kansas was on the minds of many black Texans. Hundreds left for what they hoped was a better life.

Something like a year ago, a colored woman going by the name of Madam Walker, delivered two addresses at Nolan Hall, "On the political destiny of the colored race in the U.S."

On each evening the hall was packed to overflowing, among the number a sprinkling of whites. The woman was eloquent and interesting, and highly spoken of by the press throughout the state.

After leaving Denison, she swung around the circle in the Indian territory and then went to "Bleeding Kansas."

Document 102
A Prominent Radical
[Carolyn Ashbaugh, *Lucy Parsons: American Revolutionary* (Chicago: Kerr Publishing Co., 1976), p. 30]

Lucy Gonzales Parsons, a native of Waco, was a leader of the Chicago working-class movement, a writer, an editor, an orator, and a founder of the Industrial Workers of the World. Her husband, Albert Parsons, was executed for his role in the Haymarket Riot. In her poem "The Parody," based on one by Lord Byron, she condemns capitalism and war. "The Parody" was published first in the Socialist *in 1878.*

A PARODY

"I had a dream, which was not all a dream." . . .
And men did wander up and down the cheerless earth,
Aimless, homeless, hopeless. . . .
As, by fits, the realization of their impoverished condition passed like a
    vision before them.
Some laid down and hid their eyes and wept
As the cries of their hungry children
And prayers of their despairing wives fell like curses upon them;
And some did rest their chins upon their clenched hands
And swear to help abolish the infamous system that could produce such
    abject misery. . . .
And some did gnash their teeth and howl, swearing dire vengeance
    against *all* tyrants.

And War—which for a moment was no more—did glut himself again;
A meal was bought with blood (tramps' blood),
And each sat sullenly apart, gorging himself in gloom.
No love was left;
All earth, to the masses, was but one thought—and that was:—Work!
    Wages! Wages!
The pangs of hunger fed upon their vitals.
Men, in a land of plenty, died of *want*—absolute—
And their bones were laid in the Potter's Field.

Document 103
Musician Cancels Segregated Performance
[Maud Cuney Hare, *Norris Wright Cuney: A Tribune of the Black People* (1913; reprint, Austin: Steck-Vaughn, 1968), p. 215]

After graduating from the New England Conservatory of Music, Maud Cuney Hare, a Galveston native, lived for a time in Austin, where she directed music for the Deaf, Dumb, and Blind Institute for Colored Youth. In 1897, she refused to perform in the city's segregated opera house. She later returned to Boston and became a noted music historian, folklorist, pianist, and playwright.

Programs were in the hands of the printer when it dawned upon the management of the Opera House [in Austin] that it would not do to allow seating of white and colored patrons together. They telephoned that it would be necessary to sell tickets to colored patrons for the balconies only. Mr. Ludwig [her teacher] and I indignantly canceled the contract for the House. No hall being available, the recital, with the kind assistance of Mr. Ludwig, was given at the [Deaf, Dumb, and Blind] Institution.

Document 104
A Human Torch
[Alfreda M. Duster, ed., *Ida B. Wells, Crusade for Justice: The Autobiography of Ida B. Wells* (Chicago: University of Chicago Press, 1970), p. 84]

Nationally known journalist Ida B. Wells spoke to an 1893 meeting of leading Washington, D.C., women about the impact a Texas lynching had upon her.

The next morning the newspaper carried the news that while our meeting was being held there had been staged in Paris, Texas, one of the most awful lynchings and burnings this country has ever witnessed. A Negro [Henry Smith] had been charged with ravishing and murdering a five-year-old girl. He had been arrested and imprisoned while preparations were made to burn him alive. The local papers issued bulletins detailing the preparations, the schoolchildren had been given a holiday to see a man burned alive, and the railroads ran excursions and brought people of the surrounding country to witness the event, which was in broad daylight with the authorities aiding and abetting this horror. The dispatches told in detail how he had been tortured with red-hot irons searing his flesh for hours before finally the flames were lit which put an end to his agony. They also told how the mob fought over the hot ashes for bones, buttons, and teeth for souvenirs. . . . He had no trial, no chance to defend himself. . . . For that reason there will always be doubts as to his guilt.

4

EDUCATION

The Freedmen's Bureau established a series of schools immediately after emancipation which became one of the most visibly successful of its endeavors. As African-Americans increased their years of education, they demanded farther-reaching, more advanced courses. Private schools were absorbed into public school systems as these developed and, later, colleges came into being. Although the educational opportunities offered to blacks never equaled those available to whites, education was one means by which black women could get higher-paying jobs and enlarge their vision. Many became teachers, principals, professors, deans, and even college presidents.

Document 105
Education
[*Flake's Bulletin*, Galveston, November 11, 1865]

We saw fathers and mothers [freedpeople] together with their grown up children all anxiously engaged in the pursuit of knowledge.

Document 106
Self-Respect
[*American Missionary* 12 (August 1868): 177, as cited in Robert C. Morris, *Reading, 'Riting, and Reconstruction: The Education of Freedmen in the South, 1861–1870* (Chicago: University of Chicago Press, 1981), p. 210]

The recitation of the following poem by a black student in Hempstead reportedly evoked a hearty laugh from the audience, which included several leading merchants and former slaveholders.

Dr. Inez B. Prosser was one of the first black women in the United States to receive a doctoral degree. She received her doctorate in educational psychology from the University of Cincinnati in 1931. Her dissertation was one of the first on the social development of elementary school children. She was a graduate of Prairie View Normal Institute and received a B.A. from Huston College in Austin in 1925 and an M.A. from the University of Colorado in 1927. She served as dean and registrar at Tillotson College in Austin from 1921 to 1930. (University of Texas Institute of Texan Cultures)

Izola Fedford Collins graduated from Galveston's Central High School in 1944 and fifty years later, was elected president of that system's school board. With degrees in music from Prairie View A & M University and Northwestern University, she taught music and led award-winning choirs and bands in Galveston, Goliad, Hitchcock, and Bay City. She also taught band instruments privately and was a jazz and lounge pianist for social events. She was elected to the Galveston School Board in 1986, served as vice president, and as president from 1994 to 1995. She was awarded Galveston's Teacher of the Year award in 1987, and named one of Galvston's finest educators by students of Stephen F. Austin School in 1988. (Photo by Manny Chan, Creative Photography, courtesy Izola F. Collins)

1

Pray look at me
Why don't you see
How tall and strong I am?
I stamp my foot
And shake my fist
Just like a great big man.

2

I clap and sing
Like any thing,
And when I grow some bigger,
I'll read and spell
So very well
You'll never call *me* nigger.

Document 107
"Let me go to school"
[George P. Rawick, ed., *The American Slave: A Composite Autobiography*, Suppl., ser. 2, IX, pt. 8, Clarissa Scales (1937), pp. 3461–3462, reprinted with permission of Greenwood Publishing Group, Inc., Westport, Conn., copyright © 1979]

My ambition was to be a teacher, but daddy always kept me busy in de fields. Daddy was a good fahmer, and dat's all dat he knowed. He always told me dat it was enough learnin' fo' me if I could jes' read and write. He never even had dat much.

"Dat's mo' dan I ever got," he said. "Yo' kain't go to school today. I kain't spare yo'. Go out and chop dat cotton."

"But daddy, let me go to school: I wants to get my lessons good and be a teacher."

"Clara, it look lak rain and we got to git dat cotton chopped. Now go on out to de field."

I'd go into de fields and chop de cotton. Sometimes I'd git to thinkin' in de field, and wonder if I'd ever become a teacher. I never did git to be a real teacher. . . .

Den a colored teacher, Hamlet Campbell, come down f'om de nawth. He rented a room in dat big house and made a school out ob it. De trustees hired him and paid him. De chillun didn't have to pay to go to school. I always tell my granddaughter how I used to be at de head ob my class.

Document 108
Self-Education
[George P. Rawick, ed., *The American Slave*, Suppl., ser. 2, VII, pt. 6, Maggie Whitehead Matthews (1937), pp. 2624–2625, reprinted with permission of Greenwood Publishing Group, Inc., Westport, Conn., copyright © 1979]

We never was showed our A B C's. We couldn't even be caught readin'. Jes' to be caught lookin' at a clean sheet of paper was enough to get a scoldin', but to look at a piece of paper dat had writin' on it and if we made lak we knowed whut was wrote on it we sure got a whoopin' fo' it. I couldn't read at dat time but many was de time dat I was caught lookin' at a piece of paper wid writin' on it and I got a whoopin' fo' it. I had told 'e dat I could read whut was on it.

I haven't been to school one day in my life. De only time dat I was in a schoolhouse was when my parents was invited to a closin'-day pahty at a school. I enjoyed de pahty very much, but I jes' never went to school. I learned to be a good speller, 'cause fo' twenty cents I bought me one of dem blue back spellers. Dere was many a time dat I could out spell de folks whut had sent to school. Dey was small words but I could spell 'em. I never did learn how to write though. Many was de time dat I wished I could write, 'cause I wanted to write about my life. I've lived a long time and seen a lot of devilment, yo' know.

Document 109
"I learned fast"
[George P. Rawick, ed., *The American Slave: A Composite Autobiography*, Suppl., ser. 2, V, pt 4, Mary Anne Gibson (1938), p. 1472, reprinted with permission of Greenwood Publishing Group, Inc., Westport, Conn., copyright © 1979]

I can read and write. I went to school after slavery fo' three winter terms. De teachah, Isabella Shaw—a light colored woman, said dat I was swift. I learned fast.

Document 110
The Duties of a White Schoolmarm
[The Diary of Sarah M. Barnes, typescript, March 14, 1868, Rosenberg Library, Galveston, courtesy of James W. Hosking]

Many northern women, black and white, came South to teach the freedpeople. One such white missionary was Sarah Barnes from Connecticut, founder of the Barnes Institute in Galveston, with thirty girls and thirty-three boys on her class rolls. In addition to teaching at the Day School, she and her assistant made house calls and taught Bible Class and Sunday School.

Galveston, Texas, March 14, 1868.
Was up quite early this morning, because there seemed much to be done during the day, and although we manage to crowd a large amount of work into twelve hours . . . no time must be wasted. . . . First came house calls which consumed the time until eight o'clock, then donning hats we hastened out to make calls among our charges. Two of the children from the first house we entered we found were attending our Day School, and we were warmly greeted by their parents. They seemed perfectly delighted because the "School Mistis" had come. We introduced our Bible Class which they had already heard about from some one attending . . . and by way of compliment to us added "we is mighty proud of you." . . .

We could not refrain from spending a little of our time in looking around [in the city cemeteries]. . . . One side is called the "Yankee Ground." Here are the Union soldiers and friends of the union. . . . Sometimes I hope to give a half day to these graves for the sake of some bereaved mother, mourning sister or friend who may be far away. . . .

Home again, and at two oclock we are waiting for the arrival of two ladies, (from England visiting a sister here). . . . One is an authoress and is in favor with the Royal family. She brought an autograph book where we traced our names. . . .

As soon as their call was over, we started out to see an Old Auntie we feared was ill. . . . We made the other calls on our way home, both pleasant and profitable ones I hope. . . . And thus closes another week of work here among this people.

Document 111
"Please let me hear from you"
[Julia Caraway to Sarah Barnes Rathbun, typescript, July 30, 1871, Sarah Barnes Collection, Rosenberg Library, Galveston, courtesy of James W. Hosking]

After Sarah Barnes married Captain Rathbun and moved to Connecticut, Julia Caraway, the mother of a former student, wrote to her.

Galveston, Texas
July 30th, 1871
Dear Mrs. Rathbun.
Please accept this ring for little Florence [Sarah Barnes Rathbun's baby], as a slight token of my love for you and her. I wanted to send something, and thought this would be nice because she could keep it always. The next time your husband comes to Galveston, I hope you will come with him, and bring the baby, for I want to see both of you so much.

Primus [a former student], Cora, and Maggie send their love to you. Cora is attending school now, near our house.

Please let me hear from you, and don't forget to send the baby's picture. . . . I wish, too, that you would send me a little piece of some of her dresses. Remember me to your Mother, and all your friends, and accept much love for yourself from your friend.

Julia Caraway

Document 112
Progress of the School
[Reprinted in the *American Missionary* (May 1867), pp. 103–104]

Although it is unsigned, Sarah Skinner, Sarah Barnes's assistant, is probably the author of this report to the American Missionary Association.

Galveston, March 29, 1867.
As to the progress of the school, I think under the circumstances it could not be better. On the first of January my most advanced class was only part way through the First Reader. Now I have a large class in the Second Reader, and one in Spelling, beside three large classes in Mental Arithmetic. I never knew a class of white children with the same advantages, make more rapid progress than one of the arithmetic classes has. The first of January they began addition and are now through multiplication; beside, they are now able to write any number given them on their slates, up to one thousand. We have no conveniences for writing, other than slates; but it is really remarkable to see with what accuracy the children will copy from the blackboard. There are now four day schools and three large night schools in Galveston. All are attended with marked interest, and a great desire is manifested by the colored people to be educated. There are seventeen teachers in the Freedmen's work in Texas, seven of whom are from Wisconsin. Mr. Allen, our agent, is constantly traveling through the county, preparing places for teachers to hold schools, and, also, finding places to board them. The latter is, however, by far the most difficult matter. Were it not for the loyal Germans throughout the State, there would be very few places where they could board. As it is, in almost any town of importance, at least one family can be found who will take a "Yankee teacher" in.

In some places, however, teachers have to board at hotels, and submit to very disagreeable treatment. One of our teachers, a Mrs. Dickinson from Beloit went to a small town called Hempstead, and obtained board in a private family, where she was doing very well, when a rebel son came home. On learning a *teacher* to the Freedmen was an inmate of the house, he became very indignant; and going to her room, he ordered her out of the house. She went to a hotel, and fared little better. Though not ordered to leave, she was seated at table alone, with Northern people at one end of the room, and Southerners at the other. In writing me she said she supposed she was not deemed worthy to sit with either company. But amid all of her persecutions she seemed very cheerful. . . .

Document 113
Miss Kate Emmons Has Seventy-six Scholars
[*Free Man's Press* (Austin), August 22, 1868; Center for American History, University of Texas at Austin]

It is not known if the teacher referred to, Miss Kate Emmons, is black or white.

Mr. Anthony Culbreath, writes us from Sumpter, Trinity County, as follows: I send you the above list of thirty-six subscribers, and inform you that the money is subject to your order.

Send the paper also to Miss Kate Emmons, and to Parson Lakey. Miss Emmons is teaching our school; She has seventy-six scholars, and they are improving very fast.

Those names marked, are her scholars, all of whom have learned to read since they were set free. Some people here do not like to have Miss Emmons teach school, and even threaten to run her off, or whip her.

Document 114
"Send us teachers"
[W. V. Tunstall to the *National Era* of December 14, 1871, reprinted in Dorothy Sterling, ed., *The Trouble They Seen: Black People Tell the Story of Reconstruction* (Garden City, N.Y.: Doubleday, 1976; reprinted by Da Capo Press), p. 300]

Creswell, Texas, November 29, 1871

To the Editor:

We need immediately five hundred teachers for colored schools in Texas. The colored people in this State cannot supply the demand. There are but few white Republicans who can engage in the profession of teaching and rebels will not teach them. Therefore our only prospect is to get teachers among the educated colored people of the North or Christian white people who are willing to endure privations among the heartless whites of the "sunny South." . . . Send us teachers.

Document 115
"De boys is going to college"
[George P. Rawick, ed., *The American Slave: A Composite Autobiography*, Suppl., ser. 2, V. pt. 4, Betty White Irby (1937), p. 1862, reprinted with permission of Greenwood Publishing Group, Inc., Westport, Conn., copyright © 1979]

After freedom, Betty White Irby was determined that her children would receive an education. When she remarried, she held her ground against her new husband.

"De boys is going to college. I ain't goin to run my chilun away, and drive 'em to destruction and to de penitentiary. If anybody has to git out, Robert, it'll be you." It wasn't long befo' he left.

Document 116
Resistance to School Integration
[*Houston Telegraph*, May 31, 1870]

We may let our children work in the fields or shop with the children of our former servants. They may hunt, or fish or play together, but to attend the same school never!

Document 117
Fisk Graduate Teaches in Galveston
[Herbert Aptheker, ed., *The Correspondence of W. E. B. Du Bois, Selections, 1877–1934* (3 vols.; Amherst: University of Massachusetts Press, 1973), vol. 1, pp. 8–9]

Miss L. A. Bowers graduated from Fisk University in 1888, a fellow classmate of W. E. B. Du Bois, and immediately obtained a position with the Galveston public schools. She and Du Bois were both nominated for the presidency of the Fisk Class of 1888 Club.

Galveston, Texas, Nov. 14, 1890

My Dear Classmates:
    . . . I am working still in the Public Schools of this city. This is my third year in this work, as I have worked here ever since my graduation. The work is pleasant; we have a pleasant set of teachers. I am teaching the Eighth and Ninth grades in our High School. My grades study higher Arithmetic and Grammar, Physical Geography, Physiology, History, Philosophy, Geometry, Algebra, Rhetoric, General History and Latin. I enjoy the higher work more than I did the work of the lower grades. The schools are good here, we will have our first graduating class this year. There are five who will finish our High School. We end up with the Eleventh grade. . . . We need two teachers. . . . I receive a salary of fifty dollars [per month] now

but hope to be promoted this year and receive ten or fifteen dollars more. I do not do a great deal of studying now but I find I am kept busy most of the time. I do not get [home] from school until three o'clock and then I must give several music lessons before dark.

I do not take a very active part in society. . . . I am interested in my work and give most of my attention to that. I wonder what are the marriage prospects of the class. . . . For my part I have made up my mind never to enter such a contract. . . . I extend a hearty invitation to every member of the class to sometime visit me in my home at Galveston. We are very plain and poor but should any one of you wish to come to our city I will throw my doors open to you and entertain you as long as you wish to stay. I am sure that all of us have been very proud of Mr. [W. E. B.] DuBois as one of us. . . . As I read of his success in the paper I felt proud to be able to tell persons that he was a classmate of mine. . . .

Your loving classmate
L. A. Bowers

Document 118
Christine B. Cash—Seventy Years an Educator
[To the Administrative Staff, Bishop College, Dallas, Texas, and Friends and Former Fellow-Workers Elsewhere, from Christine B. Cash, Marshall, Texas, December 21, 1969, courtesy Meredith C. Beal]

Christine B. Cash began teaching at age seventeen in 1906 in rural East Texas and later went on to public school administration and college teaching at Bishop and Jarvis Christian colleges. In 1947, she became one of the first native black Texas women to earn the Ph.D. degree—from the University of Wisconsin. She concluded a distinguished career at eighty-six in 1975 after a decade as an educational consultant and lecturer.

. . . It was in October 1903 that I first arrived at Bishop College campus having been transferred from my rural home in Marion County, Texas by my father in a wagon drawn by two mules. I had been a constant visitor to Wiley College from the time I was eight years of age until my matriculation at Central School in Jefferson, Texas. The older girls in my home community were Wiley College students who resided in the King's Home Dormitory for girls. An older half-brother of mine was also a Wiley college student. So at the end of my four years of study in the Central School in Jefferson, my mother, who was an ardent Baptist and a loyal member of the New Zion Baptist Church, which was then one of the founding churches of the Texas and Louisiana Baptist Association, decided that she would send me to Bishop College at the opening of its 1903 session. My father preferred that I matriculate at Wiley. My mother, knowing that my father would do what I wanted, coached me to say that I would prefer attending Bishop College. So they compromised on the issue by agreeing that I would determine the school. I decided on Bishop College. On my arrival I was questioned regarding my classification: I had completed Grade 8 in the public school system, but was required to pass an examination in Grammar, Grammar Analysis and Reading, Civil Government and United States History, Arithmetic, Geography: Descriptive and Physical, and Physiology. From this humble beginning my first great surprise was accorded by the Faculty of Bishop College, May, 1906, at which time I was designated on the graduating program of both the Scientific Preparatory and the Normal Departments as being First Honor Graduate and the recipient of two diplomas. I cherished those diplomas for years and strove to perform to the best of my ability as a teacher.

My first certification was achieved in June of 1906 when I took the State and County Examination in Jefferson, Marion County, Texas. On the basis of the appraisal by the County Board of Examiners, I was awarded First Grade County Certificate. On my request the papers were forwarded to the State Board of Examiners, where all papers were assigned passing marks with the exception of Geometry and Physics. However, a Second Grade State Certificate was awarded me.

The failing grade in Geometry and Physics given by the State Board of Examiners served as a stimulation. I resolved to do independent study until I could achieve an average grade of 85 in all of the twenty-five subjects which were required for a State Permanent Certificate authorizing an individual to teach any subject in the Public Schools of Texas from Grade one through twelve. I met that requirement in 1916, but not without challenge. . . .

During the span of those ten years of independent study for those examinations I prepared myself vigorously and thoroughly. After completing one examination during the span of the years mentioned, I had an occasion to challenge the State Board of Examiners regarding a grade of 75 given to me on an algebra examination. I had given the same problems to an algebra class which I was teaching at the time. In a formal letter of protest to the State Examiners, I explained that I had taught my solutions of the problems to my students and if I had taught them incorrectly I humbly requested that they send me the correct solutions so that I would correct the errors which I had made. The reply was a change of the grade to 100. In the year 1916 the State Department of Education of Texas awarded me this Permanent High School Certificate on the basis of a series of examinations in twenty-five subjects with a general grade of 85+. Therefore when the B. A. degree was awarded by Bishop College in 1926, I made no application for a permanent certificate based on four years of college study. . . .

Document 119
"I am now at this place teaching"
[To Mrs. L. J. Rhone, My Dear Sister, from her sister A. L. Ransom, October 22, 1906, Rhone Family Papers, Box 3U171, Folder 2, Center for American History, University of Texas at Austin]

Warranton Tex.
Oct 22, 06

Mrs. L. J. Rhone
    My dear sister, I now write you, I am now at this place teaching. I open school on the 15 inst and getting along farely well. Hope you and family are well. Guess you all heard of Walter Nobles death. He was buried at Brenham Monday the 15 inst, died (away from his family,) with a himerage from lungs. I haven't my children up here yet, I shall go for them Saturday. The children, being so much expense to me, and trouble trying to teach and trying to support them at all times.
    For this reason I have decided to marry for better, though it may be worse. What do you all think about it? Should I marry it will be between this time and Xmas. Say to Mr. Rhone, that I sent my contract to LaGrange Monday the 15 inst. Supt, not being there, left it there so he could approve it. He sent it out Saturday dated 20 inst. Now I taught one week before or ahead of date. I began teaching the date I sent it to his office. May I make my voucher out from date I began work? or not. Tell me just what to do. I'll teach hear 5 mos. If you all know of any school I can get let me know. I'll be through here in Feb. Did Lilian go to school? I left my horse and buggy in Brenham. Let me hear from you all soon.

Your sister
A. L. Ransom.

P.S. I have a $200.00 Policy from the Courts of Calanthe Lodge and a $200.00 Policy from the Daughters of tables of the Tabernacle made to my children. Now in case of my death I want you and husband to see that my funeral will come from the Daughters which is to be $50.00 and the $50.00 from the Courts that should go on funeral, go to support children. And at my death would like for you to take children. The money from Courts will be paid to you all in 6 mos. time. The money from Tabernacle in 3 mos time, providingly you all be Guardians for them. You'll get money in that time, I shall sure keep financial in both.

Hope you both will do this. It have worried me so much of late to ask you all this. That is why I write.

Document 120
"I just want you to teach"
[To Urissa E. Rhone from her mother, L. J. Rhone, March 20, 1921, Rhone Family Papers, Box 3U171, Folder 5, Center for American History, University of Texas at Austin]

Urissa Rhone Brown's parents were both educators—her father, Calvin Rhone, taught in Fayette County public schools, and her mother, Lucia Knotts Rhone, was also a teacher.

Addressed:
Crawford Hall
Prairie View, Tx.
LaGrange Texas 3-20-1921

My dear daughter
    This come to say we are all well. I am quite lonesome today Son and B. went to West Point to church today. I had a letter from Mancy yesterday Jessie was a little ill with her eyes. Urissa[,] Son says they carry on that way every year at P.V. [Prairie View]. I just want you to get a certificate so you want [won't] be in the state son was[,] not because I want you to teach. I mean to send you back if I live and keep my good health I know you are smart enough I don't doubt that the last bit. I believe my prayers is what put [?] son to the front. Well be sweet.

Lovenly your mother
L. J. Rhone

P.S. Butts Mackentire trying to play bad at WP last night stuck a knife in Viola Watson's leg Beulah will tell you all about it

Document 121
"See if you can get an answer book"
[Urissa Rhone Brown to her mother, Lucia J. Knotts Rhone, September 11, 192?, Rhone Family Papers, Box 3U171, Folder 2, Center for American History, University of Texas at Austin]

While attending Prairie View, Urissa Rhone Brown received assistance from her mother, who helped out with books and clothing. After graduation, Urissa had a successful career in Central Texas that included teaching and serving as principal of the "Colored" Round Top-Carmine High School.

P.V. Texas [Prairie View]
Sept. 11, 192[?]

Dear mother,

How are you all? Hope you are well. Guess you arrived home O.K.

I got everything all right today. I got two books today. The others are not here yet.

Mama go to both of the drug stores and see if you can get an answer book to George Wentworth and David Eugene Smith's School Algebra book.

There's nothing strange to tell.

When have you all heard from Son? Tell me where he is when you write.

Love to all,
Urissa

M. E. Hall, Room 35
[written on paper with algebra equations]

Document 122
"I will send them as soon as possible"
[Mrs. Lucia J. Knotts Rhone to her daughter Urissa Rhone, September 19, 1920(?), Rhone Family Papers, Box 3U171, Folder 5, Center for American History, University of Texas at Austin]

LaGrange Texas 9-19-1920[?]

Miss Urissa Rhone:

My dear daughter

How goes everything by this time? We are all well. I got home all right; found everything moving smooth. they picked one bale of cotton whilse I were gone; and we picked two last week Maurice picked (92 [pounds?]) one day they are paying .75 and board in here for picking we can't get any help we have about 4 open. Now about the answer books the man says he will have some in about tuesday if he does I will send them as soon as possible. I will send you some cloth to make you an apron. If I don't send the apron. Well Son is still in Townley Ala. Have you got an answer from B.L. and C.C.? Well good luck to you and simply push on is the wishes of your dear mother.

L. Rhone

P.S. What did Lucile say about coming down there to school?

Margaret is here with Beulah today our collection on Sunday was $143.44.

Document 123
A Former Student Appeals for Help
[To Mrs. U. E. Brown from Irma Lee Anderson, November 8, 1957, Rhone Family Papers, Box 3U172, Folder 1, Center for American History, University of Texas at Austin]

Room 5 Crawford Hall
Prairie View A&M College
Prairie View, Texas [November 8, 1957]
Mrs. U. [Urissa Rhone] E. Brown

Dearest teacher,

How are you? I am fine only I have been so busy.

I have just finished my mid-term examinations. I had four yesterday and two today. I think I did pretty good in all of them. Our instructor gave us our average grades for the Mid-term in Business. My grade is an A. I was really glad to hear that and I am going to strive to keep it up there.

Mrs. Brown, I have to write a term paper in science on Sunspots. It is a very narrow topic and it will be kind of difficult. I didn't know until after I had selected my topic and we can't change. I talked to my instructor about it and he told me I still would have to write on it, but it wouldn't matter if it doesn't be so long, as long as it takes in everything concerning Sunspots. I'd like to ask if you would help me with it. I plan to come home for Thanksgiving and I will get all the information that I can and come over to your home and let you help me to arrange it, also show me how to foot note, if you will. It will be appreciated very much.

How is school? Are you still planning to come down here for Homecoming? I hope so. Come on down and see us win.

Mother, Daddy, Freddie, Rutha Mae, L. W. and Cynthia were down to see me Sunday. I really was glad to see them.

I must close. I hope to see you on Homecoming.

Your student,
Irma Lee Anderson

Document 124
Aspirations
[Merle Yvonne Miles, " 'Born and Bred' in Texas: Three Generations of Black Females," Ph.D. diss., University of Texas at Austin, 1986, p. 139]

Sociologist Merle Yvonne Miles found in a study of three generations of black Texas females that a strong commitment to education was passed on from one generation to the next.

My mother insisted that all of her children get a college education. She was a teacher herself, and two of her other sisters and two brothers were teachers also.

Document 125
Women Go to College
[Merle Yvonne Miles, "'Born and Bred' in Texas: Three Generations of Black Females," Ph.D. diss., University of Texas at Austin, 1986, pp. 133–134]

My grandmother, on my mother's side, worked very hard. When my mother got her first job as a teacher in 1890 she paid for a home for her mother. My grandmother had sent my mother off to college . . . and she sent five more of my mother's younger brothers and sisters off to college.

Document 126
"My mother's mother was a college graduate"
[Merle Yvonne Miles, "'Born and Bred' in Texas: Three Generations of Black Females," Ph.D. diss., University of Texas at Austin, 1986, p. 137]

Nobody in our family was going to miss going to college. . . . My mother's mother was a college graduate. She had her Master's Degree. . . . She was a teacher. . . . My mother is a teacher and has a B.A. degree and has done some graduate study; my aunt has her Master's Degree in Physics and I'm working on my B.A. degree.

Document 127
Mothers Club
[Dorothy Robinson, "Interview with Christia Adair," April 25, 1977, Radcliffe College, in *The Black Women Oral History Project*, vol. 1, pp. 58–59, with permission of K. G. Saur Verlag, a Reed Reference Publishing Company, and the Schlesinger Library, Radcliffe College]

Christia Adair helped organize black and white women in Kingsville before World War I. She also worked for women's suffrage there and after moving to Houston became a leader in the National Association for the Advancement of Colored People and the civil rights movement.

I ran into a problem of a big gambling house that seemed to be one of the first things you got to when you got to the little Negro Town [ca. 1918]. . . . But it looked like we were helpless because the authorities, the sheriff department and like that, was getting rake-offs, and they were not concerned about it. But one day I came along by that building and one of my teenage boys, Sunday School boys, was coming out. And it just put war-fire in me . . . and I found out that he wasn't the only teenager that they were using at the tables, to make this money. . . .

I told the Negro women who were working with me, I said, "We just can't do it alone, and white women who have sons and daughters ought to be interested in this project." Well, I knew one white woman who was the president of a Mothers' Club. . . . So we went to this woman and told her what was what and she just became fired up with it, too. . . . She suggested that we organize a Mothers Club in our community and we did. But it was really an interracial Mothers Club, but we didn't recognize it in those days like I would now, or could appreciate it like I could now.

. . . This sheriff became very frightened when he found out that the thing [mothers organizing] was rolling. Then he subpoenaed a lot of women to come to his office and held court. . . .

The women went to his office but said nothing.

And when we told the District Attorney what had happened . . . he didn't know what had been going on. But at any rate, he called real court then with authority. . . . And it ended up with this sheriff having to go and nail up the building himself. . . .

Document 128
Curriculum at Prairie View
[*Prairie View State Normal and Industrial College Catalogue 1899–1900*, pp. 33–35]

FEMALE INDUSTRIAL DEPARTMENT.

Harriett F. Kimbro, Preceptress and Instructor in Sewing.
    Leonora Avay, Assistant Preceptress and Instructor in Cooking.

SEWING ROOM.

The department is in charge of a special teacher, who instructs the girls in different kinds of sewing, both by hand and on machines; in drafting, cutting, basting, and fitting, in garment and dressmaking, laundry and general housework.

A large room is well fitted up for this important department, and furnished with different styles of sewing machines, tables, forms, patterns, charts, and other necessaries, to afford an excellent opportunity to learn domestic economy. Text-books are used in every branch of this department. Nursing and hygiene are taught theoretically and practically in the care of the sick. The especial aim of this department is to properly qualify the students for the duties and responsibilities of home and social life, as well as for those of the school room. We desire them to render useful service to the people by introducing better and healthier ways of living, and more rational methods of caring for the sick wherever they may live and work.

N.B.—Every young lady must bring with her to the school a pair of rubber overshoes and a waterproof cloak.

FIRST YEAR—FIRST TERM [Also SECOND AND THIRD TERMS]

Turning, folding, basting, hemming, overcasting, backstitching, proper wearing and use of thimble in connection with needle, right length of thread, threading needles and making knots, holding of work by left hand, position of work and needle taught in connection with stitch given; also, beginning, joining, and fastening of threads; hems, narrow and wide.

SECOND YEAR—FIRST TERM. [Also SECOND AND THIRD TERMS]

Review previous year's work; overhanding on folded edges; overhanding on selvages; wide hems; fell, darning, running; drill given in cleaning needles; position of the fingers in making stitches; also, teaching the pupils to use the side of the thimble.

THIRD YEAR—FIRST TERM [Also SECOND AND THIRD TERMS]

Review previous year's work; gathering, laying or stroking gathers, putting gathers into bands by backstitching and hemming; French fell, straight fell; reversible seam; darning, patching, button holes commenced; four-hole buttons sewed on; feather and herring-bone stitches.

FOURTH YEAR.

Review button holes and sewing on buttons; putting in gussetts; darning tear with ravelings; patching on calico and woolen goods; stocking darning; cutting bias bands, and joining same; tucking and suffing. Some garments to be made. Instruction given in the combing of stitches, and in cutting and putting together the parts of the garment.

DEPARTMENT OF MUSIC.
M. J. Isabelle.
FIRST YEAR.

Beyer's pianoforte course. Books 1 and 2. Major scales in one and two octaves. Finger and wrist exercises. Catechism.

SECOND YEAR.

Kohler, op. 162. Duvernoy, op. 176.—Schumann, Album for the Young. Major and minor scales in two and three octaves. Finger and Wrist exercises. Catechism.

THIRD YEAR.

Courney, op. 139. Clementi, Sonativas, Hellar, op. 47. All major and minor scales, and arpeggios.

[Fourth through eighth years of study included Mendelssohn, Bach, Haydn, Czerny, Mozart, and Chopin.]

Document 129
An Educated Woman
[*The Red Book of Houston: A Compendium of Social, Professional, Religious, Educational and Industrial Interests of Houston's Colored Population* (Houston: Softex Pub., ca. 1915), p. 108]

Burgess, Mrs. Desdemona W.—Wife of G. O. Burgess; is a daughter of Mr. and Mrs. Dennis Bryant. She was born and reared in Grimes County, Texas, near Navasota, where she attended the public schools. In a competitive examination she won a scholarship in Prairie View where she graduated with the class of 1903. She also attended one term at Bishop College. She has been an active teacher in the State before and after her marriage. She is now editress of the Independent Record, a newspaper published weekly in the interest of Independence Heights. She has been a consistent Christian for a number of years and now holds membership in Trinity M.E. Church. She is an active member of the Order of Eastern Star and holds the friendship of her sisters and neighbors. In her public career she has never ceased to be a careful housekeeper and devoted wife.

Document 130
"Conduct becoming ladies is insisted upon"
[*Prairie View State Normal and Industrial School Catalog for the Year 1906–1907*, p. 29]

We strive to use such discipline as will develop a *high type of womanhood*. Girls are encouraged to do right from *principle*. They are placed on their honor, and *conduct becoming ladies is insisted upon*.

The Preceptress lives with the female pupils and is present to advise and direct them.

Since we believe a knowledge of the details of household economy is essential to the education of every woman, each female pupil is required to spend some time every day in caring for the dormitories.

What to bring.—Two blankets or quilts; three sheets, each two and three-fourths or three yards long; three pillow cases; one white bed spread; four towels; four table napkins; two yards unbleached domestic for clothes bag; one pair rubber overshoes; one mackintosh rain cloak; one umbrella.

Document 131
Scientific Cooking
[*Prairie View Catalog 1906–1907*, pp. 24–26]

DEPARTMENT OF COOKING
Mabel A. Bohannon.

Cooking is the art of preparing food for the nourishment of the human body. Within the past few years much interest has been taken in this branch of Domestic Science. The rapid and marked improvement in cooking utensils, valuable research along the line of food economy, the establishment by the government of food experimental stations and the introduction of cooking into the public schools, even in universities, have all helped to bring the matter before the public so that scientific cooking is no longer a mere fad but a demand of the present age.

Course I. *First Year Class*, 3 hours a week.
Fall Term.—1. Simple Meats and Vegetable Dishes. Making pies. Measurements.
2. Fuels. Range. Chimney. Canning and Preserving.
3. Making Soups. Yeast. Plain Breads.
Winter Term.—1. Study of Beef, Mutton, Pork and Venison, with diagrams of cuts.
2. Study of Milk, Butter, Cheese and Fish.
3. Study of Fowls, Eggs, and internal organs of the animals used for food.
4. Plain Confections: Cakes, Pastry.
Spring Term.—1. Composition of the human body.
2. Mineral matter. Impure water and foreign matter.
3. Food principles. Practical lessons on preparing fish, eggs, meat and fruit.
4. Adaptation of food to climate, occupation, etc.
Course II. *Second Year Class*, 4½ hours a week.
Fall Term.—1. Study of Desserts, Extracts and Baking Powders.

2. Way in which food supplies the wants of the body.

3. Nutrition, Absorption and Digestion.

4. Making Jellies, Pickles, Marmalades, etc.

Winter Term.—1. Composition of food. Practical lessons in fancy confections.

2. Study of preservation of food condiments.

3. Practical lessons in rolls, fancy desserts, cakes, etc.

4. Study of fungus plants and other vegetables.

Spring Term.—1. Jellies, Salads, Puff Pastry, Practical lessons in Salads, dishes with gelatine fruit, etc.

2. Dietaries. Fermentation. Invalid cooking.

3. Review of work in study of food composition.

4. Plain creams and sherbets.

Course III.—*Third Year Class*, 6 hours a week.

Fall Term.—1. French terms and cooking. Symbols and chemical terms.

2. Fancy fruits and desserts.

3. Study of obaginous seeds, farinaceous and saccharine preparations.

4. Care of cooking utensils. Setting tables.

Winter Term.—1. Pastry cooking. Special work in Breads. Pastry, Cakes.

2. Study of alcoholic beverages and non-alcoholic beverages.

3. Review of work of department.

4. Selection, care and arrangement of kitchen furniture.

Spring Term.—1. Special work in breads, pastry and cakes.

2. Complete Inventory.

3. Care of Dining Room.

Course IV. *Senior Class*, 6 hours a week.

Fall Term.—1. Study of Menus. The usual and average American dinner consists of:

	Dinner.	
Soup.		Celery.
	Roast.	
Potatoes.		Tomatoes.
	Salad.	
Crackers.		Cheese.
	Dessert.	
	Coffee.	

This should be served in five courses. Attention must be given to the following points:

1. The care of the dining room before dinner.

2. The setting of the table, side table and side board.

3. Preparation of relishes, bread, water, etc.

4. Serving the meats.

Winter and Spring Terms.—Etiquette of serving and carving. An essay of not less than 800 words. All books submitted neatly copied. Correct all first year students' books and paper. Prepare meals and serve to board.

Document 132

Personnel of Prairie View

[*The Red Book of Houston: A Compendium of Social, Professional, Religious, Educational and Industrial Interests of Houston's Colored Population* (Houston: Softex Pub., ca. 1915), pp. 180–183 (excerpts)]

Twelve of the total thirty-seven faculty and staff listed are women, a number of whom received their education in the North.

Cox, Miss Ruth E.—Born in Mexia, Texas. Graduate of the Literary and Industrial Department, Sewing and Millinery Department, Prairie View Normal 1909. Teacher in the Domestic Art Department, Prairie View. Taught one year in the public schools of Freestone County, Texas. Member of the A.M.E. Church.

Crawford, Mrs. N. R.—Teacher in Prairie View Normal. Born in Houston in 1865. Graduate Prairie View in 1908. Owns city and farm property. Member of the Trinity M. E. Church, Houston. Member Eastern Star and A. O. O. P. Teacher of Science Prairie View, and teacher 10 years in Houston public schools.

Evans, Miss Annie L.—Teacher and Dean of Women's Department, Prairie View. Associate Professor and Head Preceptress. Member of the Methodist Church, U. B. F. and King's Daughters. Student of Oberlin College and University of Chicago.

Fulton, Miss Katie V.—Teacher. Born Fayetteville, Tenn. Graduate of Domestic Arts, Prairie View. Past three years teacher of Domestic Art, Prairie View. Three years Supervisoress of the Jean Fund in Lee County, Texas, with the best record of any teacher. Took summer course in Industrial Arts. Member A. M. E. Church. Home, Belton, Texas.

Hancock, Mrs. S. E.—Teacher, Prairie View. Born at Austin, Texas. Student of Oberlin College. City property in Austin. Member of Congregational Church, A. M. W. and F. I. H. Head matron three years Domestic Science.

Howard, C. Gertrude—Born in St. Paul, Minn. Took course in the University of Minnesota and the College of Agriculture. Taught one year at Tuskegee Institute and for the past two years in the Domestic Science Department, Prairie View Normal and Industrial College.

McCall, Mrs. Saphronia—Head Nurse, Prairie View Hospital past three years. Born 1877. Native Texan. Graduate of the Provident Hospital, Chicago, Ill., 1911. Owns home. Member of the M. E. Church.

McGee, Mrs. Ethel—Widow. Born at Wilberforce, Ohio. Educated in the Wilberforce University. Graduate in Domestic Art and Domestic Science. For past two years teacher in Domestic Science Department, Prairie View Normal. Member of the A. M. E. Church.

Moxley, Miss Martha C.—Teacher, Prairie View. Born at Corsicana, Texas. Graduate of Prairie View in 1914. Member Missionary Baptist Church. For past year assistant music teacher.

Patterson, Miss W. B.—Teacher, Prairie View. Born at Calvert, Texas. Graduate of Washington Normal and Washington College of Music in 1909. Member M. E. Church. Music teacher and directress of Prairie View chorus.

Robinson, Miss O. A.—Born in Jackson County, Texas. Educated in the public schools of Victoria, Texas, and graduate of Mary Allen Seminary. Taught in Mary Allen Seminary and rural schools for 12 years. Teacher in the English Department, Prairie View, for the past three years. Member of the M. E. Church and Farmers' Improvement Society. Owns home.

Simms, Miss M. J.—Teacher, Prairie View. Born in Austin. Graduate of Prairie View in 1890. Property consists of nice home. Member of Missionary Baptist Church. Member of U. B. F., S. M. T., Young Women's Christian Association; Assistant Preceptress Young Women's Christian Association.

Document 133
National Recognition
[A. W. Jackson, *A Sure Foundation: A Sketch of Negro Life in Texas* (Houston: Yates Publishing Co., 1940), pp. 162–163]

Mrs. Fannie A. Robinson, who served as secretary of the Colored Teachers' Association of Texas from 1918 to 1926, has had a varied and distinguished career in the educational field. She is a native of Hempstead, where she received her elementary training; also at Hearne Academy. She taught at Hearne and Palestine, being head of the English department of Lincoln High School at the latter city. She holds a bachelor of science degree from Prairie View State College and has done post-graduate work at the University of Colorado. . . .

At the 1920 Baltimore session of the National Association of Teachers in Colored Schools, Mrs. Robinson served as a member of the finance committee; also in 1921 at Oklahoma City. In 1922, she was elected assistant secretary of the national organization in Hampton, Virginia. . . .

Becoming a member of the Colored Teachers' Association of Texas in 1910 in Galveston, Mrs. Robinson has been identified with the organization ever since, giving eight years of gratis and unselfish service and playing no small part in formulating and executing the associational program during the period. . . .

Document 134
Mary Allen Seminary

[*Fortieth Annual Catalogue: 1927–1928, Mary Allen Seminary, Crockett, Texas* (n.p.: n.d.), pp. 8, 23–27]

Mary Allen Seminary was founded in 1886 for the education of black girls and young women. Students came from all over Texas and Oklahoma. Classes were offered for grammar school, high school, and college.

REQUIREMENTS FOR GRADUATION

Students who complete ninety-five (95) Quarter hours of work will receive the degree of "Associate in Arts" or Science. Candidates for graduation are required to complete the following courses of study:

English—25 Quarter hours
Education—20 Quarter hours
History—10 Quarter hours
Science—15 Quarter hours
Mathematics—5 Quarter hours
Religious Education—3 Quarter hours . . .

A WORD TO PARENTS

Please do not visit your daughter more than once during the year and then only for one day, unless she is sick, for just as long as you are here her mind is not on her school work. Only Parents, and kin folks can visit. Girls are not allowed to leave the campus except in company with a teacher or with parents. They may write four letters each week, but these must be to home folks. All mail inspected before leaving. . . .

Each girl should bring with her, for her own use, a comb, hair brush, needles, pins, clothes pins, a desk dictionary, a Bible, 3 sheets for her own bed, 3 table napkins, 3 pillow cases, 3 towels, 1 bed comfort, a water proof coat and rubber overshoes. Every article should be plainly marked with the owner's name. Also bring small mirror and drinking cup. Every girl should have at least 3 pairs of broadheeled shoes.

Have your girl's teeth and eyes examined before she comes.

It is very important that girls be here for the first day and that they remain until the last day of the term. Students who come in a month or so after school opens and who leave a month or so before the close cannot be expected to retain their class standing.

Girls do not go home for Christmas, as we have no vacation. . . .

REGISTER OF STUDENTS 1927–1928

College

[Excerpts]

Sophomore

Artie Mae Fleeks	Crockett
Lois Mae Hankins	Camden, Ark.
Ellen Frances Lincoln	Tyler
Corrine Reba Lindsey	Lovelady
Maggie Lee Smith	Crockett
Vergie Beatrice Wade	Bland Lake
Charles B. Wallis, Jr.	Camden, Ark.
Eva Beatrice Woods	Crockett

HIGH SCHOOL
Second Year

Juanita Alexander	Texarkana, Ark.
Elizabeth Byrd	Madisonville
Eva Cornelius Brown	Tyler
Cecile G. Crawford	Huntsville
Minnie Dansby	Kilgore
Roberta Davis	Brookshire
Dorothy Dupree	Alto
Otis Etta Denby	Houston
Ruby Flewellen	Brenham
Mae Etta Garrett	Trinidad, Colo.
Gertrude Graves	Independence
Laura Adine Mable	Washington
Alberta Perry	Crockett
Kate Agnes Patterson	Voth
Ruth Roberts	San Augustine
Mattie Mae Robinson	El Reno, Okla.
Helen Wiley	Galveston

. . .

ALUMNAE MARY ALLEN SEMINARY

[Excerpts]
Name—Married Name   Address
*Deceased

1891

*Lucinda Bates—King
*Mary Bryant—Alexander
*Addie Biggs   Tyler
Susie Cowan—Fields   Cotton Plant, Ark.
Katie Neal—Evans   Clay Station
*Laberta Warren—Sparks

1893

Minnie Dansby—Hamilton   Rt. 6, Kilgore
Annis Taylor—Johnson   Midway
Juanita Woodward—Clark   Houston
Susie Wofford—Pirtle   Muskogee, Okla.

1894

Fannie J. Clark—Cox   Memphis
Lola M. Douglas   Tyler
Clara Jackson—Brown   Austin
Clara Hemphill—Benton   Carthage
Georgia Rhome—Mitchell   Los Angeles, Cal.
*Huldah Ryan
Louise Schermack—Moore   La Grange
Maudesta Shaw—Barnes   Dallas
Mattie Shotwell—Dickens
*Hattie L. Sledge—Morgan
Alice B. Williams   Cuero

Document 135
A Teacher in the Family
[Dorothy Redus Robinson, *The Bell Rings at Four: A Black Teacher's Chronicle of Change* (Austin: Madrona Press, 1978), pp. 3–7]

Dorothy Redus Robinson began teaching in a segregated one-room school in the South Texas town of Markham in 1928. She later moved to Anderson County, where she spent the next forty years as an elementary teacher, homemaking

Dorothy Redus Robinson, the first teacher on either side of her family, is pictured during the 1929–1930 school year, shortly after she began her career in Hallettsville. "I was a precious symbol," she recalled. "Through me the family were pushing their boundaries farther from the field work and domestic chores, which to my parent's generation still held deep connotations of slavery." Robinson described her teaching experiences over forty-seven years in her autobiography, *The Bell Rings at Four: A Black Teacher's Chronicle of Change.* (Courtesy Dorothy Redus Robinson; quotation from *The Bell Rings at Four,* p. 3)

Members of the Pine Hill PTA in East Texas are pictured after taking a break from clearing stumps from the school campus ca. 1934–1935. In the days of segregation, schools for African American youth received few services from local school boards. Frustrated by the numerous stumps on the school's campus, Dorothy Redus Robinson and the parents established Campus Improvement Days. Robinson recalled, "The men appeared early with spades, axes, hoes, scoops, scrapers, and mule teams. The housewives appeared later with box lunches . . ." (Courtesy Dorothy Redus Robinson; quotation from *The Bell Rings at Four,* p. 129)

teacher, coordinator and teacher of special education, and principal. In 1969, she
was appointed by the governor to the Advisory Council for Technical-Vocational
Education. In this reminiscence, she recalls her first days as a teacher.

School would begin on Monday, October 3, [1928,] but the independence
of my professional life was born on this particular morning when papa
placed the train ticket in my hand at the San Antonio and Aransas Pass
depot, told me that my trunk was checked to Hallettsville, Texas, and assured me that Uncle Benja and Aunt Baby would surely meet me there. To
say goodbye, we shook hands. To have kissed in public would have
embarrassed papa.

On the train I gave some thought as to how I would approach my work.
Yes, I had had a year's study at Prairie View College, and my courses had
included psychology; but as I recall now, I, in planning my year's work,
relied more on what I had seen my elementary teachers do than on what
I had learned at Prairie View. This in no way indicates the quality of instruction at Prairie View; rather, it bespeaks my lack of background to accept meaningfully the offerings of the college.

. . . I was the first teacher from either side of the family. I was a precious
symbol. Through me the families were pushing their boundaries farther
from the field work and domestic chores, which to my parent's generation
still held deep connotations of slavery.

. . . I was to live with Uncle Benja and Aunt Baby without paying any
room or board. This was a blessing of inconceivable magnitude, since my
salary was to be $52.50 per month for the school term of four and one-
half months. . . . [Their] farm . . . was located about half a mile from the
one-room schoolhouse that had been built around the turn of the century
with funds collected by local blacks among themselves and dedicated to
"school and church purposes." . . .

Lacking both in architectural beauty and utilitarian aspects, the small
building, about twenty by thirty feet, stood in stark ugliness in one corner
of a cemetery bordered on two sides by dark, thick woods. . . . The schoolhouse had never been touched by a paint brush. The wooden walls had
never been planed. To touch the surface with the hand or any other part
of the body was to risk picking up a painful splinter. The seats—there were
no desks—were long enough to accommodate five or six pupils and were
built of the same rough lumber used for the walls. Continued use by rest-
less bottoms had proved to be an effective planing device, and the danger
of splinters was reduced to near zero. Four small windows were the only
source of light.

In the back of the single-room building was a raised platform and a crude lectern, which itinerant ministers used as their pulpit. The school children used a shelf in this structure to store their lunch pails. . . .

There was no playground equipment, no plantings to enhance the landscape, and only one ramshackle outdoor surface toilet. There was not even a source of water supply. There was a rusty wood-burning heater but no wood.

. . . parents responded to my call and took turns bringing loads of firewood, and the children took turns bringing drinking water from home.

My enrollment totaled nineteen. Few of my charges referred to me as "Miss Redus." "Cousin Dorithy" (long *i*) was the more frequent title. Indeed, I was related to many of them. . . .

With available textbooks, pictures, discarded magazines, nuts, sticks, grains of corn, and creative games, the children were taught. . . .

The fact that my school term was short was a blessing in one respect. It enabled me to return to Prairie View for the third quarter, which began in March.

For the most part, the $236.25 that represented the total of my first year's earnings, was spent as it was collected. Monthly I sent money to my oldest brother who was attending Prairie View. I had assembled a meager personal wardrobe suitable for both the spring quarter and the summer session, which I also planned to attend. I had given Uncle Benja $7.50 to help pay his taxes and I had, of course, bought Christmas presents for papa, mama, and other members of the family.

So upon the closing of school, I borrowed some ninety dollars from the First State Bank in Yoakum, Texas to help finance my second venture at Prairie View. . . . I again became a coed.

Document 136
"She is also a great teacher"
[Dorothy Redus Robinson, *The Bell Rings at Four: A Black Teacher's Chronicle of Change* (Austin: Madrona Press, 1978), frontispiece]

The following note was written in 1974 by second-grade student Tracy Sumrall as a tribute to Dorothy Robinson, who was retiring.

Well I think Mrs. Dorothy R. Robinson is about the best woman there is. She is also a great teacher, if I do say so myself. She works very hard. She has two jobs and she is very good at both. I love her very much. The End.

Document 137
Exceeding Expectations
[B. Ann Rodgers, "African-American Seminole Women: Leadership in Isolation," unpublished paper presented at Texas State Historical Association Annual Meeting, Austin, March 5, 1994, pp. 7–8]

A group of African-American Seminoles settled in Brackettville shortly after 1914 when their band of Scouts lost the protection of the military at Fort Clark. After they moved to the village, women—and Rebecca July-Wilson in particular—rose to positions of leadership. July-Wilson founded the Mothers Club and owned and operated a restaurant. Her daughters, Dorothy and Charles, attended high school in Giddings and Elgin and earned degrees in education in Austin. Charles Wilson related this anecdote in an interview with the author.

The day [ca. 1916] the state inspector came stands out very clearly in Charles Wilson's mind. By this time Charles Wilson was principal of Carver. She had to drop everything she was doing to spend the day being driven from house to house while the inspector tried diligently to prove that she had "padded the [attendance] records." . . . But Wilson knew that [such] subterfuge at Carver was hardly necessary since she and Dorothy Wilson had managed with Herculean efforts to get most of the Brackettville Seminole community to send their children to school on a regular basis. The good attendance at Carver was what caused the problem—the attendance was "too good" for a black school according to the state inspector. But as the day wore on, it became very apparent that the records were impeccably legitimate. At that point the inspector drove to the white campus in a huff. The superintendent, Marion Wills, was outside and saw Charles Wilson in the state inspector's car and asked her what she was doing. "Oh, just going for a ride," she responded. There was no question that Wills did not know who the inspector was and why he was in town, yet he just smiled at Wilson and wandered off across campus, never questioning her rather flippant answer nor bothering to acknowledge the state inspector's existence. The scene was not lost on the state inspector who "softened a bit . . ." at what clearly amounted to a vote of confidence by the superintendent in Wilson. "I wouldn't say he apologized," but Wilson remembered that he also never came back.

Dr. Dorcas D. Bowles was inaugurated as dean of the School of Social Work at the University of Texas at Arlington on January 3, 1993. She was interim president of Atlanta University from 1987 to 1988, a professor of social work there from 1986 to 1987 and Acting Dean and Professor of Social Work at Smith College from 1972 to 1986. (Courtesy Dorcas D. Bowles)

Dr. Barbara W. White is the first African-American dean at the University of Texas at Austin, appointed in 1993 to head the School of Social Work. From 1990 to 1992, she was Associate Dean of the School of Social Work, Florida State University. She was president of the 140,000-member National Association of Social Workers from 1991 to 1993, and the editor of *Color in a White Society*. (Photo by Deborah Cannon)

Dr. Carol D. Surles was installed as president of Texas Woman's University in 1994 by Dr. Jayne Lipe (left) and Dr. Don Reynola (right). She is the first African American woman and third woman to serve as chief executive officer at the nation's largest university primarily for women. TWU's enrollment is about 10,000. Surles was formerly vice president for administration and business affairs at California State University-Hayward. She said, "People don't really care what you know until they know that you care." (Office of Public Information, Texas Woman's University, Denton)

Ada C. Anderson of Austin, left, and Dr. Ruth Simmons of Houston, right, are pictured at the Lyndon Baines Johnson Library and Museum in Austin on March 11, 1995, at the "Women Who Did, A Celebration of Achievement" awards ceremony and book signing for Ruthe Winegarten's *Black Texas Women: 150 Years of Trial and Triumph.* Anderson is a certified real estate broker and an investment consultant. She was a trustee of the Austin Community College  from 1972 to 1976. In 1989, she founded LEAP (Leadership Educational Arts Program) under the auspices of the Austin Lyric Opera to provide cultural enrichment opportunities for black youth. Simmons assumed the presidency of Smith College in 1995, the first black woman to head one of the elite Seven Sisters schools and the first to head a top-ranked college or university. She is a native of Grapeland, Texas, one of twelve children in a sharecropping family which moved to Houston when she was seven. She was formerly vice provost of Princeton University and provost of Spelman College. She is a graduate of Dillard University, and received a master's degree and a doctorate in romance languages from Harvard University. (Photo by Sharon Kahn)

Document 138

UT Students Face Integration

[Linda Lewis, "Young, Gifted and Black," in Daryl Janes, ed., *No Apologies: Texas Radicals Celebrate the '60s* (Austin: Eakin Press, 1992), pp. 65–66]

Linda Lewis attended the University of Texas in the early days of integration—the 1960s.

[In 1967–1968] I lived in a "fully integrated" women's dormitory financed by the Methodist women of Texas—so the brochure said. The reality of the living arrangements placed six Black coeds in a facility housing 200-plus young women. Not surprisingly, we were assigned as three sets of room-mates on each dorm floor. Clearly, part of the unofficial job description was for the six of us to represent an unknown class and gender in a labo-ratory setting—coed dormitory living. After our first month of integrated living, my roommate and I were doubly exhausted: the routine demands and pressures of freshman activities were evident, and we had been con-stantly barraged with questions about any and every detail of our lives and our thoughts.

In the bathroom: "How do ya'll get your hair to do like that?" In the dining room: "Do you eat this kind of food?" . . . So at eighteen, I and my peers cautiously began the life-long nuisance activity of quoted Black per-sons. Many late nights ended with several white friends in our room dis-cussing everyday racial differences. It was truly a living, learning experi-ence for all of us. But my roommate and I grew weary of what we termed "dumb white folks' questions." This integration mission business meant we had responsibilities beyond good academic performance.

. . . We suffered from the fish-bowl syndrome: every little thing a Black did was noticed. It was during my freshman year at UT that I became more appreciative of many things in my own culture that were absent on cam-pus. At least monthly, someone would declare the need for a sanity break, which entailed time out with only Black people. It may have required only going across town to HT's [Huston-Tillotson's] campus to learn the latest dances or a weekend trip to home and family.

. . . For instance, many joined one of the national Black sororities on campus. The one I selected, AKA, had some notoriety because of the Bar-bara Smith [Conrad] Incident. Barbara Smith was a UT music major who gained national media attention because she was denied the lead in a cam-pus opera production opposite a white male. When reporters came to campus to interview her, all AKAs and most Black coeds claimed to be Barbara Smith. Although Barbara had left UT for New York by the time I came to school, the knowledge that I was asked to join a social organiza-tion that had already made a material impact on campus life was thrilling. Personally, it was a joy to belong to an all-Black, all women's organization. Ultimately, only my sisters could really understand the constant battles to maintain respect and a clear sense of self-worth in this unique situation. Somehow we knew that as women we would be forever different from most women—because this was possibly one of the first times in Texas that daughters of former slaves lived, shared, and competed with the daughters of former slaveowners.

5

THE ARTS

The state's black female artists—poets, musicians, painters, writers, dancers, and actresses—have enriched the lives of their communities and the nation. They have given voice to the experiences and aspirations of generation after generation. Both a sampling of the art and reminiscences of these women's lives are included here.

Document 139
"Ethiopia Speaks"
[Bernice Love Wiggins, *Tuneful Tales* (El Paso: by the author, 1925), pp. 38–39]

Austin-born Bernice Love Wiggins published her collected poems in 1925. She spent her first forty years in Austin and El Paso before moving to California, where her trail becomes lost.

Lynched!
Somewhere in the South, the "Land of the Free,"
To a very strong branch of a dogwood tree.
Lynched! One of my sons,—
When the flag was in danger they answered the call
I gave them black sons, ah! yes, gave them all
When you came to me.

You called them the sons of a downtrodden race,
The Negro you said, in his place must stay,
To be seen in your midst is deemed a disgrace,
I remembered, oh yes, still I gave them that day
Your flag to defend.

The orchestra of the New Hope Baptist Church in Waco, pictured here ca. 1900, performed for both church and social functions. (Photo courtesy Irene C. Cobb and the Texas Collection, Baylor University, Waco; print from University of Texas Institute of Texan Cultures)

And knew when I sent them to your fields of battle,
To suffer, to bleed, to be hewn down like cattle,
Not to them be the plaudit, should victory they win,
History scarcely records it,—too dark was their skin,
'Twas truth I spoke in.

    My sons:
How it grieves me for I taught them, 'tis true
That this was their country and for her to die,
Was none less than loyal, the right thing to do,
Brave and loyal, they proved and now they ask why
Their country ill treats them, because they are black,
Must I take it back?

Why not take it back?
Until in the South, the "Land of the Free,"
They stop hanging my sons to the branch of a tree,
Take it back till they cease to burn them alive,
Take it back till the white man shall cease to deprive

My sons, yea, my black sons, of rights justly won,
   'Til tortures are done?

Mary wept for her tortured son, in days of yore,
Ethiopia weeps for her sons, tortured more,
Mary forgave, 'twas her Savior son's will,
Ethiopia forgives, but remembers still,
And cries unto God with uplifted hands,
"Innocent bloods bathe the lands."

Lynched!
Somewhere in the South, the "Land of the Free,"
To a very high branch of a very strong tree,
Lynched! One of my sons,—
When the flag dropped so lowly they headed the call,
I gave them, my black sons, Ah, yes, gave them all,
When you came to me.

Document 140
"Women's Rights"
[Bernice Love Wiggins, *Tuneful Tales* (El Paso: by the author, 1925), pp. 56–57]

I jus' don't 'prove ob wimmen
   Runnin' 'round fum place to place,
A talkin' 'bout dey want dey rights
   Hits jus' a plum disgrace,
Dey mos' all got mo' rights right now
   Den dey can carry straight;
Hits awful how de wimmen folks
   Is carrin' on ob late.
Deys trying to pile mo' on dey backs
   Den what deys gw'ine to tote
Ain't dey got 'nough 'sponsebilities!!
   How cum dey wan'na vote?

T'ree thousand years now, mo' or less,
   de men's been doin' fine,
A runnin' all de politicks,
   An' t'ings along dat line.
Dey'd better let 'em keep hit up
   Lord nos hits fo' de bes',
When wimmen starts to runnin' t'ings,
   Dey mos'tly starts a mess.

Take Adam fo' example,—he
  Was doin' fin' alon'
Den up stemps him a 'oman
  An' he was made to moan.

I reckin' I'se ol' fashin, but
  Deres mo' den me will say
A 'oman's place is in de home,
  An' dere she ought to stay.
In dis wurld dere mus' be chillun,—
  If de wimmen lac' de men,
Gw'ine hang erround de ballot box,
  Who's gw'ine to raise 'em den?
Hit jus' simply wasn't 'tended,
  Take de beasties ob de wood,
de she beast min' de younguns an'
  de he beast bring de food.

Day say dat wimmens gw'ine to rule
  Dis entire wurld sum'day,
I truly hope dat time won't cum.
  'Till I'se been laid away.
No, 'oman don't no what she want
  She change jus' lac' de win'
An' if she gits to be full boss
  What will dis wurld be den?
I'se sick ob all dis talk about,
  de rights whut wimmen want,
I speck dey'll git 'em do' because
  Hits seldom dat dey don't.

Document 141
"The Poetical Farmwife"
[Bernice Love Wiggins, *Tuneful Tales* (El Paso: by the author, 1925), p. 55]

In Bernice Love Wiggins's poem "The Poetical Farmwife," she explains why it is difficult to write while doing housework.

I think about all those sweet nothings
  I read, that the magazines buy,
I know I can write some that's better
  And so I sit down just to try.

I hear Billy call from the barnyard,
    "Ma! One of them hens got away,"
You can't mix up love lays and chickens,
    They don't go together, no, nay.

I've wandered away down the hillside,
    Carrying my book and my pen,
And there I would write just like lightning,
    To get all the pretty thoughts in.
The thoughts get all mixed up with turnips
    That Billy wants for dinner today,
You can't mix the cook pots and poetry,
    They don't go together, no, nay.

One day Billy came from the dairy,
    I said with my prettiest smile,
"Now, Billy dear, please don't disturb me,
    I really must write for a while."
"Come skim this milk, Janey," he blustered,
    "I've got to go help with the hay,"
You can't mix the sonnets with churning,
    They don't go together, no, nay.

Document 142
"A Plea for Higher Living"
[Josie Briggs Hall, *Hall's Moral and Mental Capsule for the Economic and Domestic Life of the Negro, as a Solution of the Race Problem* (Dallas: Rev. F. S. Jenkins, 1905), p. 88]

Josie Briggs Hall may have been the first black female to publish a book in Texas. Her book includes her own work as well as that of other black Texans and Americans. In the following excerpt, Hall pleads that women of all races be treated with respect.

Let no race respect their women
    More than we respect our own;
Let us learn to honor Virtue,
    Place our women on a throne.
Let us treat the sisters, daughters,
    And the wives of other men,
As we'd have our own be treated;
    Naught would clog our progress then.

Julia K. Gibson Jordan (left) and Charlie Mae Brown Smith (right) are coauthors of *Beauty and the Best, Frederica Chase Dodd: The Story of a Life of Love and Dedication* (Dallas: Dallas Alumnae Chapter, Delta Sigma Theta Sorority, 1985). The holder of a master's degree from North Texas State University, Julia K. Gibson Jordan has had a long career in the field of education. She wrote a weekly newspaper column and is the author of a history of Booker T. Washington High School in Dallas and a history of the Dallas Chapter of the Links, Inc. Charlie Mae Brown Smith, a librarian by profession, has worked with the Zale Library of Bishop College, the Martin Luther King Branch of the Dallas Public Library, and in the Dallas public schools. She received a Master of Library Science degree from Texas Woman's University. She was responsible for the first printed directory of the Beta Delta/ Dallas Alumnae Chapter, Delta Sigma Theta, and was chair of the Dallas Alumnae Chapter History and Archives Committee for the National Convention in 1985. Frederica Chase Dodd was a national Delta Sigma Theta sorority founder and leader. (Courtesy Julia K. Jordan and Charlie Mae Brown Smith)

> May our women e'er endeavor
>   To attain the highest good:
> Strive to be, in real merit,
>   Models of true womanhood.
> Dress, accomplishment, wealth, beauty,
>   Virtue's place can not supply:
> As the woman is, the race is:
>   If she fail us, Hope must die.

Document 143
"To a Dark Girl"
[Gwendolyn Bennett, "To a Dark Girl" (1927), in Erlene Stetson, ed., *Black Sister: Poetry by Black American Women, 1746–1980* (Bloomington: Indiana University Press, 1981), p. 76]

Gwendolyn Bennett was born in Giddings but left the state at a young age. Her Texas girlhood influenced aspects of her writing. The first woman to receive a Guggenheim Fellowship, she played an active role in the Harlem Renaissance of the 1920s as a painter and poet.

I love you for your brownness
And the rounded darkness of your breast,
I love you for the breaking sadness in your voice
And shadows where your wayward eyelids rest.

Something of old forgotten queens
Lurks in the lithe abandon of your walk
And something of the shackled slave
Sobs in the rhythm of your talk.
Oh, little brown girl, born for sorrow's mate,
Keep all you have of queenliness,
Forgetting that you once were slave,
And let your full lips laugh at Fate!

Document 144
"Sonnets"
[Gwendolyn Bennett, "Sonnets" (ca. 1930), in Langston Hughes and Arno Bontemps, eds., *Poetry of the Negro, 1746–1949* (Garden City, N.Y.: Doubleday, 1949), p. 109]

2

Some things are very dear to me—
Such things as flowers bathed by rain
Or patterns traced upon the sea
Or crocuses where snow has lain . . .
The iridescence of a gem,
The moon's cool opalescent light,
Azaleas and the scent of them,
And honeysuckles in the night.
And many sounds are also dear—
Like winds that sing among the trees
Or crickets calling from the weir

Or Negroes humming melodies.
But dearer far than all surmise
Are sudden tear-drops in your eyes.

Document 145
"Life"

[Lily Bell Hall Chase, "Mamshe," typescript, undated, Lily Bell Hall Chase biographical file, Texas Women's History Project Resource Files, Texas Woman's University Library, Denton, courtesy Merchuria Chase Williams]

Lily Bell Hall Chase lived a modest life as mother, wife, and writer. She graduated from Crockett Colored High School as class poet and enjoyed writing verse throughout her life. Although her work was never published, her daughter, Merchuria Williams, preserved it. An excerpt from Chase's diary is also reprinted below (Document 152).

Life is a keyboard
Upon which we press
Black keys of sorrow
White keys of happiness.
But as we learn to play
The entire keyboard through
We learn that the black keys
Hold music too.

Document 146
"Our Own Daughter, Little Ruby Joyce"

[Annie Mae Hunt, in Ruthe Winegarten, ed., *I Am Annie Mae: The Personal Story of a Black Texas Woman* (Austin: Rosegarden Press, 1983), p. 61]

Annie Mae Hunt, a Dallas domestic, seamstress, and saleswoman, wrote the following poem of grief in the 1940s following the death of her daughter.

1.

She were born in to the world
    Those she never open her eyes
But we love her so much
Our own daughter, little Ruby Joyce

2.

Daddy an I will never forget you
    Altho it's so hard to fear

But we will try to meet our darling
    Little Ruby Joyce over there

3.

Dear lord, we want you to help us
    An to stand by us each day
So we'll be able to meet her
    Our own daughter little Ruby Joyce

4.

Mother an Daddy will always love you
    Just long as we live in this world
An in that great judgement morning
    We'll meet our own daughter little Ruby Joyce

Document 147

"Question to a Mob"

[Lauretta Holman Gooden, in J. Mason Brewer, ed., *Heralding Dawn: An Anthology of Verse* (Dallas: by the author, 1936), p. 16]

Lauretta Holman Gooden, born in Sulphur Springs but raised in Texarkana, began writing poetry at about age ten. As an adult, her time was divided between writing and operating a grocery business with her husband in Dallas.

O, cruel mob—destroying crew,
Who gave the life of man to you?
Why have you gathered, small and great,
To murder, more through sport than hate?

Do you not feel the pangs of shame?
When on your heads is placed the blame?
O, cruel mob—unpitying crew,
Who gave the life of man to you?

Has Heaven commanded you to take
Humans and burn them at the stake?
O, cruel mob—think what you do:
Who gave the life of man to you?

O, fiends of earth that God gave breath,
Why do you love the sound of death?
What will you answer in Judgment? Who
Will say, God gave man's life to you?

Document 148
"A Dream of Revenge"
[Lauretta Holman Gooden, in J. Mason Brewer, ed., *Heralding Dawn: An Anthology of Verse* (Dallas: by the author, 1936), p. 16]

Ah! How the wind raves this bitter night,
How the waves roar as they break upon the beach!
Not a star is out.

Rave on, Winds—
Thunder on, Sea.
My heart beats time to the fierce music of your voices:
My heart feels the cold, maddened
Between the deeply suppressed conflicting passions
Of wounded love and outraged pride.

Ah! It suits me—this savage coast and water.
I like the howling chaos of wind and water;
A plan of vengeance comes to my darkened mind.
Yet why should I mourn the loss of love I never possessed?
What devil whispered vengeance to my soul?

The passionate tenderness is gone;
I plucked it from my heart as I would have torn a thorn from my flesh.

Document 149
Remembering Childhood in Galveston
[Maud Cuney Hare, *Norris Wright Cuney: A Tribune of the Black People* (1913; reprint, Austin: Steck-Vaughn, 1968), pp. 79–80]

In the biography of her father, noted musician Maud Cuney Hare wrote about growing up on the Texas Gulf Coast in the 1880s.

The twelfth ward in Galveston, in which we always lived, was in the East End of the city, near the beach. Our house, which was a modest one, was in every sense a home.

My mother was not strong and spent much time out doors with her flowers. There were roses—red, pink and white, and the yellow Marechal Neil; borders of violets, daffodils and jonquils in the spring, and asters and chrysanthemums in the fall, with cape jasmine, well known in Texas, but now rare and precious to me, after years of life in the Northeast.

Back of the house were orange trees, plum and pomegranate, the purple fig and mulberry trees, where we used to read perched upon seats among the branches. Mother cared zealously for her flowers until Easter, when the yard, awakened by the spring, would be stripped and the flowers carried to the hospital.

Our home life was particularly happy. The three married brothers lived within a radius of three blocks. There were seven cousins, and as we were near the same age, we were companionable and always warm friends. We found much pleasure on the beach and in the surf. Father, who enjoyed surf bathing, went often with us.

Christmas and New Years were of course our gayest holidays. There was always a generous Santa Claus, but father gave his personal gifts on the first day of the year. The night before, we always had a family party enlivened by the visits of intimate friends. Father enjoyed reading aloud the poems of the old year, always closing with "Ring out the old, ring in the new." As midnight approached, we would guess the minute and all troop out doors to see the stars shining on the new-old world.

"Open house" was held on New Years Day, with the reception for the grown-ups.

Christmas with the children's party and the candle-lighted tree, always brought us books galore. Our first introduction to New England was through a treasured Christmas book—"A Family Flight Around Home," by Edward Everett Hale and his sister.

Father cared but little for current fiction. He read deeply, preferring early Hebrew, Greek and Roman history. He was fond of the classics, and in poetry, enjoyed Byron, perhaps next to Shakespeare. He often read aloud to us, and we liked to listen, although there were many things which we could not understand.

Document 150
On Being Black
[Ada DeBlanc Simond, "The Discovery of Being Black: A Recollection," *Southwestern Historical Quarterly* 76, no. 4 (April 1973), p. 477, reprinted with permission of the Texas State Historical Association, Austin]

Ada Simond of Austin was a historian of the black experience and author of a series of children's books, Let's Pretend: Mae Dee and Her Family. She worked for the Texas Department of Health for a quarter of a century before "retiring" to several years as a court bailiff and a recorder of local black history. She was living in Port O'Connor when this discussion took place.

Mama rounded up all five of us [ca. 1914] and told us a long story, some of which I don't think I ever heard. But she made us understand that some people are white, some are colored, and that some white people hate colored people. The point that she made sure we understood was that in the sight of God we were exactly like Him in every way except perfection. God is perfect: further that we were all beautiful, good, and smart; and that God loved us more than anyone could ever hate us. She assured us that we were such precious things to her and to Papa that they would never let anything ever happen to us, nor would they ever let anyone harm us. . . . From that day I knew what it was to be different, to be black.

Document 151
Etta Moten on Her Early Musical Career
[Monroe Anderson, "A Singer Recalls Her Career," Chicago *Tribune*, February 5, 1980]

Etta Moten was a stage and screen performer who became famous for her starring Broadway role as Bess in **Porgy** *and* **Bess** *from 1942 to 1945. In later years, she was a popular lecturer on Africa and the African American heritage and represented the Links, Inc., at many international conferences.*

If you were a minister's daughter like I was, then you were in theater. Being born in a church [in Weimar] is almost being born in theater, because there were church theatricals. My mother used to put on plays and I was in them. The choir is a showplace for you, and it's a place where if the bug is going to bite you, it will. And that is where it was for me.

The Associated Negro Press and its members, for a time there were 212 newspapers across the country, were important because the papers had theatrical pages. And through the Associated Negro Press many an artist's career was started and fostered. . . .

The white papers just simply did not write about . . . Negroes, unless they were criminals. Claude [her husband and founder of the Associated Negro Press] told me there was a code, a rule, a silent rule, an understood rule, that there were no pictures of Negroes in the white papers. But the Negro newspapers had large sections on the theater and this was a godsend for many, many big stars of today. It made me, it made my career, and I had a good career.

. . . And then when you were good enough you would get money to go to Europe. If Europe said you were great, you could come back and the American audiences would say you were great.

Document 152
"During my pregnancy"
[Typescript, Lily Bell Hall Chase file, Texas Women's History Project Resource Files, Texas Woman's University Library, Denton]

Etta Moten (Barnett) is pictured as the lead, with Todd Duncan, in the 1953 Broadway production of *Porgy and Bess* at the Ziegfeld Theatre in New York. She found success in New York and Hollywood singing the role of Bess in the George Gershwin musical in the 1940s and '50s. The daughter of an AME preacher from Weimar, Texas, Moten also made two movie musicals, *Flying Down to Rio* with Ginger Rogers and Fred Astaire and *The Gold Diggers of 1933* with Joan Blondell and Dick Powell. In 1946, she had the title role in the Broadway production of *Lysistrata*. Moten became a popular lecturer on Africa and the African-American heritage and has represented the Links, Inc., at numerous international conferences. (Courtesy Theatre Collection, Museum of the City of New York)

Just after World War II, Lily Bell Hall Chase moved from Crockett to Los Angeles, where she awaited the birth of her daughter in December 1946.

First week of June: Still energyless. . . . I pat my stomach and talk baby talk to it. . . .

Second week of June: Coming back to life again (Haven't been nauseated as yet). Do work better, not pepless anymore, but still easily aggravated and upset. . . .

August 5th: Went to Crockett ([son] George Marvin and I) to help Grandmaw and Grandpaw and Aldereen get packed for moving to California. . . . I'm going with them to help them travel. . . .

Wednesday [Aug.] 21st: Arrived fresh as a daisy. . . . Expectant's kicking strong. Mary says aren't you pregn Lillye Belle? I said do you really have to ask? (Couldn't it speak for itself in other words) July and August was good to me. Everything easy now. . . .

December 30th: Mary and I rode the trolly (train) to the clinic in Watts. Oh! brother how the doctor pushed and examined. I'm fed up. He says I want [won't] make it back for another exam. He's right for he pushed the baby out almost, (grins and ugly faces), and I felt so good when I came. Just the same Mary and me skipped, sang and bought fruit and candy bars and come home. Gee, I'm beat though. . . . I didn't stay home and hide when pregnant either time. I dressed beautiful, felt beautiful and went same as before my pregnancies. Deliver me from a tackie ill kept lady, especially a pregnant one. . . . The enchantment of my pregnancies and endearment of caring for the helpless tiny life is a beautiful rewarding experience I thoroughly am grateful and look forward too. . . .

Results: December 31 at 8:48 a.m. a 7 lb. 1 oz. girl was born to the proud parents of Mr. and Mrs. George R. Chase—Merchuria Ann Chase.

Document 153
"My opera . . . began with an overture"
[Barbara Conrad, "Comment," reprinted from *Discovery: Research and Scholarship at the University of Texas at Austin* 12, no. 3 (1992): 2, 3]

While a student at the University of Texas in 1957, Barbara Conrad of Cass County was forced from a leading operatic role. Her casting opposite a blond male student raised political ire in the Texas legislature. Her performances were later acclaimed in London, Vienna, Hamburg, and the Metropolitan Opera in New York.

An opera usually opens with an overture, has one, two or more acts, and concludes with a grand finale.

My opera began at The University of Texas at Austin with an overture entitled "A Dream." What I mainly dreamed about was to be a student in the classic sense of the word—to be part of the student life of the university. I was denied that experience. My overture culminated in a controversy so well publicized that it is known to this day, and my dream became a nightmare that haunted me for years. Yet what was it like in those days for me to sit in the classrooms on the extraordinary campus of The University of Texas and be part of the institution? It meant the opportunity to acquire the kind of education that I had dreamed of all my life, to be exposed to the kind of teachers and facilities that I had only read about in books and heard other people talk about. At The University I found some of the finest teachers and best friends I have had in my life, and I have never forgotten that. . . .

One of the things I learned on The University of Texas campus is that if you have a dream, no one and nothing can stop you or strip it from you. It is an integral part of you; it is in your blood, in every cell. I realize that the fabric of my being is strong indeed, for it has withstood some incredibly intense assaults. But I was meant to be a singer.

Document 154
Studying Music

[Anne Lundy, "Conversation with Ernestine Jessie Covington Dent," *Black Perspective in Music* 12, no. 2 (Fall 1984): 244, 263]

As a teenager in 1915, Jessie Covington Dent played the violin in the Ladies Symphony Orchestra in Houston (organized by her mother), composed of black women and girls. After graduating from Oberlin Music Conservatory and the Juilliard School of Music, she became a concert pianist in the late 1920s.

I was supposed to have been under some kind of pre-natal influence. My mother was taking piano lessons as she was carrying me; Mama was getting me ready for the piano. When I was four years old I began to take my first lessons. And when I was five years old I started taking lessons from Madame Corilla Rochon.

My only piano teacher was Madame Rochon. I studied with her until about the time I went to Oberlin. On the other hand, when the ladies wanted to form this orchestra . . . I find that my mother was instrumental in getting the orchestra started—the women's orchestra. They decided that I should have violin lessons so that I could be a part of the orchestra.

. . . After my first graduation [from Oberlin Music Conservatory] in 1924, I went to New York. In competitive examinations at the Juilliard Musical Foundation, I was fortunate to win four fellowships for a period of four consecutive years, studying two years with Madame Olga Samaroff and two years with Mr. James Friskin. I must say that those four years of my training were filled to the brim with the finest in training class work, private lessons and advanced theory; wonderful contacts through privileges and experiences for hearing and seeing great personalities and performances on the concert and operatic stage and exposure to the finest musical culture—the broadening effects of which could only be reaped with maturity.[1]

Document 155
Alma Gunter, Primitive Artist

[*Remembrances of Two Artists—The Stitchery of Ruby Yount; The Paintings of Alma Gunter*, exhibit program, intro. by Rudolph V. Pharis; Karen Wittliff, exhibit coordinator (Lufkin: Lufkin Historical and Creative Arts Center, 1980), unpaginated; copy at Texas Women's History Project Files, Texas Woman's University Library, Denton]

Alma Gunter of Palestine was a nurse until her retirement in the 1970s. Then she began painting in earnest and became a nationally recognized visual artist.

I paint at any hour, day or night whenever the urge strikes me. I paint what my mind photographed and recorded over all the years of my life. I think in pictures, and that defeats forgetting. . . .

In the following, Gunter comments on her painting Waiting Games.

In cities, where so many people are lonely, there are many waiting games. As depicted here there is the little boy we would call a key child (both of his parents work and the child wears the house key on a chain around his neck), who sits on the step with his dog, ball, bat, and mitt waiting for someone to come along and play ball with him, the salesman across the alley who sits dejected facing another day of "No Sales," his bottle and sample case at his feet, the woman in the window who watches the mail box. The woman in the doorway who waits for whatever the day might bring, and the man with lunch box who waits for his ride to work.

Document 156
"Roar upon roar of applause"
[*Dallas Express*, March 5, 1927, cited in Ruth Ann Stewart, *Portia: The Life of Portia Washington Pittman, the Daughter of Booker T. Washington* (Garden City, N.J.: Doubleday, 1977), pp. 96–97]

In the 1920s, Portia Washington Pittman gave private piano lessons in Dallas, supervised educational programs for the Texas Association of Negro Musicians, and taught music at the high school named for her father, Booker T. Washington. In

1927, she conducted the Booker T. Washington High School choir for the visiting convention of the National Education Association.

600 VOICE HI SCHOOL CHORUS CHARMS
N.E.A. CONVENTION.
CONVENTION HALL PACKED AS STUDENT
CHORUS OF 600 FROM BOOKER WASHINGTON
HIGH SCHOOL, DIRECTED BY DAUGHTER
OF ILLUSTRIOUS EDUCATOR, GIVES THIRTY-
MINUTE PROGRAM OF SPIRITUALS . . .

Not only did roar upon roar of applause from 7,500 pairs of hands greet every number rendered by the 600-voice mass chorus of The Booker Washington High School when it appeared before the National Education Association in the Auditorium of the Fair Grounds on last Tuesday evening, but President Randall J. Condon, Master of Ceremonies for the evening, went into the wings as the program closed and Mrs. Portia Washington Pittman, conductress, left the stage, urged her to return and requested that she lead the whole assembly in singing the old familiar tunes of "Swanee River," "Old Black Joe" and "Carry Me Back to Old Virginia." And never before in the history of the association has there been such harmony produced to the rhythm as beat by the baton of this conductress. They all sang with the chorus; then sat again in utter silence until the last golden echoes of "Couldn't Hear Nobody Pray" had died away, burst again into applause as the students began to move from the stage, and members of the official family rushed to the wings to meet and congratulate Mrs. Pittman. . . . Said Principal Peterson, member of the Executive Committee and head of one of the largest High Schools of Los Angeles, ". . . I have never in my life been so affected by the evident soul of music as I have been here with this chorus. And you can never know just how much this chorus has done to encourage real study of the needs of the Negro. The impression will be a lasting one." . . .

It was a complete success from the moment that Mrs. Pittman was introduced as the daughter of Booker T. Washington, until the last student had left his place on the stage.

Years later, Portia would still flush with pride and happiness in telling of her triumph: "White people in the South had never heard Negro spirituals sung like the way I taught them. Because I had a German training that gave me the artistic part and I added things. For instance, there was a song called 'O Mary Don't You Weep Don't You Moan.' White people had never heard the song before and they put it in the school textbook the following year as a new beautiful Negro spiritual."

Document 157
Ethel Ransom Art and Literary Club, Houston
[Ethel Ransom Club Minutes, 1927–1935, Houston Metropolitan Research Center, Houston Public Library]

Like most women's clubs of the period, the Ethel Ransom Art and Literary Club combined programs of cultural enrichment, such as book reviews and art exhibits, with attention to current events and service to the sick and needy.

Houston, Texas
February 13, 1932

The Ethel Ransom Club met with Ms. Hoggatt on Junes St. on the above date.

Opening hymn Blessed Assurance with Mrs. McKinney at the piano.

The chaplin, Mrs. Carrie Atkinson, then led the 22nd Psalm with all members joining in after which she prayed a prayer that reached the hearts of all present.

Those present were Mrs. C. A. Atkinson, Mrs. V. H. McKinney, Mrs. Kay, Mrs. Hoggatt, and Mrs. Ellison. Mrs. Atkinson paid 10 cts. club dues.

Mrs. Grigsby reported having sent a basket of roses to Mrs. Coleman who has been ill in the Houston Negro Hospital. All expressed a wish for her speedy recovery.

Communications were read from the president of the State Federation of Negro Women's Clubs. She called attention to the petition for Disarmament. Ethel Ransom Club through the president's efforts sent a petition signed by (100) one hundred citizens of Houston.

Attention was called to our paper, "National Notes" [publication of the National Association of Colored Women] and a request made that all members subscribe for same.

Other communications called attention to Negro Author's Week and Club Day the 4th Sunday in April.

By suggestion of Mrs. Ellison the club decided to have flower exchange meeting the same to be held at Mrs. Forde's residence.

The president urged that a trip to the Old Folks' Home on Crosby Road and the T. B. Hospital. Mrs. McKinney made a motion that we visit the T.B. Hospital the 2nd Sunday in March. Mrs. Kay seconded the motion. Carried.

Mrs. Hoggatt took the club in hand and served a wonderful repast that was quite refreshing.

L. H. Grigsby, Pres.

E. C. Ellison, Sec.

Document 158
"Jo's Jottings"

["Jo's Jottings," *San Antonio Register*, June 22, 1934, microfilm at Institute of Texan Cultures, University of Texas at San Antonio]

The cultural life of San Antonio's black community was highlighted for many years by Josephine Bellinger in her regular column "Jo's Jottings" in the **San Antonio Register.** *She and her husband, Valmo Bellinger, were co-publishers of the newspaper from the early 1930s until its sale in the late 1970s. Josephine Bellinger performed many functions at the paper—from writing, rewriting, and layout to photoengraving.*

WELL!

Now that the glorious "JUNETEENTH" is OVER, let's talk about it . . . From all indications it was a BIG day . . . with lots of things goin' on . . . F'rinstance there was the Junior Women's Progressive Club celebration at Central Playground . . . the big FREE barbecue and dance at Leon Park which drew quite a crowd . . . and still ANOTHER dance at Smart Set Auditorium . . . while those preferring the wide open spaces formed merry parties and motored to their favorite fishin' holes and spent the day getting a nice painful sunburn . . . NO, there wasn't much work goin' on . . . Even MY boss BROKE DOWN and gave me the day off . . . So I folded up my little tent and together with the "GANG" went down on the banks of Guadalupe River and spent a DELIGHTFUL . . . LAZY day . . . But for every JOY I 'spose there must be corresponding SORROW . . . MINE came the following morning when I had to do TWO days work . . . SO-OOO you see the boss got his REVENGE after all . . . SUCH IS LIFE!

POSSIBLY one of the PRETTIEST of the very pretty parties of the season was given last week when the chawmin' Missus Nat Winchell entertained on her beautiful lawn complimenting Anna Mae Walker and Mary Byars-Richardson . . . Bridge was the fav'rite game . . . and aside from the very lovely score prizes there were precious gifts for the honorees, who have since departed for New York and Boston, Mass., respectively.

SPECIAL NOTICE TO ALL CLUBS!

The Register staff is making a series of visits to the social, literary and charitable clubs of the city. Please call Cathedral 1721 and leave the name, date, place and time of meeting of your club.

. . . The DELIGHTFUL refreshments were served Buffet style . . . and there was such a varied . . . and bounteous assortment . . . YES'M Mrs. Winchell . . . you REALLY know your parties . . . It's the TALK O' TOWN! O'TOWN.

Speaking of cards . . . I hear that a bunch of the local gals have formed a sorta' POKER CLUB . . . and are playin' for MONEY! . . . Yeah they think they're THAT GOOD . . . But why not? . . . Doesn't the Bible say "As a man THINKETH so IS he? . . . And I guess that goes for WOMEN TOO!

ELNORA HAYES . . . and WILLIAM JAMES JEFFERSON tied the OFFICIAL KNOT last night . . . and decided that TWO could live happier than ONE . . .

THE WEEKS PUSSONALS

Mrs. R. O'Hare Lanier, a very comely young matron of the Bayou City has spent several days in the city visiting friends . . . Mrs. Lanier's hubby heads Houston Junior College and they're both very popular . . . The W. H. Brown's are visiting relatives and friends in Fort Worth . . . Dallas and Texarkana . . . They are accompanied on the trip by their son and daughter, Mr. and Mrs. Willie K. Brown . . . Deepest commiseration to Mr. and Mrs. Aaron Handy who were called to Kansas City Wednesday to kneel at the bier of Mrs. Handy's mother, who passed Wednesday morning . . . Gardenias . . . to lovely Nell Gray Washington for being chosen as representative from the San Antonio Branch N.A.A.C.P. to the National meet at Oklahoma City . . . she leaves Monday night . . . Hope you have a big time Nell . . . and bring us back LOTS OF NEWS! . . .

G'BYE.

Document 159
"Aaronetta Pierce Is . . . a National Treasure"
[Tom Walker, "Champion of Black Art," reprinted from *Images*, the Sunday magazine of the *San Antonio Express-News*, March 6, 1994, pp. 5, 7]

Aaronetta H. Pierce, art patron and civic leader, went from being a San Antonio Art Museum docent to co-creator of the Southwest Ethnic Arts Society, member of the Texas Commission on the Arts and the National Endowment for the Arts, and chair of the 1988 San Antonio Blue Ribbon Committee on the Arts.

What drives Pierce to champion black art in San Antonio? "Actually, I've been involved with every kind of art," she replies. "I've been on every local arts board imaginable. And I've done it not because it's 'chic' or 'cute' or 'fun' but because of what art can do for people, for communities—their quality of life.

Aaronetta Pierce "is a Southwestern wonder, a national treasure, and a knock-out sister friend," says writer Maya Angelou. "Her knowledge and love for the arts, her intelligence and humor beyond measure make her valuable to us all." A member of the Texas Women's Hall of Fame, Pierce is founder of Premier Art-works, Inc., which markets the work of African-American artists. In 1985, she be-came the first black woman appointed to the Texas Commission on the Arts, and in 1987, then-Mayor Henry Cisneros named her first chair of the Martin Luther King Memorial City/County Commission. In 1988, she chaired a committee whose report resulted in the creation of the San Antonio Department of Arts and Cultural Affairs. She also served as a panelist for the National Endowment for the Arts. (Photo by Al Rendon for *Images,* the Sunday magazine of the *San Antonio Express-News,* March 6, 1994, p. 5; quotation from same source)

"But," she adds, "I focus on black art because it's been systematically ignored in America's cultural history. It's less a problem of discrimination than of simple ignorance. People just don't know about black art. That's changing, though."

Pierce is married to Dr. Joseph A. Pierce, Jr., a local anesthesiologist and her partner in Premier Artworks. They are parents to two sons. Joseph Aaron, 24, a 1991 Georgetown University graduate, is an international investment analyst in Chicago. Michael, 21, is a senior marketing major at Morehouse College in Atlanta.

This past year, Pierce chaired the arts committee for the Martin Luther King Commission. As chairman of San Antonio's first King celebration in

1987, she brought here two African-American legends of the civil rights movement: Rosa Parks and the Rev. Joseph E. Lowery. Parks ignited the movement in 1955 by refusing to surrender her seat near the front of a public transit bus in Montgomery, Ala.; Lowery was a fearless president of the Southern Christian Leadership Conference, one of the early vanguards of the movement.

HUD Secretary and former San Antonio Mayor Henry Cisneros says of Pierce's appointment as first chairman of the MLK Commission: "I was searching for someone with broad acceptability, a high degree of professionalism, the ability to organize and work well with people. The person had to be a stickler for detail and be knowledgeable of African-American leadership issues. Luckily for us, we found the perfect person: Aaronetta Pierce."

Says the chairman for the 1994 MLK Celebration, Nancy Bohman: "Aaronetta set a standard of excellence that year. Her successors, me included, have found it hard to live up to.

"If I don't, though," she adds with a chuckle, "it'll be hard to face her again."

In 1986, a member of the San Antonio Museum Association board, Pierce led the first important survey of black art ever shown in San Antonio. Titled, "Hidden Heritage: Afro-American Art, 1800–1950," it brought to the city the great black art curator David Driskell; muralist Elizabeth Catlett, who studied in Mexico with such giants as Diego Rivera; and venerable artist/professor Lois Mailou Jones.

"Aaronetta is tremendously strong," says Institute of Texan Culture Executive Director Rex Ball, who worked with Pierce in bringing to the institute the famed Walter O. Evans black art collection from Detroit. "She knows how to keep her eye on the goal while hurdling a multiplicity of obstacles."

Maya Angelou, the renowned poet who read an original work at the inauguration of President Clinton, calls Pierce a treasure.

"Aaronetta Pierce is a Southwestern wonder, a national treasure, and a knockout sister friend," Angelou says. "Her knowledge and love for the arts, her intelligence and humor beyond measure make her valuable to us all."

Pierce grew up in Nashville and attended Tennessee State University, then predominantly black, where her father was associate dean. In 1963, she earned a bachelor's degree at the University of Iowa, majoring in English and the social sciences.

In Nashville, Pierce says, she was introduced to black culture through programs and lecture series at Tennessee State and nearby Fisk University.

"I'll never forget seeing the great contralto Marian Anderson and U.S. Supreme Court Justice Thurgood Marshall," she says.

Pierce views her corporation, Premier Artworks, as allowing great works of black art to become a part of American history. She markets them with slides, photographs and an extensive file of literature, exhibition catalogs and documentaries. The works include original paintings, drawings, sculpture and limited edition prints.

"The pieces sell for as much as $300,000," she says, "and for as little as $300.

"Most African-American painting continues to be realistic in style," she says. "That's because it's so often visual histories with black subjects. It depicts African-American life and culture. These days, however, I am finding more and more abstract African-American art."

Pierce exhibits black artwork in public fixtures like Cappy's Restaurant on Broadway.

"It's working," she reports. "There are now local collectors, other exhibits, articles being written. The city is responding. It's starting to celebrate its diversity, to build self esteem among its unacclaimed citizens."

She adds that San Antonio now hosts a growing community of black artists—one in which they can survive, be recognized, sell their works and communicate with one another.

"It also creates an environment in which young black people who want to become artists can grow up," she says.

Among the local African-American artists Pierce has exhibited, she cites John Coleman, F. L. "Doc" Spellman, Edward Jackson and Jones Perkiness.

Pierce also is proud to have served as a panelist for the controversial National Endowment for the Arts.

"Art is so important," she says. "As a country, we all need to be proud of our cultural heritage. If we deny the cultural contributions of any of our people, they become alienated, disenchanted, disconnected from our society. We all lose."

Pierce vividly recalls the day she committed herself to championing black art.

"It was in 1980," she recalls, "and I was a docent at the San Antonio Museum of Art. A little black girl gazed up at me in the portrait art gallery and said, 'Mrs. Pierce, there's something wrong here. Why don't I see pictures of black people?'

"There are days when I wake up wishing I'd never heard the child say that. My commitment changed my life. It's been exhausting.

"But," she adds, "I love it."

6

CHURCHES, CLUBS, AND
COMMUNITY BUILDING

Many women have invested themselves in community life through church and club activities. From religious missionary work in the nineteenth century to the contemporary period, they have formed groups to help neighbors; build and support hospitals, orphanages, homes for the aged, and schools; and nurture a spiritual life for their communities. The church was often the training ground which prepared black women for public activities. Many of these church leaders gave life to the black women's club movement and later the civil rights movement.

Document 160
"They appoint Sister Milly to help raise money"
[J. Mason Brewer, *The Word on the Brazos: Negro Preacher Tales from the Brazos Bottoms of Texas* (Austin: University of Texas Press, 1953), p. 68]

Women have figured prominently in the black church, particularly in Protestant denominations. They organized for Bible study, music, missionary work, and community service. The fictionalized Sister Milly of the 1860s typifies the enthusiasm that many women contributed to their volunteer church work.

So when freedom come in a bulge before you could say, "Amen," and they start the Baptist church down to Wild Hoss Slew, they appoint Sister Milly to help raise money to build the church house, so she calls a meeting of the sisters and asks them what can we do to raise some money to help build the church house? She say, "I ain't no woman for dancing; we don't want to do that." Then she say, "I knows what; everybody can get some hens and we'll have a hen barbecue and sell them to the white people down to Calvert."

Dr. Claytie Odessa Searcy is an ordained minister in Dallas. As chair of the Women's Division, she was responsible for raising more than $100,000 to re-locate Bishop College from Marshall to Dallas. She is president and founder of the Searcy Youth Founda-tion, which has sponsored the Child Development Center, a private day care facility. (Courtesy Texas Black Women's Archives, African American Mu-seum, Dallas)

So the sisters pay heed to Sister Milly and they sells a hundred dollars worth of chickens and raises the first hundred dollars on this church down to Wild Hoss Slew, and they calls it to this day "Hicks Chapel" after Sister Milly.

Document 161

Negro Woman's Christian Temperance Union

[*Houston Daily Post*, April 5, 1900]

After the Civil War, alcoholism became a major problem for many Texas families. Thousands of women joined the Woman's Christian Temperance Union, founded in the state in 1882, to eliminate drinking and the sale of alcohol. The WCTU was the state's first female biracial group. Under the leadership of Mrs. Eliza Peterson, a Texarkana music teacher who took office as head of the Thurman (or black) Texas WCTU in 1898, the membership grew rapidly. A popular speaker who attracted large audiences and hundreds of converts, she went on to become national super-intendent of "colored work" for the WCTU.

Mrs. Eliza Peterson, president of the Negro Women's Christian Temperance Union, is in the city and will organize a branch of the WCTU among the colored women of this place at the African M.E. church on Wall Street on Thursday night, April 5. An interesting program will be rendered.

Document 162
College WCTUs
[*Dallas Morning News*, March 6, 1905]

Mrs. [Eliza] Peterson, president of the Texas work among colored people, is very busy organizing college YWCTUs and holding medal contests. She has spoken in seven of the thirteen colleges in Texas and will speak in the others as rapidly as possible. Mrs. Peterson commands the respect of both white and black in her work.

Document 163
Waco WCTU
[*Dallas Morning News*, February 11, 1907]

Mrs. E. E. Peterson, president of the colored (or Thurman) unions of Texas, has recently organized a W.C.T.U. in Waco with seventeen regular and four honorary members. The meeting for organization was so crowded that many had to leave the church. About 200 pledges were signed. Mrs. Peterson has studied the work thoroughly, and as she is an educated Christian woman, her work is well done. When last heard from she was in the country, a few miles from Waco, organizing. Mrs. Peterson lectured in the Second Baptist Church before 400 people and when the opportunity to express themselves on the temperance question came 350 stood up. This was in the midst of a great revival, but the minister thought a rousing gospel temperance meeting would help the revival, which it did. Mrs. Peterson has special hours for prayer and fasting.

Document 164
Organizing WCTUs
[*Dallas Morning News*, February 18, 1907]

The mass meeting held Sunday, Feb. 3, drew a great crowd. The day was cold and rainy, but the colored people are interested in the W.C.T.U. in Waco. One of the Baylor students gave an excellent address. Mrs. Lucy Thurman, National superintendent of colored work, will be in Texas soon. Dates are as follows: Marshall, 15–20; Tyler 21–22; Waco 23–1, Austin 2–8, Seguin 9.

Document 165
WCTU Convention
[*Dallas Morning News*, January 25, 1909]

The recent convention of the Thurman [black] W.C.T.U. held by Mrs. E. E. Peterson in San Antonio was the best in the history of their organization. Large crowds were present at every session, and among these many white people. Over 6,000 pages of temperance and prohibition literature were distributed. . . . Many white ministers were introduced and made speeches encouraging the negroes in their efforts to free Texas of the saloon.

Document 166
" . . . Colored Union Organized by Carrie Martin"
[*Texas White Ribboner* (magazine of the Woman's Christian Temperance Union), March 1944, p. 4; copy at Center for American History, University of Texas at Austin]

L.T.L. [Little Temperance League] Organizations
   Austin, San Marcos and San Antonio.
   I have ordered the picture Dollars and Sense. We are working hard to carry out the program outlined by the departments, L. T. L. and Y. T. C.
   Our goal is to organize a State Negro W. C. T. U. organization in 1944.
   We have launched a membership campaign in each of the reported organizations.
   Any little help the State members would like to contribute we will appreciate. To help the work progress, I need stamps, envelopes, stationery, postal cards, organizing packets, literature and pledge cards. I have a splendid projector.
   The State has very little funds, I know, to appropriate for this work and I do not have anything to give but my efforts. So, "press on" in faith and I know the Lord will direct me to secure the tools with which to work.
   Pray for the work with the Negro people of Texas, and write me a word of encouragement.

                                                    CARRIE E. MARTIN

Document 167
Baptist Home Mission
[Mrs. A. D. Hill biographical information, Armstead Papers, Box 6, Folder 6, Rosenberg Library, Galveston]

Church women have deepened their collective strength and broadened their influence through religious missionary societies since they began at the end of the nineteenth century. These societies have provided aid to the poor and needy; donated money, bedding, clothing, and Bibles to college students; and supported missionary efforts in Africa. They have also provided important leadership opportunities for women as they gathered annually for socializing and networking.

Report to the Women's Mt Olive District Convention of Texas
Mrs. A. D. Hill, President

The Good Will Baptist Home Mission Society of Brenham, Texas, the 5 day of August 1917 sends Christian greeting.

Report for the year ending	$3.00
Society organized	1898
with 40 members. Present membership	6
Children in Starlight Band	None
Meetings held during the year	8
Number of times Pulpit decorated	4
Number who have given up snuff	None
Number who have given up beer	All
Gathered into the S.S.	7
Backslides restored to the Church	None. 1
Amount given during the year for Church improvement at home	4.25

We send to this meeting for woman's work C. A. Gilmore

Document 168

Returns of Eastern Star Chapters

[*Proceedings of the Tenth Annual Session of the Masonic Grand Chapter, Order of the Eastern Star, Austin, Texas, July 9–12, 1901*, Eastgate Eastern Star Collection, Texas Woman's University, Denton]

Female Masons, the Order of the Eastern Star, came to Texas around 1891. Within ten years, their organization had spread throughout the state.

Name, Location	No. Members	Sus- pended	Rein- stated	Initi- ated	Grand Chapter Revenue
Electa, No. 1 Galveston	20		1	3	$9.05
Bethlehem, No. 2 Marshall	13				5.20
Queen of Sheba, No. 3, Austin	28		4	6	13.30

Name, Location	No. Members	Sus- pended	Rein- stated	Initi- ated	Grand Chapter Revenue
Adah, No. 4 Dallas	43			12	17.20
St. Mary, No. 8 Bonham	25	1		4	11.20
Sunlight, No. 9 Victoria	32		3		12.80
Silver Queen, No. 12, Paris	24	2		6	11.60
East Gate, No. 15 Denton	8		1		3.20
Ellah, No. 19 Cleburne	10			3	5.05
Jewel, No. 24 Bryan	12	3		3	5.85
Bryan, No. 30 Greenville	19			4	9.00
. . .					
Total State Membership					635
Total State Revenue					$233.70

Document 169

"Lifting as we climb"

[Dorothy Robinson, "Interview with Christia Adair," April 25, 1977, in *The Black Women Oral History Project*, vol. 1, pp. 77–78, with permission of K. G. Saur Verlag, a Reed Reference Publishing Company, and the Schlesinger Library, Radcliffe College]

The white General Federation of Women's Clubs made an open display of racism in 1900. During its national biennial convention, it rescinded accreditation of the first black club in the organization, the Woman's Era Club of Massachusetts, and subsequently published a racist story in which a white clubwoman invites a (light-skinned) black woman into her club, then dies of shock after her son marries the black woman's daughter and their baby is born "jet black."[1] Christia Adair, a member of the Texas Association of Colored Women's Clubs, reviewed the legacy of slavery in explaining the rationale for the founding of the National Association of Colored Women in 1896.

Well, these women [National Association of Colored Women] decided that they would try to start out with an effort that would make the white woman out a liar first about them being immoral because of the color of their children. But at the same time, they wanted to educate our women to know that it would be better not to have a lot of things than to lay down your principle and your chastity and your virtue. . . .

This organization is a group that has never had any barriers. Our motto is "Lifting as we climb." Which means that we have not tried to major [focus] on the woman who has already reached her zenith, who has had all kinds of opportunities and advantages, but the woman who needs us, the woman who hasn't had any advantages, the woman who is down and needs to be lifted. . . . We feel like if it takes recognition to give her a push and a start in life, we give it.

Document 170
"War, war, grim-visaged war"
[Eastern Star, *Proceedings*, 1917, 18–19; copy at Texas Woman's University, Denton]

In 1917, the Masonic Grand Chapter, Order of the Eastern Star, State of Texas and Jurisdiction, held its 27th annual session in Fort Worth. Grand Matron Mrs. W. E. Thompson of San Antonio gave a stirring address on July 17.

We must lift up our eyes and look on the fields, for they are white already to harvest. For the past twelve months we have been in a swing of watchful waiting. Swinging with hope as our foremost point of ascent. We hoped and prayed that the door by which our forces entered Mexico be left ajar; that no conflict be encountered to blacken the historical records. Fates were kind, and thanks for the friendship on the border.

Now comes a world war and we still hope. For what? For equal rights and protection, "o'er the land of the free and the home of the brave?" With our troops already in France, we are planning ten thousand ships and one hundred thousand aeroplanes. We foresee a dismal future. "Not interested," some one has whispered. Well, for your own sake and the well being of the race we represent never give utterance to such an unworthy thought.

We have over one thousand bright, healthy and capable young men in training in the Des Moines training camp. This is one promotion worthy of recording. In sending our boys to the front, we do not entertain the thought of them being massacred, no, for to the noble brave-hearted, no thought of annihilation is entertained. Think of him returning to his home and state with a deeper interest in all affairs pertaining to a well-regulated and an illustrious life.

Our girls may be useful in many ways. The Red Cross is in need of their services; they may make bandages at home that suffering may be relieved upon the field. Think of the rich society young women in training and graduating in motor transportation, being able to adjust and mend tires with lightning speed. They have forgotten their wealth, their beauty, their femininity, are donning overalls and giving service. While capable men are at the front the energetic and thrifty women will pursue professions heretofore considered out of her line of work.

War, war, grim-visaged war; we have a distaste for war, but after the call of thousands to arms, after the firing of many double powered machines, after the sacrifice of our dear ones and loved ones upon the field of battle; then, when the aeroplane has ceased to drop into the waters of the Rhine her deadly bomb and the mists have rolled away, will we understand each other better, and a better service be prepared to give to the great cause of humanity.

Sisters, we must get interested, for all that is human must retrograde, if it does not advance. Our race must strive to increase in wisdom and in stature and in favor with God and man. Serve your church, your home, your country; this service will redound to racial betterment, social uplift. From these three heads all useful tributaries of union merge. We want in our ranks the best material in the race for the fabric of the institution is greatly handicapped by the entrance of the unworthy.

Document 171
The Texas Association of Colored Women's Clubs
[Mrs. L. A. Carter, "A Brief History of the Texas Association of Colored Women's Clubs," typescript (ca. 1950s), George and Jeffie Conner Papers, Texas Collection, Baylor University, Waco]

The National Association of Colored Women (NACW), organized in 1896, was an umbrella organization that took existing groups into its membership and incorporated new groups in the twentieth century. By 1905, there were enough clubs in Texas to form a state association.

The Texas Association of Colored Women's Clubs (formerly the Texas Federation of Colored Women's Clubs) was organized by Mrs. M. E. Y. Moore in the city of Gainesville, in 1905. A few women from clubs over the state responded to her call to organize a federation aiming to improve the homes, the moral and social life in the communities of Texas. Mrs. Moore was elected President; . . . She served three years until she was forced to give up the Presidency because of ill health. . . .

Mrs. Inez Scott of Paris succeeded Mrs. Moore. . . . More women were interested and the number of clubs increased.

In 1910, Mrs. [Mary] Alphin of Waco was elected the third President.

The first printed minutes was given the State under her Administration. . . . Leaving the State, she resigned in 1916 at the meeting in Greenville.

Mrs. Carrie Adams of Beaumont was elected and being a very enthusiastic person, she had a little difficulty in laying the foundation for establishing a home for delinquent girls. Four years later, Mrs. R. A. Ransom of Fort Worth followed Mrs. Adams as President. The intensive drive for the girl's home was such a success that a ten acre tract was bought in San Antonio for $5,500, with $2,000 down and $700 a year. At this session in San Antonio, Mrs. Ransom resigned as her health was impaired. The Vice-President, Mrs. H. E. Williams of Corsicana, was elected and the balance due on the property was paid in full during her Administration.

Mrs. A. E. S. Johnson of Marlin, was then elected President [1927]. Along with a general improvement in the work of the Federation, she made appeals to the rail road companies of the state for better accommodations. Travel became more enjoyable and comfortable.

Mrs. A. B. Dement of Mineral Wells, was the next President. She put emphasis on the program of the organization making each phase of the work more practical and insisted that we bring into our fold more members and more clubs, and that we be great in the number of members we attract, the host of friends we cultivate. Keep in earnest, and diligent in lofty accomplishment.

Mrs. C. H. Christian of Austin followed Mrs. Dement; her efforts were much the same as her predecessor, creating a larger interest among the women of the state.

Mrs. W. E. Brackeen of Fort Worth, being the next President, ardently advocated the need of a Camp Site since the State was now sponsoring a home for delinquent girls. She recommended using the San Antonio property which was eventually sold and a site between Dallas and Fort Worth was purchased.

Mrs. V. C. Fedford of Galveston, for many years Treasurer, was elected to the Presidency. Her efforts were directed toward a larger and more intense interest in federation through out the State. Because the last property bought was being surrounded by Military establishments, another location for a Camp Site was sought.

Mrs. I. W. Rowan of Dallas succeeded Mrs. Fedford. Greater stress was put on departmental work which resulted in more efficient accomplishments. During the next session of the Association in Marlin, Mrs. A. X. Robertson of that city was elected. A Scholarship to rotate among the Districts was inaugurated. The district receiving the scholarship was to select the candidate or recipient.

In 1955, Mrs. J. O. A. Conner of Waco was elected. She put forth special efforts to improve the record system of the organization and to give informative entertainment to the group. For the latter services of Carrie P. Hines was secured in the presentation of the Lily of the Valley, a historical play. Mrs. Hines as author, director and Producer has raised more than $2,000 at the presentations in Galveston and Waco.

Ladies, this ends our early period of Presidents—Better Known as the Trail Blazers, for indeed they paved the way for our Latter period of Presidents.

Respectfully Submitted
Mrs. I. A. Carter

Document 172
"CHARITY FUND NEARLY $1000"
[*City Times* (Galveston), May 25, 1918, p. 1]

Mrs. L. A. Pinkney was a leader in the Galveston Women's Progressive Club and in charge of publicity for the National Legislative Council of Colored Women in 1925. She spearheaded interracial efforts to establish an old age home for blacks in the Galveston area.

The committee of colored people who assisted the United Charities in an effort for funds to be used for old indigent colored people of Galveston reported last Sunday to President Robt. G. Street of the United Charities that the pledges and cash collections in the recent drive amounted to about $1000. The effort of the colored citizens in this matter has been highly commended.

Mrs. L. A. Pinkney, chairman, said several churches and other organizations have not yet reported.

The following names and cash have been added to the subscription list:

Union Guiding Star No. 5, $5; Ladies' Auxiliary, I. L. A., 851, $12; T. W. Patrick, $6; Miss C. E. Scull, $1; Conway and Profits, $2.37; Progress No. 3, $25; D. H. Taylor's Cafe, $1.50; Lawrence Joseph Cuney, $1; E. H. Taylor, $1; St. Luke Baptist Church, $6.13; Progressive Club, $5.25; Progress No. 1, $20; Brothers and Daughters of Jeptha [?], C. H. O'Donald, $1; Damon [?]; Mr. C. A. Bailey [and several others—illegible]; Lizzie Anderson Juvenile, No. 3, #1; Wright Cuney Lodge, No. 1, $5; Mrs. M. G. Burney, 50¢; F. E. Stewart, 50 cents; Ave. L. Baptist Church, $2.50; Charlie Smith, 25 cents; T. Bridges, 25 cents; Business League, $2.

Document 173
On the Home Front
[*City Times* (Galveston), October 27, 1917, p. 1]

Mrs. L. A. Pinkney of the Progressive Center, 2807 Avenue M, wishes all ladies and representatives to meet today from 1 to 5 p.m. to assist in the matters, etc., of the comfort bags for our soldier boys who expect to leave next Tuesday.

Document 174
"At 16 years old, I was Sunday School Superintendent"
[Dorothy Robinson, "Interview with Christia Adair," April 25, 1977, in *The Black Women Oral History Project*, vol. 1, pp. 50–51, with permission of K. G. Saur Verlag, a Reed Reference Publishing Company, and the Schlesinger Library, Radcliffe College]

We had a Sunday School Superintendent in our little church in Edna, named Miss Beulah White. You see, when I left home to go to school, I was between 15 and 16 years old, which meant that I was still a little girl. But I had been active in my Sunday School and things like that, and my Sunday School Superintendent fell ill with tuberculosis and she, after so long a time, wanted to talk to me. . . . [She said,] "I wanted you to be Superintendent of the Sunday School." Well, it just took the breath out of me because I couldn't understand how she could ask that of me and I said, "Oh, Miss Beulah, I don't know how to be a Superintendent." "You can learn. I know that's what I want to happen to the Sunday School, when I go. I want you to be the Superintendent of the Sunday School." And she kept plugging after me about it and pressing me and she said, "Will you promise me that you'll be the Sunday School Superintendent?" And I said, "Yes, Miss Beulah." So then she sent me home.

When I got home and told my mama about it, Mama said, "Well, what did you say?" I said, "I couldn't do anything but say 'yes.' She's a dying woman." Mama said, "All right, if you told her yes, you would be Sunday School Superintendent, you are Sunday School Superintendent." I said, "No, Mama, I . . ." She said, " . . . You made a promise that you can't break." And so, that meant that at 16 years old, I was Sunday School Superintendent of Scruggs Chapel Methodist Church in Edna, Texas.

In September [1909], when I went back to Sam Huston [College], I told Professor McNealy, who was the religious education director of our school, what had happened. He said, "All right. We're going to put a lot of time in our class work when we go back after vacation. Edna's going to have a good superintendent." The whole class became interested in that fact, that

Christia Daniels was Sunday School Superintendent, and everybody was leaning toward helping me be a good superintendent. And when I went back to Edna in vacation time, I felt that the children wouldn't love me. They would kind of feel like they had been set aside and I had been selected to do something that maybe I wasn't equal to. [But] . . . the children were glad. Instead of saying, "Christia's superintendent," they said, "We're superintendent of our own Sunday School." And together we had a Sunday School.

Document 175
Church Suppers

[Clara Stearns Scarbrough, *Wesley Chapel, AME Church, Georgetown, Texas* (Georgetown: Don and Clara Scarbrough and the *Williamson County Sun*, 1986), p. 11]

I especially remember the Saturday night church suppers [ca. 1930s]. Various church departments and clubs would bring forth their respective bills of fare to raise ever needed money for Wesley Chapel. Mrs. Hattie Tanksley could make the best homemade ice cream in the world. You could buy a small bowl of it for 15 cents. Mrs. Mary Bailey could make the best chicken and dumplings.

Document 176
"What book shall we study?"

[Mrs. N. L. Perry to Mary Church Terrell, November 11, 1925, Mary Church Terrell Papers, Container #7 (Correspondence April–November 1925), Library of Congress]

Women across the state looked to Mary Church Terrell, the first president of the National Association of Colored Women, for leadership and inspiration.

1012 E. Collin St.,
Corsicana, Texas., Nov. 11, 1925

Mrs. Mary Church Terrell,
    Washington, D.C.

Dear Madam:
    I have just read your article, "An Appeal to Colored Women," in National Notes. I think it is an excellent article. I wish to ask what book shall we study? In the schools here there is a book—"Our Community," shall we study that, or just what would you recommend? I belong to a club and now we are making up our Year Book, and we usually study some book.
    Please let me hear from you soon.

Yours very truly,
Mrs. N. L. Perry

Document 177
YWCA
[Typescript, Maria Morgan Branch Archives, Young Women's Christian Association, Dallas, reprinted with permission of the YWCA of Metropolitan Dallas]

SETTING UP CONFERENCE
MARIA MORGAN BRANCH Y.W.C.A.
DALLAS, TEXAS
OCTOBER 6, 1928
10 A.M. TO 4 P.M.

1. Devotion .... Mrs. J. C. Frazier 10:15–10:30
2. 10:30–10:50. . . . The Committee Woman and Her Job
   . . . Mrs. Spence
3. 10:50–11:10. . . . The Secretary and Her Job . . . Miss F. A. Lynes
4. 11:10–11:30. . . . The Dallas Y.W.C.A . . . Mrs. W. C. Proctor
5. 11:30–11:50. . . . The Branch Conference . . . Miss M. E. Davis
6. 11:50–12:05. . . . The By-Laws of the Branch
7. 12:05–12:15. . . . Regular Meeting Day
8. 12:15–1:30 . . . . Lunch
9. Program for Year:
   a. 2:00–2:10. . . . Employment . . . Mrs. H. D. Winn
   b. 2:10–2:20. . . . Education . . . Mrs. T. Tubbs
   c. 2:20–2:30. . . . Finance . . . Mrs. Charles Jones
   d. 2:30–2:40. . . . Girl Reserve . . . Mrs. F. Dodd
   e. 2:40–2:50. . . . Hospitality . . . Mrs. C. R. Boswell
   f. 2:50–3:00. . . . Health (Mrs. Cowan) [handwritten]
   g. 3:30–3:10. . . . Membership . . . Mrs. Eva Weems
   h. 3:10–3:20. . . . Publicity . . . Mrs. H. G. Hardin
   i. 3:20–3:30. . . . Religious Education . . . Mrs. McKay Turner
10. Calendar for year. . . . Miss Wooten 3:30–3:45

PURPOSE
The purpose of the Young Women's Christian Association shall be to associate young women in personal loyalty to Jesus Christ as Savior and Lord; to promote growth in Christian character and service through physical, social, mental and spiritual training, and to become a social force for the extension of the Kingdom of God.

Dr. Dorothea W. Brown recalled that as a child growing up in Austin, she always played the teacher, "lining the other children up, being in charge." That sense of responsibility carried into adulthood as she assumed leadership positions in education and community organizations. She earned a B.A. from Huston-Tillotson College, a master's degree from John Carroll University in Cleveland, and a doctorate in Educational Administration with a special cognate in Urban Studies from the University of Akron, Ohio. She has been a teacher, an assistant principal, and a guidance counselor, as well as Dean / Director

of Instructional and Instructional Personnel Development at Cuyahoga Community College in Cleveland and Associate Director, National Institute of Staff and Organizational Development for the College of Education, University of Texas at Austin. Dr. Brown has been a national leader of the Links, Inc., and the Girl Scouts of the USA. (Photo by General Marshall, courtesy Dorothea W. Brown)

Document 178
Day Care and Welfare
[Mary Yerwood Thompson, "Howson Child Development Laboratory: A Human Relations Agency," master's thesis, University of Texas at Austin, 1958, pp. 29–36]

During the Depression, Mary Yerwood Thompson became the director of the WPA nursery school for children of parents on relief, founded by the Community Welfare Association, a group of Austin black women. The CWA was an outstanding example of an organization which built and sustained a major community institution over decades, generating support across race and gender lines. In order to obtain a graduate degree in social work, Thompson was forced to leave Texas. She graduated from Atlanta University in 1943.

People were in need everywhere . . . just plain ordinary people, were unemployed, hungry, sick, improperly clothed, and poorly housed. . . . Heads of families were heard to say, "If I just had somewhere to leave my babies, I believe that I could get out and find a job." . . . Their desperate urgent cries were for such material things as oil for their lamps, food, clothing and shelter for their families and employment for themselves. . . .

The emergency nursery schools were established for the benefit of children from families who were either on direct relief or who were on the work-relief program. They also served as a measure to provide employment for adults as staff members. This was the first large-scale grant of public funds in the United States for group programs for young children. Hence, major impetus was given to nursery education which included recreation, a guided educational program, nutrition, and service. . . .

The program was adequately housed, and food for the children was to be furnished by the government, but there was absolutely no equipment with which to work. So, while the nursery school was still in a pioneer stage of development, . . . the writer and Mrs. Caldwell amassed such gifts as a gas range, an electric refrigerator, tables, chairs, utensils, play equipment, small cots, linens, and other necessities for operating a nursery school. A program was then mapped out peculiar to the needs of the group. The uniqueness of this nursery school was soon realized; though there were limitations, they were certainly overshadowed by good community relationships and worthy purposes.

Document 179

"We women want PEACE"

[Roberta J. Dunbar at the National Association of Colored Women Biennial Meeting in Fort Worth, July 25–30, 1937, NACW Minutes, 1935–39, Mary Church Terrell Papers, Library of Congress]

In 1937, Roberta J. Dunbar, chair of the NACW Peace Department, delivered an eloquent address during the organization's convention in Fort Worth.

PEACE . . . seems to be the main topic of the day. . . . The women of the national [Association of Colored Women] like the women all over the world are the mothers, wives, sisters, and relatives of the human fodder which feeds the god of war.

If you could see into the hearts of the women of China, Africa, Japan, Germany, Italy, England, and India they want Peace, for they are the helpless sufferers when the dogs of war are turned loose.

We women want PEACE, and no woman of any nation is in a better position to bring this Era than the women of America.

First, we must have a united womanhood in this country, who in turn will unite with the women of the world, presenting an International front in this great battle for Peace.

Document 180

Woman's Role in the Church

[A. W. Jackson, *A Sure Foundation: A Sketch of Negro Life in Texas* (Houston: Yates Publishing Co., 1940), pp. 11–12]

Truly, there is a place and work for [women] in the house of God, not to take the lead; neither bring up the rear, but to go hand and hand and side by side in spreading the good news of salvation to a lost world. . . . For mothers are good appointed teachers and it is their work to bring their children early to Christ. After they have been brought to train them in Christian work for the glory of God then for the service of man. . . . She should rescue the perishing, care for the dying, console the mourning, visit the sick, care for the less fortunate ones, and to give all means according to her ability to spread the mission work in all the world.

Document 181
"A Brief History of Crockett State School for Girls"
[Typescript, n.d. (late 1950s?), George and Jeffie Conner Papers, Texas Collection, Baylor University, Waco]

After years of lobbying by the Texas Association of Colored Women's Clubs and a few white allies, the legislature authorized construction of a state delinquent home for black girls in 1927, but did not appropriate funds until years later.

The Texas Training School for Negro Girls, located near Crockett, is one of the newest and most up-to-date of our state institutions. Housed in a nine-building, modern ranch-style plant, the school is designed to accommodate 100 girls. The school has 115 girls at present.

The Crockett State School was established in 1927 by act of the 40th Texas Legislature. Necessary appropriations for construction were not voted, however, until the 49th Legislature in 1945 provided for the operation of the school, which opened August 25, 1946, in a former prisoner-of-war camp about two miles east of Brady, in McCullough County.

On October 1, of that year Mrs. I. W. Rowan, the first superintendent, assumed her duties, and students were first admitted the following February. . . .

The Brady State School opened with a staff consisting of the Superintendent, a Secretary, Three Housemothers, and a Graduate Nurse, and Assistant. Later an Educational Director, Music Teacher, Homemaking Teacher, and Cook were added. Today the staff numbers thirty persons, employed full time, and three persons employed part-time.

Mrs. Emma G. Harrell, formerly the resident nurse, succeeded Mrs. Rowan as Superintendent in June, 1948, though continuing to direct the nursing duties. She is a graduate of Prairie View College. . . .

It soon became apparent that the school should be moved nearer Texas's Negro Population center and into permanent quarters. The old P.O.W. Camp was deteriorating, and expensive to maintain. Many possible sites were considered before deciding on Crockett in Houston County, where businessmen donated a $12,000 farm to the Council as a site. The new plant was designed and built in record time, and was occupied for the first time on December 30, 1950.

Each of the four cottages has facilities for twenty-five girls, twenty-two in the dormitory section, and three in the honor room. Every girl has a bed, a dresserette, and a bench of her own, this unit is called her house. There is a Housemother in the Cottage, and each cottage has its clothing room, work room, utility room, recreation room, and bathrooms.

All students, and some staff members use the same dining room. Food preparation is directed in the Central Kitchen by a Dietitian-Cook who has eight students to assist her in maintenance and serving. Girls are taught fundamental principles of cooking, and table serve as an on-the-Job part of the School's Homemaking Course, which also includes sewing, child-care, and housekeeping, and is a required course for every girl.

Cosmetology is another vocational course popular at Crockett. For twelve months the girls, who must meet physical, mental, and scholastic requirements, are schooled in methods of hair-styling and manicuring, facials, etc., and they practice on each other the techniques they learn. Many have gone on to pass the state licensing examination. Out of more than 100 students who have taken the state examination only one has failed.

In the school's laundry, a course in laundry technique helps prepare the girls for good jobs upon their release. Equipment includes washing machines, dryers, ironers, and ironing boards for hand work. The girls get experience with both commercial and household types of machines. The students over 16 are aided by the Texas Employment Commission to secure jobs in their communities.

Most of the students at the Crockett State School are from families too poor to furnish them with much in the way of personal clothing, so the school supplies each girl with dresses, brown oxfords, and varicolored socks. If she does have her own clothes, any girl is permitted to wear them, but in actuality very few receive anything from home. Each girl who has the ability is taught, and encouraged to make, and mend her clothes.

The academic school must provide a program to fit a variety of educational needs. There are girls who cannot read or write, and others ready for high school. The school attempts to help each girl according to her needs, and to prepare her for life back in the community. Every effort is made to teach girls how to live, how to make a home, and how to get along with other people in her community.

Prior to the creation of this school Texas had made no provisions for the custody and training of Negro Girls who got in trouble. The courts could do nothing to protect such a girl or protect her community from her delinquent acts. . . . One of its [the school's] main problems has been the large percentage of girls with low mentalities, whom the school should not be expected to accept.

Recreation is an important part of the program . . . for most of the students have much to learn about getting along with other people. The Physical Education Director is responsible for all recreation. Each cottage, and the hospital have recreation rooms with television, each cottage is equipped with radio. Recreation is somewhat limited because of the lack of indoor space and facilities, and [an] auditorium [and] gymnasium is badly needed; also a chapel for religious services only. Some money has been raised to erect a chapel.

A 4-H Club, organized by the Houston County Home Demonstration agent has created much interest among girls being trained in homemaking, and there is also a Girl Scout troop which has undertaken projects such as clothes repairing and lawn beautification. . . .

The students have participated in a number of off-campus activities, such as the local high school athletic activities, programs, musicals, and other activities, they also attended activities at Prairie View College. Crockett State School serves as a Training School for Sociology students for Prairie View College. There is a drill team called the "Westernettes." . . .

Parties are usually given on holidays, and the student body had a monthly party for all girls celebrating their birthdays. . . .

Medical care of the girls . . . is not overlooked. Each new arrival is kept in an isolation room in the school hospital for from eight to ten days while Crockett doctors, and dentists examine her thoroughly, and give her any treatment she may need. She is also given achievement, and mental tests, and fitted with eyeglasses if she needs them. It is not uncommon for a youngster's physical condition to contribute to her delinquent behavior. . . .

Disciplinary problems arise in any Institution where there is so much freedom, and where there is a common background of delinquent conduct. For most of the Crockett girls, discipline consists of work assignments, deprivation of privileges, and occasional assignment to the 10 room Detention Cottage, which has well-lighted rooms. Bad conduct also results in discipline which subtracts from a girls adjustment period and means a longer stay at the school. The students themselves have helped to improve the conduct in the school considerably.

On the other hand, a girl who adheres to regulations, and shows improvement can attain the honor roll, where she is allowed special privileges such as off-campus trips. Recently, for example, a group of honor students attended the 9th annual institute of Family, and Marriage Living at Prairie View College this institute is sponsored by the Dept. of sociology. . . .

The school also has a garden in which all girls work, although most of them come from cities. . . . Future plans call for some truck farming, and animal husbandry, but money so far has not been available for facilities or to buy hogs or chickens.

The school has the services of a part-time chaplain, and the officials attempt to provide a well-balanced religious program for the girls. . . .

The principal purpose of the school is to straighten out girls who have gotten in trouble, and prepare them to return to their home communities as better citizens, capable of taking their places in society, and earning a decent living. Most of the Crockett State School students who have been discharged, Mrs. Harrell reports, have secured good jobs after leaving the school. Some have completed High School, some have finished College. Many are now good housewives. The practical things they have learned at the school have proved to be a big help to them upon their return to community life, and reports from Probation Departments indicate that the number of girls making satisfactory adjustments far overweigh the number of girls who haven't done so well. . . .

Document 182
"State to Build Home for Delinquent Girls"
[*Waco Messenger*, July 11, 1941, p. 1]

Austin. (Spl)—Among the items included in the appropriations bill signed by Gov. O'Daniel last week was one appropriating $60,000 for the erection of a home for delinquent colored girls of the state. The school will be located at Gainesville in close proximity to that for white girls.

This brings to an end the fight which has been waged for several years under the leadership of the Federated clubs of the colored women of Texas.

Document 183
Missionary Societies' Duty
[Mrs. M. A. B. Fuller, *Guide for Woman's Home and Foreign Missionary Societies and Circles* (Austin: Mrs. M. A. B. Fuller, ca. 1946), unpaginated; copy at the Center for American History, University of Texas at Austin]

Maud A. B. Fuller of Austin, a member of the Ebenezer Baptist Church, was president of the Women's Auxiliary of the National Baptist Convention from 1928 to 1968. She wrote church literature, founded the first national organizations for black Baptist youth, and wrote handbooks for youth groups, church societies, and home and foreign missionary societies. She raised thousands of dollars for missions and traveled to Africa several times.

It is your duty to see that a Star Light Band is organized in your church. A Girls' Auxiliary for girls from 12 to 16 years of age; A Y. W. A. for young women from 17 to 25 years of age; A Sheperd Boys' League from 12 to 17 years of age; A Junior District Convention, and A Junior State Convention.

These are the people who will constitute the future church. It is up to you, as God's Stewards, to see that they are trained in useful service. . . .

One great need of our Missionary Societies is a Bible study revival. . . . It is hoped a year spent on the "Life and Teachings of Jesus" will broaden our vision of Christianity, deepen our spirituality and awaken our conscience to the great duty committed to us by Jesus—to bring the unsaved world to his feet. . . .

The strength to do this comes from the prayer in the next lines:

"Help me to watch and pray,
And on Thyself rely,
Assured, if my trust betray,
I shall forever die."
    By Editor . . .

Article VII
Committees

1. Enlistment.—It shall be the duty of this committee to visit every Baptist home and enlist every member in some active work for the church and enlist the women in missionary work. . . .

2. Social.—Welcome strangers and visit newcomers to your neighborhood. Plan for all the social activities of the Society.

3. Benevolent.—Visit and aid the sick and needy poor. Visit hospitals, carry flowers or good cheer wherever needed.

4. Missionary and Educational.—Encourage Bible and Missionary study and secure Missionary aid and educational offerings. Secure subscriptions for the denominational paper and distribute Missionary tracts.

5. Industrial.—Plan for sewing or other work for the needy. Try to increase interest in all church aid and support.

Document 184
Austin Council of Negro Women
[Typescript, "Report of the Austin Metropolitan Council of the National Council of Negro Women," November 10, 1947, National Archives for Black Women's History, Offices of the National Council of Negro Women, Washington, D.C.]

Although the National Council of Negro Women was organized in 1935, chapters were not founded in Texas cities until the 1940s. The Austin Council, for example, was organized on September 29, 1946. The seventeen founders included several public school teachers, three housewives, and ten women identified by their sororities—Alpha Kappa Alpha, Zeta Phi Beta, Sigma Gamma Rho, and Delta Sigma Theta. Several of these women were affiliated with Huston and Tillotson colleges, one was a physician, and one was a USO worker.

REPORT OF
THE AUSTIN METROPOLITAN COUNCIL
of
THE NATIONAL COUNCIL OF NEGRO WOMEN

The Austin Metropolitan Council was one year old, Sept. 29, 1947. During the year our activity emphasis has been centered around membership drives and selling the council to the women of Austin. The idea and work of the council have been received kindly by the ladies. And, now we have enough members to launch an active program for the year '47–'48.

ACTIVITIES OF THE COUNCIL FROM OCT., 1946 TO APRIL, 1947

Oct., 1946 — Membership Drive launched
Nov. — One delegate was sent to Conference in Washington
Dec. — Special Program presenting Mrs. Annetta Edmonds, Dallas, Texas. Subject "Social Frontiers for Negro Women." Membership effort included.
Jan., 1947 — A Panel Discussion, presenting Miss Elfida Vasquez, of Mexico and Mrs. Myra Ravel, of Council of Jewish Women "Minority Women in Action." Membership effort incl.
Feb. — International Soiree honoring Miss Saku Devanesen, of India and Miss Alice Monguia, a Spanish singer. Membership effort incl.
March — Program presenting Mrs. Homer P. Rainey—"Women of the World on the March"; Mrs. Virgie DeWitty special music
April — Presented Mrs. Keyes of the Planned Parenthood Federation of America and invited representatives from local school P.T.A.s as guests.

The public occasions culminated with the April meeting. The council has reconvened as of Nov. 10, 1947.

Submitted by
Mrs. Odalie Richardson, Pres.

Document 185
Mary McLeod Bethune in Galveston
[Typescript, National Archives for Black Women's History, Offices of the National
Council of Negro Women, Washington, D.C.]

Galveston, Texas
September 21, 1948

On Thursday, May 6, 1948, at 3:30 p.m. twenty-seven (27) ladies of the Galveston Metropolitan Council of the National Council of Negro Women met with Mrs. Mary McLeod Bethune, our Founder-President, at the home of Dr. and Mrs. E. A. Etter, 908—35th St., in an open forum. Some of the highlights of Mrs. Bethune's talk were as follows: Contact every Negro woman in your community, for the purpose of acquiring her membership in your Council; also to solicit the membership of any White woman who may be interested. . . . Don't be selfish and seek opportunity for ourselves alone, but work for the betterment of our Race as a whole. When a public official of your city does anything that is beneficial to us, write him a letter commending him for his action. If something is done that is detrimental to our Race, contact him and let him know how we feel about that too. Endeavor to have a representative sit in on any committee that is deciding anything that will affect us. A Negro can speak for himself much better than any white person can. In unity there is strength. By getting other Women's Organizations to join your Council, as well as getting the women to join as individual members, we can represent most of the women of our city, and the greater your membership, the greater your strength. An organization representing four or five hundred members will be given much more consideration than one representing fifteen or twenty members. Use the women of your Council best suited to the job at hand. If there is another group to be met, choose the woman who can meet people well and state your business clearly and intelligently. . . . Mrs. Bethune suggested that we solicit the memberships of other women's organizations at five dollars per year, allowing them two votes, their president and another member of their choice. Two dollars and fifty cents of this amount being sent to the National Council and a like amount remaining in our local treasury. She further suggested that the members tax themselves a small amount each month to swell our local treasury instead of giving so many entertainments to raise money. To stimulate a greater interest of the community in the Council, Mrs. Bethune suggested that we have regular Council meetings; Contact the heads of Religious and Civic Organizations of other races and extend to them an invitation to meet with us in order to promote better Race Relations in our community. . . . She also stressed the necessity of each Council member subscribing to the publications of the National Council. . . . At 5 o'clock pictures were made of the entire group and of all officers present. Some members had individual pictures made with Mrs. Bethune, after which open house was held until 7 p.m. At 8 p.m. the meeting opened at Ave. L Baptist Church. Beautiful music was rendered under the direction of Mrs. E. O. Coleman, including Mrs. Bethune's favorite, "Climbing Jacob's Ladder." Our Founder-President delivered a most inspirational and uplifting address to a large group, including many white friends.

Acting County Attorney Sherwood Brown offered a welcome to the city on behalf of the Mayor.

Respectfully submitted by,
Mrs. Rosalie G. McBeth, Cor. Sec.

Document 186
The Chat-An-Hour Club, Houston

[Minutes of the Chat-An-Hour Club, RG E-42, Houston Metropolitan Research Center, Houston Public Library]

After being forced from the leadership of the National Association for the Advancement of Colored People because of her left-wing political views, Mrs. Lulu (sometimes known as "Lula") B. White founded the Chat-An-Hour Club in 1949. It provided another venue for her leadership.

March 3, 1949

A small group of women met on the above date answering the call of Mrs. Lula White. The purpose was to form a Study Club which is to be under the Educational committee of the NAACP.

With the consent of all present the club was named "Chat-An-Hour Coffee Club." The time of meeting 10:00 o'clock A.M. every first and third Thursday for only one hour.

The group decided that 25 cents per month dues should be paid by each member. It was decided that we could have some white friend come in some time and discuss certain problems confronting us. We shall also study and discuss books written by Negroes and about Negro life etc. . . .

Houston, Tex. March 17, 1949

. . . Mrs. Webster told of the life of Mrs. [Mary McLeod] Bethune. Mrs. [Eleanor] Roosevelt sent her message. . . . Mrs. Dodson gave some highlights in the life of Ralph Bunche who has done such a wonderful job of statesmanship in bringing about peace between the Jews and the Arabs. . . .

Lulu B. White founded the Chat-An-Hour Club in Houston in 1949 under the auspices of the Educational Committee of the NAACP. The group's activities included social, educational, and political events. Seated left to right, Roberta Banks, Elizabeth James, Minnie Sledge, Corine Stanley, Priscilla Qualls, Vista Tryon; standing, Irene Herger, Maebelle Cosby, Mary Hinton, Annie Bell Henry, and Dolly Crawford. (Courtesy Houston Metropolitan Research Center, Houston Public Library)

Recommendations were as follows:

1. A blotter for distribution in the public schools of both races. A picture of Mr. [George Washington] Carver with a sketch of his life to be on the first blotter.

2. Use 12 Negroes (one for each month) a year on a calendar giving a short history of each.

3. Beginning a Museum of African Art

4. Ralph Bunche Day.

Dec. 8, 1949

. . . Mrs. White made the following announcements: A mobilization on Civil Rights on to Washington march sponsored by the NAACP and other organizations. There will be a conference meeting Jan. 8 in Houston at the Music Hall. Delegates from Texas conferences of Churches and Negro organizations. A planning committee will meet at Mrs. White's Friday night. The local branch is host to this meeting. Asking for sponsors and cosponsors, I.L.A. Chamber of Commerce to take to Washington to show that all of Texas is interested in the passing of the Civil Rights bill. No tickets can be sold to the meeting. Little badges "On to Washington" to sell at 10 cents each. $125 for Music Hall meeting "To Insure These Rights." Other cards 50 cents. Delegates will be elected at this conference to go to Washington. Branches have been asked to send in ten dollars for expenses of delegates. Have a patron list at $1.00 each and give a badge.

After a pleasant chat over the coffee cups all agreed to do all they could for the conference meeting.

Mrs. Dodson reviewed the book "Cry—The Beloved Country." . . .

Houston, Tex., Feb. 9, 1950

. . . A book review was given by Mrs. McCoy "The Miseducation of the Negro" by Carter Woodson

7. Suggestion by Mrs. White for a Houston's Citizen's Political Action Committee to place Dr. John Davis on the ballot for a member of the City council. . . .

April 24, 1958

. . . It was decided that on the first meeting in May we would have a memorial service in honor of Mrs. Lulu White who was the founder of the Chat-An-Hour Club.

At this point Mrs. Nannie Aycock [Aycox] our guest speaker arrived. Mrs. Aycock gave us much interesting and valuable information concerning our schools. She gave a full explanation of the new Hale-Aiken Bill which I am sure many of us had not read. She also gave us a list of the colleges in Texas that have integrated and the exact extent which they integrated.

7

EARNING A LIVING

Until World War II, most black girls and women were locked into low-wage jobs primarily in agriculture, housework, and laundry work. But when opportunities opened up in business and the professions they took advantage of them where they could.

Document 187

"Mama . . . made us do the washing and ironing"

[Jakie L. Pruett and Everett B. Cole, *As We Lived: Stories by Black Story Tellers* (Burnet: Eakin Press, 1982), Rosie Williams, pp. 78–79]

From the days of emancipation, black women could always find jobs as domestics and laundresses. This back-breaking work provided one method of survival for their families. Women could often do the laundry of other families at home while caring for their own.

Besides mama making us cook our own self something to eat, she made us do the washing and ironing [ca. 1910]. And, man, she was strictest 'bout that more'n anything else. We'd wash them outside in the yard in tubs with a ole rub board and homemade lye soap. We'd get the water to boiling in a ole wash pot to use for the washing, and we had to do ever bit of the work ourselves. And they'd better be good and clean, too.

Mama'd be watchful 'bout the ironing. If there was just one little wrinkle . . . she'd grab it and throw it back in the tub and let it get good and wet. Then, we'd have to start plumb back over with that piece. Wring it out with our hands and hang it back on the line to dry again. There'd better not be nairy a wrinkle if you didn't want to be doing it again, I'm telling you. Not one! They'd better be as smooth as your hand.

We'd use them old heavy iron flatirons that'd have to be heated out in the yard on a wood fire. She never let us heat them on the cooking stove inside. You'd get a log and set it on fire out in the yard and set your iron, turned up, beside it, so's it'd get good and hot. Then, when it was hot, you'd rub it on the grass to get most of the smoke and ashes off'n it and bring it in the house to where the ironing board was. We'd have a ole rag there to wipe it off better before putting it on the clothes. You know, so's it would get nothing on the clothes we'd washed.

We'd have a candle there, . . . and we'd kinda rub that hot iron over the side of it just when we was all ready to iron that piece. And then, when we finished, it would be all waxy and shiny from the ironing and from that candle. Oh, it'd be so smooth and glossy and nice. Real pretty looking.

Document 188
"Home Laundry"
[*Waco Messenger*, February 14, 1941, p. 5]

Miss Dorothy Ross, Prop.
Cash and Carry
High Quality work
Try Us Once
1313 Tabor Street

Document 189
"I've done four washes in one day"
[Ruthe Winegarten, *I Am Annie Mae: The Personal Story of a Black Texas Woman* (Austin: Rosegarden Press, 1983), pp. 67–68, 83–84; Naomi Carrier, "Working," from the musical by Ruthe Winegarten and Naomi Carrier, *I Am Annie Mae* (Austin: Sistuhs, Inc., 1990), p. 15]

After years as a farm worker and domestic, Annie Mae Hunt of Dallas turned her back on menial labor and became a self-employed businesswoman. She supported herself and her children for many years by sewing and selling Avon. Poet and composer Naomi Carrier captured the universal feelings of thousands of women like Annie Mae Hunt, who work all their lives and never have anything except their good names, in her song "Working."

When I was raising these first three kids in Dallas during the Depression, . . . I'd wash and iron. Like on Monday morning, I'd get up, I'd go out to Mrs. X's house, wash for her, hang her clothes up. Then I'd go on down to wash for another woman. I've done four washes in one day. I'd come on back, and these things I had just hung out for Mrs. X, they'd be ready. I'd take them down, and I'd sprinkle them and put them in a basket. And then she had other things for me to do. I could iron a shirt or a child's dress so a fly couldn't stand on the collar. A fly, he would slip off! . . .

I'd go on out and clean a stove, a bad stove. My hands'd be all messed up. Cleaning an ice box. . . . in that day you had to be at work at 7, 8 o'clock in the morning, and serve dinner at 5 o'clock in the evening. . . . And you had to do it, if you wanted a job. . . .

Sometimes I wouldn't get home till 10, 11 o'clock at night.

WORKING

I been working
And doing
And going
And giving
And all I'm doing
Ain't . . . doing no good.
I been working
And doing
And going
And giving
And all I'm doing
Ain't . . . doing no good.

I'm giving out.
I've done my best;
Still doing all I can;
I lost my child,
My mama too.
I even lost my *man*.
And what I make of my life
Only I can understand.

Why I'm working
And hoping
And giving
And living
And all my giving is . . . in vain.
Yes, I'm wishing
And waiting and hoping

And praying
And all I got is my name.
And all I got is my name.

I had cleaned houses all my life. That's all I knew. And every now and then somebody would pay me 50 cents to make a dress, cause that was a way of life, and that was money. I knew I could sew. . . .

Well, I was doing housework, working for 5 dollars a day, and I was downtown trying to wait for the Preston Hollow Bus . . . and I was on the streets slippin and slidin on ice. A girl said to me, "If you go into Seals and Grant and get you a pair of heavy socks and throw them over your shoes, like I got, you won't slip and slide no more." . . .

So I went in there and got me a pair of socks, and . . . when I got back outside, woman, I got so cold, it just went through me. . . . And my conscience, my mind begin to talk to me. . . . And it says to me, "Good as you can sew, good as you can sell Avon (I had been selling Avon and I had quit), you ought to freeze to death." My mind is saying that.

I heard my own self's mind, and I said to this girl, "Now, I'm going back home." She said, "You're not going to work?" And I said, "No. No baby, I don't have to do that." . . . And freezing cold like I am? I never intend to clean nobody's house in this town . . . as long as I live.

I come on back home that day, and I called the Avon representative. And the next day I walked up on Bexar Street, and had this man to make me a sign, "Dressmaking," to put in my yard, and I went to making dresses and selling Avon. . . .

Document 190
On the Farm
[Ruth Allen, *The Labor of Women in the Production of Cotton*, Bulletin No. 3134 (Austin: University of Texas, 1931), pp. 176–177, 181–182, 183]

Shortly before the Depression, Dr. Ruth Allen, a professor of economics at the University of Texas, interviewed 207 black women in a survey of female cotton workers in Central Texas. She found that over half the women worked as sharecroppers; others hired out for wages; some did both. Allen concluded that the women could earn more by abandoning cotton production and selling produce and poultry. The men typically collected and controlled the family wages.

The Negro man who lives in a family with several women will sometimes control the income of the entire group. One such instance was a young Negro man married to one of four sisters, all of whom lived in the house and worked together in the field. A query as to whether he did not find

Mrs. Cora Burton of Waller County was a poultry demonstrator for the Extension Service who supplemented her income in 1947 by raising chickens, ducks, geese, and turkeys. (Courtesy Special Collections Manuscripts and Archives, Texas A & M University, College Station)

himself rather lonely with so many women brought the answer, "No, I likes it." It later developed that each of the women worked regularly in the field, but not one collected her money or spent it. . . .

The burden of the Negro mothers in the bearing of children is heavy compared to that of the white women.

Twenty-five of these women . . . have families of ten or more children. Children among the colored farm group are, if they are to any group, an economic asset. Many of them work in the cotton patch almost from infancy. Two or three mothers visited in the fields had each a child of six years trudging beside her and picking his "hundred every day," as the mother proudly informed us. . . . The younger women are frankly impatient of the standards which demand the bearing of large numbers of children. . . . The older Negro, though, is a "die hard" when it comes to woman's duty. Woman after woman considered a sufficiently condemning answer the simple query, "What else did the Lord put women here for?" Unquestionably, the ignorance of proper methods of limitation of families is doing great damage to the health of Negro women. . . .

A single woman reports having a washing machine. She was left twelve years ago with eleven small children to bring up and had secured the money for accomplishing her task by doing farm labor and taking in washing. She had a washing machine, run by a small gasoline pump, which represented an outlay of $207.00, even though there was an evident lack of clothes and many times a shortage of food. She said that she was determined to have a washing machine, even if "the children do have to do without." Now she has more strength for field work. . . .

Thirty-one of these women, about one-seventh of the number, produce an income from production in the home; that is, from milk, butter, and eggs. But seventeen of them sold products amounting to less than $25.00. Seven of the remaining sold products amounting to less than $50.00, . . . and one woman sold butter and eggs amounting to more than $400.00.

Document 191
Home Demonstration Work
[Kate Adele Hill, *Home Demonstration Work in Texas* (San Antonio: Naylor, 1958), pp. 132–136]

A national movement to professionalize the homemaking role got underway around 1900, and the U.S. Congress established the Agricultural Extension Service in 1914. Mary Evelyn V. Hunter was employed as the state's first black home demonstration agent in 1915. For the next sixteen years she helped improve the lives of thousands of rural farm families.

I found a husband, wife and ten children in a four-room, crudely furnished home, with a scanty supply of food on hand. They had a measly garden and a few mongrel chickens to help support them. . . . I made several recommendations regarding home improvement and farm management. After several visits, I saw a great gain in hope and prosperity.

At the County Fair in Calvert, Texas, in the Fall of 1916, the Parrish family had the finest display of vegetables that had ever been on exhibition in the county. . . . Four hundred and fifty cans of fruit and vegetables were canned. An exhibition of the fruit, poultry, dresses, rugs, hats and other products drew comment from the largest newspapers of Texas. As a result of this and the prosperity which followed, two of the girls were sent to college and the other children completed high school training at Calvert, Texas. Three of the girls now hold permanent teaching certificates and are teaching. The parents and some of the children have purchased and equipped attractive homes. This family has taken almost a reverse attitude toward life.

Mrs. Sena Williams, a member of the Kaufman County home demonstration club in 1940, worked hard to improve her kitchen. She recalled, "We planned to change the long single window into two short ones and center the cabinet around them." Mrs. Williams and her husband financed the initial construction with the sale of a hog for $18.83. The total cost for the improvements was $210. She saved money by painting the cabinet and fixtures herself and "bought a pressure cooker for $9.25." "Now I just love to work in my kitchen and my whole family is proud of it." (Print and quotation courtesy Special Collections Manuscript and Archives, Texas A & M University, College Station)

Document 192

"My Experience as an Extension Worker"

[Mrs. Jeffie O. Conner, "My Experience as an Extension Worker," Waco, 1925, George and Jeffie Conner Papers, Texas Collection, Baylor University, Waco]

I am attempting to give some idea of the activities of the club members in women and girls work for a period of seven years.

My first duty upon entering the county was to get acquainted with the people who knew about the Extension dept. thru the Supv. Home Dem. Agent and the county Home Demonstration Agent whom I succeeded. . . .

At this time we saw the need of a more closely organized group of women and girls, even though we did have our small communities grouped into twelve large ones, we were still handicapped in getting a county wide cooperation. Therefore we perfected a county organization,

Mrs. L. E. Husk, a home demonstration agent in Washington County, gives a demonstration in comforter-making for women who are training as comfort-center supervisors. (Print from the cover of the *Prairie View Standard* 33, no. 6 (February 1942): 1; courtesy Permanent Collections—Archives/Special Collections Department, John B. Coleman Library, Prairie View A & M University, Prairie View)

which consisted of two members from each of the twelve local organizations, which gave us an enrollment of twenty-four women in our county club and since we had twelve girls clubs we also had a Junior organization of twenty-four girls. These women and girls were asked to meet each quarter. . . . Reports of the work, exhibits, demonstrations, and lectures plus games of various kinds for the girls constituted our program. The women and girls of this group became our club leaders upon returning home. . . .

Our people have bought more land in the past year than in many years. This was brought about by the influence of our work, plus a good cotton crop, last fall was the first time for some years that the farmers had very much money . . . our women had small plots of cotton which they sold and bought many things for home.

. . . The health of many families are better and they are not only looking after the food but the water as well. We find many of our people sick which cause was traced to the water supply. Another important feature of our work has been to get our people to put closets, bath rooms, and other conveniences in the home, of course we have very few homes in the rurals equipped with water works for the bath room, etc., but we are having the room just the same which makes it more convenient for sanitation. Large galvanized tubs are used instead of bath tubs at present on account of being able to move them in order to empty the water. . . .

The beauty and joy that I got out of seeing the women meet in their demonstration gardens that is scattered throughout the county to receive the various demonstrations in growing vegetables, in seeing them meet in the home meetings for the purpose of learning how to improve the home life by learning to clean and beautify the same . . . is more than ever could be realized in dollars and cents. . . .

The making of sanitary drinking cups from used tin cans has made it easy for all children to have a separate drinking cup, 1700 of these cups were made in my county last year. . . . The children not only get the idea of sanitation at school but carry this message home and in many cases families have bought more cups, glasses, etc. for the use in the home, which has played a good part in preventing the spread of various diseases. . . .

Mrs. Holloway has been a member of the women's clubs for seven years, being one of the first women to enroll in a club . . . when the work was introduced in my county. At that time she was living on a rented farm, barely existing. . . . She first began to follow up our demonstrations in gardening, poultry raising and canning, this gave her a full pantry for the next winter, which lightened her burden for food and allowed her to have a little money to spend for other necessities. She soon began to prevail with her husband to get a hog, later a cow and as things began to accumulate they soon found that if they had a home of their own they could do what we ask them in their orchard. Time went on and at last an opportunity came for them to buy 20 acres of land which they did and today they own this land with a nice five room bungalow thereon and a nice barn, poultry house, etc.

Our 1924 summary of the valuation of work done in my county will enable you to see the growth and value of Extension service to the Colored people of McLennan County. . . . the leading White and Colored citizens plus the untiring cooperation from our faithful club women and girls has made it possible for me to make the work what it was.

Document 193
Profitable Poultry
["Harris County Club Woman," January 1930, Negro Home and Farm Agents Collection, 1929–1932, MS. 210, Box 1, File 10, Houston Metropolitan Research Center, Houston Public Library, Houston]

Mrs. Will McKinney, Fairbanks Community club woman, is realizing splendid returns from her activities in poultry raising. Last September she purchased 300 White Leghorn and 100 Rhode Island Red baby chicks. . . . When the weather is good, Mrs. McKinney sells from $15 to $20 worth of eggs and chickens right at her home. . . . She has a splendid brooder house and is arranging separate laying pens and runs for her hens. Her plan is to purchase 100 baby chicks for each month during 1930.

Document 194
High School Girls
[Negro Home and Farm Agents Collection, 1929–1932, MS. 210, Box 1, File 10, Houston Metropolitan Research Center, Houston Public Library, Houston]

Reports from home demonstration agents around the state during the Depression reflect the varied activities and accomplishments of the agents and the women's and girls' clubs they supervised.

September 1932

Miss Bessie Leo Langley, 4-H Club girl of Victoria, Victoria County, Texas, and winner of the sweepstake prize in clothing, is eighteen years of age and a senior. . . . She has been a club girl for four years. . . . Each year she has exhibited some of her work at the Farmers' Meeting at Prairie View College and in the fall at Dallas, Texas. In her third year of work she took over the family sewing as her particular duty, making all clothing for the entire family and did some extra sewing for others which brought in some money to help with the family expenses. . . . She has done quite a bit of remodeling dresses, making over hats, plain and fancy sewing, and some handicraft which includes lamp shades, flower baskets, waxed flowers and rugs. The dress made by Miss Langley for the clothing contest was made in three and one half hours.

Lillie Bell Cox, winner of the steam pressure cooker, is fifteen years of age and lives with a family of six on a farm twenty miles from Marshall, Texas. She has been a 4-H club girl for three years. . . . During this year Miss Cox assisted her mother in caring for 200 chickens. Her mother has given her half of the money made. . . . She has made extra money from her neighbors by canning for those who do not have canning equipment.

Document 195
"Houston School Demonstrates Practicality of Training 'Perfect' Domestic Servants"
[*Houston Chronicle*, January 23, 1938, Negro Scrapbook, p. 14, Houston Metropolitan Research Center, Houston Public Library, Houston]

The servant problem need no longer be a nightmare to the Houston housewife if the dream of Mrs. Cecil B. Goodwin, assistant director of vocational education in the Houston public schools, is fulfilled and the project of training servants, which is still in its embryo stage, becomes a fullfledged venture.

Then not only will we have housemaids trained in neatness and dependability, nursemaids who know the fundamentals of child psychology, laundresses who are adept in the care and upkeep of fine linens and cooks who can prepare well-balanced meals, but also happy and contented workers who are conscious of doing superior jobs for satisfied employers, and Texas will have gone a long way toward solving its negro help problem. . . .

Nellie Dillon, for many years connected with the Jack Yates High School and now teacher in the vocational practice house, instills first of all in the minds of her 70 pupils the ethics of employment—what an employe owes the employer in efficiency, reliability and systematized labor, and the idea that any work, however high or low, that is intelligently done, deserves and commands respect and fair wages from the right kind of employer. . . .

Nellie, in her crisp white uniform, carries her degrees from Tuskegee Institute and from Prairie View State College, and her advanced work in the University of Wisconsin and Southern California, with modesty and dignity. Her pride seemed far more in the class of 30 girls. . . . There are three manuals to be studied, practiced, and graded. . . . The one on cooking covers the study of actual cooking and table service down to the planning of menus and the correct pronunciation of such words as hors d'oeuvres, fricassee, saute, etc. The manual on laundering instructs among other things the care of silk hose and undergarments, of table linens and ruffled curtains, fine mending, and the removal of stains. The cleaning manual deals with the proper way to make a bed, the care of furniture, how to wax floors, clean papered walls, and rid the house of insects. . . .

"Every girl has a job awaiting her," said Mrs. Goodwin, "or rather a choice of jobs, for there are far more applications for domestic workers than girls to fill them. We had 300 calls last year for these competent, well-trained servants but we had only 60 girls to send out."

Document 196
Bleach and Straighteners
[*Galveston City Times*, September 29, 1900]

Throughout the ages, women have developed, marketed, and used products and techniques designed to improve their appearance.

REDUCED TO $1.00
BLACK SKIN REMOVER
A WONDERFUL FACE BLEACH

NELSON'S STRAIGHTLINE
The latest discovery for making
Knitty, Kinky, Curly Hair Straight.

Lucille B. Moore worked as a photographic assistant in the Teal Portrait Studio. The business was owned by well-known Houston photographers Arthur C. and Elnora Teal from 1925 until 1946. Moore not only took photographs, but often did the printing and developing. (Photo by Elnora Teal; courtesy Thelma Justice)

Document 197
Beautician
[*Texas Freeman* (Houston), July 1, 1922]

THE HOME OF BEAUTY
MADAM ROSE C. WILEY WILLIAMS, PROPRIETOR
BEAUTY PARLORS
3216 NANCE STREET

POLITE AND COURTEOUS ASSISTANTS
EFFICIENT AND CAPABLE TREATMENT
ALL THE LATEST REQUIREMENT FOR HAIR AND BEAUTY WORK
Six weeks trial treatment with all necessary ingredients
Face and hair preparations for sale
The System Taught at parlor or by mail
Write today for any information

As a special inducement to those who wish to begin the use of the Rose C. Wiley Williams Hair Grower, we will mail to your address a six week treatment, consisting of:

One box of hair grower
One box of pressing oil and shampoo
With full instructions all for $1.00.

MADAM R. C. WILEY WILLIAMS

3216 Nance St.   Phone P TON 1608

Document 198

Businesswomen

[*The Red Book of Houston: A Compendium of Social, Professional, Religious, Educational and Industrial Interests of Houston's Colored Population* (Houston: Softex Pub., ca. 1915), pp. 164–165, 170–172 (excerpts)]

Many ambitious women launched businesses in a variety of fields, sometimes in addition to a full-time job.

Classified Business, Professional and Industrial List of Afro-Americans in Houston, Revised to May 1, 1915

BOARDING HOUSES.

Brown, Rebecca   1206 Rice Street
Peters, Rosa   1603 Jackson Street, Hadley 4244

CEMENT BLOCK MANUFACTURERS.

McGowan, Hattie, Mrs.   1810 Velasco Street

CLOTHES CLEANERS AND PRESSERS.

Allen, Della   1017 Dowling Street

MANICURES.

Manning, Sarah   Basement Union National Bank Bldg.
Taylor, Pearl   1017 Prairie Avenue

MIDWIVES.

Hagen, Annie   609 Hobson Street, Preston 6728

NURSES.

Burr, Louvenia	2402 Dallas Avenue, Preston 8263
Butler, L. E.	2502 Holman Avenue, Hadley 536
Foster, Dona	Fulton Avenue and I. & G. N.
Hagen, Annie	609 Hobson Street, Preston 6728
Johnson, Bessie	609 Hobson Street, Preston 6728

RESTAURANTS.[1]

Booker, Viola	90 Gable Street
Brown, Clara	31st Street and Houston Avenue
Carter, Mattie	3418 Dowling Street
Council, Cora	5519 Washington Avenue
Crahan, Flida	813 San Felipe Street
Figgins, Martha	1220 Paige Street
Guiton, Sarah	85 Marsh Street
Hunter, Elizabeth	3204 Washington Avenue
James, Charlotte	1909½ Whitty Street
Lewis, Ella	Independence Heights
McDonald, Adeline	742 West 22nd Street
McGee, Delphia	316 Walker Avenue
McGowan, Elizabeth	2812 Dallas Avenue
Mason, Annie	2604½ Washington Avenue
Matthews, Eliza	1418 Matthews Street
Pardell, Cora	2515 Prairie Avenue
Perry, Lula	3010 Cline Street
Vinson, Mattie	2603 Engelke Street
Washington, Hattie	5506 Washington Avenue
White, Effie	801 West 6th Avenue
Williams, Dolly	2712½ Odin Avenue
Williams, Lillie	2806 Odin Avenue

Document 199

Ann's Hat Shoppe

[A. W. Jackson, *A Sure Foundation: A Sketch of Negro Life in Texas* (Houston: Yates Publishing Co., 1940), pp. 102–103]

Ann Robinson was a college graduate and a teacher before opening a well-stocked shop featuring women's hats and clothing.

Mrs. Ann Robinson, the proprietor of Ann's Hat Shoppe, is a native Texan, and was born in Wharton County. She attended public schools in Victoria, Texas, and finished her high school training in the above city. She did her college work in Prairie View College, finished in the summer of 1917. She taught school in Fort Bend County in the session of 1917–18, and married Mr. Wm. Robinson in 1919 and opened the Ann's Hat Shoppe on the first floor of the Odd Fellows Temple, Houston, Texas in 1925 and in 1934 moved to her present location, 807 Prairie Avenue. She has one of the best equipped ladies' ready-to-wear stores in Texas, manned and conducted by our group. She carries a line of stock consisting of all kinds of ladies' ready-to-wear such as coats, dresses, suits, underwear, hosiery, bags and hats.

Mrs. Robinson is destined to continue her successful career in this type of business for she is congenial, affiable, agreeable, accommodating, approachable, and has a business tact that enables her to meet and greet all types of people, the learned and unlearned, the high and the low, the hearty and the humble, and whatever happens to be the disposition of the customer, she has that unique technique that makes the customer soon discover that she is his or her friend.

Document 200
"I was the first black woman pilot in America"
[Henry M. Holden, "Brave Bessie the Barnstormer," *Sisters* (National Council of Negro Women) (Spring 1989): 6–8]

Bessie Coleman, of Atlanta and Waxahachie, was one of the first licensed female pilots in the world and the first black woman aviator and barnstormer in the United States. After failing to locate an American flying school, she traveled to France to fulfill a lifelong dream. She earned a pilot's license from the Fédération Aéronautique Internationale in 1921. During an exhibition flight in 1926, her plane crashed and she was killed.

I guess it was the newspapers reporting on the air war in Europe during World War I, that got me interested in flying. I was an avid reader, and I searched the libraries looking for information on flying. I think all the articles I read finally convinced me I should be up there flying and not just reading about it. . . . I decided I would not take "no" for an answer. . . . My mother's words [to become somebody] always seemed to give me strength to overcome obstacles. . . .

I returned to the U.S. in 1922 with my air-pilot license from the Fédération Aéronautique Internationale. I was the first black woman pilot in America. I had grand dreams but I was a realist. If I could create a minimum of my desires, I would have no regrets. My achievement was of no significance unless I could share it with others. Having attained my first goal, I set a new one [to open a flying school to teach other African-American women to fly].

Document 201
Stunt Flying
[*Houston Informer*, July 1925; reprinted in Doris L. Rich, *Queen Bess: Daredevil Aviator* (Washington, D.C.: Smithsonian Institution Press, 1993)]

ANOTHER BIG FLYING CIRCUS
Featuring
BESSIE COLEMAN'S
FAREWELL FLIGHT IN TEXAS
SUNDAY, JULY 12, 3:00 P.M.
HOUSTON AERIAL TRANSPORT FIELD

Document 202
"A wonderful womb medicine"
[Correspondence, 1873–1903, Norwood Papers, Center for American History, University of Texas at Austin]

Toward the end of the nineteenth century, women bought patent medicines like Lydia Pinkham's Vegetable Compound to treat gynecological diseases. Newspapers carried advertisements for the product, including testimonials from satisfied customers.[2] Some black women earned extra money by marketing similar products.

Austin October 14, 1894
Miss Norwood

Dear Friend as it has been quite a while since I heard from you I write you so I know about your health and to tell you of a wonderful womb medicine that I am now handling. I like it much better than the Pestiles that I use to sell I have supplyed quite a number of Ladies in this City who are great sufferers with female trouble and all are delighted with its consequences the name of the medicine is Olive Branch and if you are still troubled with womb disease I would like to cure you. . . . I would also be glad to have you act as Agent for me in selling the medicine after you like it and get well you would then be glad to sell to ladies who are afflicted and cure them write me if you need the medicine and I will take great pleasure in supplying you it is 1.00 one dollar per box and their is one months treatment in a box.

hopeing to hear from you soon I am
Very respectfully
Mrs. E. S. Reeves
207 East 4th St.
Austin Texas

Document 203
"Negro Public Health Nursing in Texas"
[Annie Maie Mathis, "Negro Public Health Nursing in Texas," *Southern Workman* 56, no. 7 (July 1927): 302–303]

The need for health care practitioners was crucial at the turn of the century, and the public health nurse became a life-saving professional. Miss Annie Maie Mathis was the first black on the staff of the Texas State Board of Health, hired in 1922 as a maternity and infancy nurse.

After a three year's program of public health nursing in Texas the decision was reached that the most definite need for the continuation of efficient work was the addition of a Negro itinerent nurse to the staff of nurses of the State Board of Health, the idea being that the Negro nurse would visit the counties in which there were nursing services, and project a program which the white nurse could supervise until the return of the Negro nurse. In 1922 a Negro nurse was added to the staff of State nurses, and in 1925 a second nurse was employed. . . .

The State Negro nurse goes into a county, gets in touch with the leaders of her race, organizes a committee whose purpose it is to assist her with the work and to carry the work on under supervision of the county nurse after she leaves the county. She also organizes adult classes, prenatal and child health conferences, doing school work in the lower grades so as to get contacts in the homes and holds additional midwife classes.

She finds many deplorable conditions; flies innumerable, poor housing, as many as six and seven people living in huts of one room. These huts are usually poorly drained locations and many of the people drink from polluted wells and stagnant streams. Contagious diseases are prevalent, such as typhoid, malaria, and consumption. Clean-up week, also Negro health week, have done much to improve these conditions.

Each year a delegation of Negro women is sent to [a] conference where they receive instructions, the most essential being health instructions. These women return to their various homes to put into execution suggestions given them at the conference. This year's meeting was held at Prairie View State School, April 30 to May 6. Delegates from five towns gave reports on how they were helping to promote health education among their people. . . . The State Negro nurse has been of much help in this program and work has been most effective. The demand for the State Negro nurse in different communities has grown to such an extent that the schedule of the Negro nurses is planned weeks ahead. All city health departments of the State have at least one Negro nurse on the public health nursing staff. . . .

The midwife problem had to be reached as midwives were not under any supervision. Very little attention was given to birth registration, the midwives were ignorant and superstitious, very set in their beliefs and careless as well as filthy. It is estimated that there are 4000 midwives in the State of Texas, the larger number being Negroes. In 1925, 1473 Negro midwives were reached. Classes were held to instruct these women, the chief aim of these meetings being to teach cleanliness, proper care of the mother and infant, use of prophylactic drops in the eyes of the newborn and how to register births. It was found, by way of comparison, that one out of nineteen white children died before reaching one year of age; one out of eleven Negro children died before reaching one year of age and one out of every five Mexican children died before reaching one year of age. One per cent of all the deaths in Texas during 1927 was due to causes relating to child birth.

The value of the Negro public health nurse in Texas is inestimable. The people are very grateful and respond in every way when called upon.

The nurse is doing much in decreasing contagious diseases and improving housing conditions in the homes and schools. Health education as a whole has advanced through this and similar agencies more in the last five years than in the previous twenty-five years in Texas.

Document 204
"My grandmother was a midwife"
[Ruthe Winegarten, ed., *I Am Annie Mae: The Personal Story of a Black Texas Woman* (Austin: Rosegarden Press, 1983), pp. 19–21]

Until World War II, over half of all babies born in Texas, regardless of ethnicity, were delivered by midwives, who were important health care workers in their communities. According to historian Ada Simond, "The wisdom and judgment of these women was trusted and respected." Further, they were usually "familiar with home remedies, herbs, teas, and roots, as well as methods and practices of practical nursing." They were "strong women" and "looked upon as authority figures."[3]

My grandmother [Matilda Boozie Randon] was a midwife [ca. 1880s–1910]. Every white man or black man born in that country that's my age, my grandma *caught* him. They called it *catch em*. Yes, a many a one down there [in Washington County] right today.

Grandma would go and stay three and four weeks with a family, according to how rich they was. The Hodes, the Yahnishes, the Wobblers, they all were rich people, Bohemian, German, Polish people. . . .

She was woke up many a night, and stayed right there with that woman until she got up. There wasn't nothing they could do for pain. Grandma kept quinine. . . .

And Grandma had another little medicine in a bottle, real dark red. I don't know what it was. Grandma kept also a black bag, just like a doctor did, she kept it. And we wasn't allowed to touch it. We couldn't even look at it too hard, cause everything she needed was there. She had her scissors and her thread that she cut the baby's cord, and she had it right there. . . . Grandma had big number eight white spools of thread, and she kept it in this bag. . . .

She had a name for herself. She was good and she was recognized!

Document 205
"I could not use the restroom"
[Kay Powers, "Doctoring and Earning Respect," *Austin American-Statesman*, March 2, 1986, pp. D28–D29]

Although Dr. Connie Yerwood was a life-saving physician with the Texas Department of Health, having been hired in 1936, she faced discrimination in the use of public facilities until the passage of civil rights legislation in the 1960s. She and her sister, Joyce Yerwood, were forced to leave the state to obtain medical training in the early 1930s.

I had to come home to use the restroom. Our office at that time was on the first floor of the Land Office building. . . . I could not use the restroom. That's unbelievable. You couldn't use the restrooms at the filling station. I don't usually like to talk about this because it's so far back, and you don't like to play up the bad things, but in traveling, we had to select certain filling stations where we knew we could use the restrooms, so that is where we went to get our gasoline and get our service.

Sure. And you couldn't eat in any place. Some of the drive-ins wouldn't even serve you. The fast-food places, some of them wouldn't even. The young people today that didn't have to go through this, they don't realize it actually existed. . . .

I couldn't take my medical training south of the Mason-Dixon line. The only medical school in Texas . . . was right down near Galveston. . . . When I got ready to file my license with the county clerk here in Austin, at that point the person waiting on me was a man, and he said, "Oh, a lady doctor. Where did you go, Galveston?"[4] . . . I said, "Now you can look at me and tell that I didn't go to Galveston, can't you?"

Marguerite Armstrong, pictured here ca. 1950s, and her husband, T. D. Armstrong, were owners of a successful Galveston drugstore. He was the first black elected to the Galveston City Council in the twentieth century. (Courtesy Rosenberg Library, Galveston, Black History Collection #60)

Document 206
"Medicine was in her blood"
["She Chose Medicine for a Career" [Dr. Connie Yerwood Odom], *Negro Achievement* (Fort Worth) 6 (June 1952): 16, 54]

Negro Achievement, *one of a family of magazines targeted for black readers by the Good Publishing Company of Fort Worth between 1943 and 1982, paid significant attention to women, focusing on their role as workers. Another of their better-known magazines was* **Sepia.**

Here is one doctor who works for months without seeing any results of her work.

And she is happy about the whole affair.

Dr. Connie Yerwood Odom is employed by the Texas State Board of Health as consultant with the division of maternity and child health. As her work is of preventive rather than curative nature, she knows that she has done a good job when she sees nothing but good health.

Asked for an example, she tells about the time she was working in a small country town. "All the Negro children were immunized against diphtheria but the white children would not consent to get shots. An epidemic of diphtheria broke out."

"Not one of the Negro children caught it."

"In our work we can only suggest that people do a certain thing but we have no power to make them do anything," she said.

MEDICINE IN HER BLOOD

Choosing a career was no problem for Dr. Odom. Medicine was in her blood, since she came from a family of physicians. Her father was a physician and her sister, who lives in Old Greenwich, Conn., is also a physician.

Immediately upon graduation from high school in Austin, she enrolled in Sam Huston College. From there she went to Meharry Medical School in Nashville, Tenn., and upon graduation enrolled in the University of Michigan for a postgraduate course in public health.

Dr. Odom said there is an acute shortage of Negro doctors in the South

These young women were Galveston secretaries in the Lloyds of Great State Insurance Company in 1952. (Courtesy Rosenberg Library, Galveston, Black History Collection #60)

because so many were lost during the war and a large number did not return to civilian practice but stayed in the army.

She also mentioned the fact that there are only seven other Negro women doctors in Texas—two in San Antonio and five in Houston. However, it appears that more women are becoming interested in medicine. During the time she was attending Meharry Medical School, there were only four girls enrolled, and today there are about 30 or 40 in attendance.

WORKS IN HARMONY WITH WHITE STAFF

She loves her work which carries her all over the eastern and southern part of the state. It is her duty to set up infant and pre-school clinics and maternity clinics in towns where there are none for Negroes.

Although the staff on which she works is white, she has never encountered any unusual situations and has done well in her position. She was the only Negro to appear on the program of the Texas Academy of Science at the University of Texas in 1946. However, at the last meeting there were about 50 Negroes to appear on the program.

Dr. Odom has an off-duty schedule that alone would tire a less energetic person. She instructs classes three hours a week in health education at Sam Huston College; works with the PTA, clubs, or any group that asks for lessons on her type of work; is on the national field committee of the Girl Scouts; is an active member of Alpha Kappa Alpha sorority; is president of her college alumni association and the United Negro College Fund.

Looks belie Dr. Odom's age. She is very youthful looking.

"Are you like most women—you don't tell your age?" she was asked.

"No," she answered slowly, "I don't mind."

But, like most women, she didn't say.

Document 207
Social Work
[Ellie Walls Montgomery, *Juvenile Delinquency among Negroes in Houston, Texas: The Need for Institutional Care* (Houston: Department of Sociology, Houston College for Negroes, 1936), pp. 7–8; copy at Houston Metropolitan Research Center, Houston Public Library, Houston]

Ellie A. Walls Montgomery from Houston was one of the first two fellows of the Urban League, graduating from the New York School of Philanthropy (later part of Columbia University) around 1913. She returned to Houston to become a prominent educator and social scientist. In 1935, she surveyed court, hospital, and school records to gather data to support the need for a residential facility for young offenders.

The court case group comprises 139 girls arrested over a period of twelve months, January, 1935, to January, 1936. . . . [These] girls are charged with 293 complaints; over two complaints for the girls. For instance, one girl is charged with wandering the streets, associating with immoral persons, and running away from home. Another is charged with the above three complaints and truancy, and disorderly conduct; five charges in all. . . .

The ages of the girls range from eleven to seventeen with one eighteen years old. Approximately 60% of the girls are between fourteen and sixteen years old. Fifty out of 139, or 35.9%, were guilty of wandering the streets; 73, or over half, associated with immoral persons; 17 had venereal disease, 40 ran away from home, while 29, or 20.8%, were pregnant. Of this last group, two were 12 years old and two were 13 years old.

Sundry reports include fighting, drinking, threatening life, and soliciting. It will be noticed that 19 cases of truancy were so pronounced as to be brought to the attention of the court. Truancy is generally handled by the truant officer through the census office of the public schools.

Document 208
Volunteer Work and Philanthropy
[Eliza Johnson Home for Our Aged Negro Citizens program, Anna Dupree Collection, Houston Metropolitan Research Center, Houston Public Library]

Through hard work and diligent saving of their earnings, Anna Johnson Dupree and Clarence A. Dupree were able to invest in real estate and eventually to return money to build community institutions in Houston.

In March, 1944, Anna Dupree, well known beauty operator and wife of C. A. Dupree, owner of the Eldorado Ball Room startled not only the community, but the whole United States with a gift of $20,000 for the construction of a building for underprivileged Negro children. This represents one of the most liberal spirited gestures made by any Negro person. There were no strings attached to Mrs. Dupree's donation. It was voluntary and unsolicited.

In order to provide a University for Negroes in Texas, Mr. and Mrs. Dupree gave of their own free will, $11,000 to help construct Texas Southern University.

Negro Girl Scouts were without a camp site until Mr. Dupree and a few other men bought 200 acres of land in Willis, Texas now known as Camp Robinhood. The Duprees then launched out to get a home for the aged humbled, and forgotten Negroes. We have always wanted to do something to help those who start out in life with the cards stacked against them, this humble couple once said. . . .

The Eliza Johnson Home for the Aged opened its doors in late August of 1952. . . . Mr. Dupree also assisted in cooking for the aged people. . . . Mrs. Dupree made fruit cobblers and baked them in the oven. Sometimes she'd make fruit and boiled dumplings. Don't suppose you know anything about that kind of food, but the old timers know.

Document 209
"I am a widow"

[To Mr. District Director from Lucia Knotts Rhone, Jan. 4(?), 1937, Rhone Family Papers, Box 3U-171, Folder 2, Center for American History, University of Texas at Austin]

After the death of her husband, Lucia Knotts Rhone tried to run the family farm as best she could. Like many other farm families during the Depression, she was plagued by natural disasters.

Carmine Tex. Jan 4[?]—1937.

Mr. District Director.

Sir,

Your letter of Old Age pension [?] Dec. 19 was received by me on Jan.[?] 12. I tried hard to not write you but being unable to come talk the matter over with you I am writing to you about the matter. I was borned in the year of 1866—Jan. 24. I will be 71 years old on the 24th of this mo. I live in the Ledbetter road 3 miles from Round Top. I farm but for three year in succession Comings [?] creek and ceder creek has overflowed my crop which did great damage to my crops. Overflows 1934—in 1935 and in 1936. These overflows damage me greatly. I worked harder that year than I worked in all of my life I am older and [last 4 words are scratched through] made less I need [help] worse than ever Now if you can help me in gettin the pension I haven't a grain of corn of help please help me. Please consider my letter. I am a widow.

(Mrs.) Lucia Knotts Rhone.

Document 210
Desperate for Work

[Records of the Works Project Administration, Record Group 69, Texas, File 690, cited in Julia Kirk Blackwelder, *Women of the Depression: Caste and Culture in San Antonio, 1929–1939* (College Station: Texas A & M University Press, 1984), pp. 68–69]

New Deal programs like the Works Progress Administration (WPA) and the National Youth Administration (NYA) assisted thousands of blacks, but in a discrimi-

natory fashion. The Women's and Professional Division of the WPA in Texas employed some 4,500 black women by November 1936, but they accounted for only about three percent of the total in the period 1935–1941.⁵ Nor were black women hired for administrative positions in the WPA or NYA. Some, like Lulu Gordon of San Antonio, complained in writing to President Roosevelt.

I am a Negro woman. I am on the relief. I have three children. I have no husband and no job. I have worked hard ever since I was old enough. I am willing to do any kind of work because I have to support myself and my children. I was under the impression that the Government or the W.P.A. would give the Physical fit relief clients work. I have been praying for that time to come. . . . I need work, and I will do anything the government gives me to do. . . . Will you please give me some work.

Document 211
"Work and food are what we are asking for"
[Mrs. S. E. Boone and [Miss?] I. M. Howard to Mrs. [Eleanor] Roosevelt, November 30, 1938, Records of the Works Progress Administration, Record Group 69, State Series, Texas 693.0, National Archives]

> 1014 Dealaware [*sic*]
> San Antonio, Texas
> November 30, 1938

Dear Mrs. Roosevelt:
. . . We are a group of Negro women who for months, some for a year have been trying to get some relief from the local officials of the Texas Relief Commission and the W.P.A. officials. Work and food are what we are asking for, for our children; they treat us very bad at the W.P.A. offices, minor clerks tell us that there are no jobs for Negroes. There are [jobs] for white people and Mexicans. We learned that about $100,000 [in] W.P.A. funds were available for a household service school where women could be trained as maids. We asked for that school but were refused. . . .

You perhaps have heard, Mrs. Roosevelt, that Negro women here can get only the most menial jobs, such as maids, charwomen and the like. We cannot ever be drygoods store clerks or saleswomen in stores or factory workers.

WPA officials spend money training white and Mexican maids who have other jobs open to them, but categorically refuse to help us Negro women who comprise more than 80% of the maids now employed and have practically no other avenues for a livelihood.

In the WPA sewing rooms we are discriminated against and those of us who do get work are so abused that we can hardly stay on the job. We have attempted time after time to get to see Mr. H. P. Drought State Administrator, but he refuses to see us.

Respectfully yours,
S. E. Boone, President
I. M. Howard, Vice President
WORKERS ALLIANCE OF AMERICA
COLORED LOCAL #3

Document 212
Protests Continue
[Ruth Wallace and Emma E. M. Hutchinson to Mrs. F. D. Roosevelt, September 24, 1940, Record Group 69, State Series, Texas 693.0, National Archives]

Conditions had not improved by 1940. The local WPA trained black women for two kinds of jobs—as matrons in public school restrooms, gyms, and lounges and as seamstresses.

307 N. Monumental Street
San Antonio, Texas
September 24, 1940

Mrs. F. D. Roosevelt
White House
Washington, D.C.

Dear Madam:-

I am writting you concerning condition of the W.P.A. of the San Antonio district in behalf of the colored women.

Mrs. Roosevelt I thought the W.P.A. was for all unemployed people regardless of race, colored or creed. It seem as if the heads of woman's W.P.A. project (where women are employed) have gotten together and decided that the Negro women do not need the aid of W.P.A. They are refusing to employ colored on any of the woman's project this fall. In the Sewing room they are only eight colored women working. When the cut came in April, they layed them all off but thirteen (13). The Matron project use about twenty (20) or twenty five (25) colored women will not use more than eight (8) colored women this fall. It employed a total of about 109 to 115 women. . . .

[A supervisor] said we have to wait until we can here from Washington, they told us not to hire you Nigger women any more, get out and get you a job or take the maid training that is for you all. . . .

We are poll tax and tax payers as well as the other races. We are law-abiding citizens of the U.S.A. This is a free country. Then why are we not given our shares of the W.P.A. . . .

I did not know our beloved President had given orders to hire only whites and Mexicans women on woman's project.

It's also the same way on the N.Y.A. project, not a one for our young unemployed colored girl. . . . Mrs. Roosevelt do you think this is fair? Please help us our children are hungry and winter is coming and wood is need[ed], the rent man is knocking and we are being denied our jobs. Mrs. Crawford is a mother of 12 children, she lost her husband and instead of giving her W.P.A. . . . she was given a $4 week job now she is always being set out doors. Churches help her once in a while. Her children are naked and hungry. There are white women working on W.P.A. with husband with good salaries and some women own several rent house yet they are working and they told a bunch of the colored women about it. . . .

Our Protest

As loyal tax payers and as citizen of the U.S.A.:—

We the Negro women of San Antonio, Texas protest the denial of employment of colored women on the various W.P.A. project and of denial of employment to our children on various N.Y.A. project because we are a dark race of people. This is unconstitutional and a violation of the constitution of the U.S. of America. The land of the brave and the home of the free. We demand that we be given jobs on W.P.A. that we are best suited to. (That is the way others are treated).

Signed Ruth Wallace—307 Monumental St.

Ex-Matron Project

Emma E. M. Hutchinson—706 N. Centre

Sewing Room

Document 213

National Youth Administration of Texas

[Faith Smith to Mr. C. P. Little, Jr., May 3, 1938, NYA Papers, Administrative Project, Lyndon Baines Johnson Library and Museum, Austin]

The NYA was the most beneficial part of the WPA for black Texans. It provided part-time jobs and vocational training for needy high school and college students ages sixteen to twenty-four. Mary Elizabeth Branch, president of Tillotson College in Austin, and Jeffie O. A. Conner, a McLennan County home demonstration agent, served on the Texas Negro State Advisory Committee.

NATIONAL YOUTH ADMINISTRATION OF TEXAS
Fort Worth
May 3, 1938

Mr. C. P. Little Jr.
NYA District Supervisor
Fort Worth, Texas.

Dear Mr. Little:

One of the negro girls who was employed last fall on the NYA project which operated at the City-County Hospital, has been given employment for three months and perhaps longer, by Miss Bess Carr, Dietitian of the hospital.

This youth will earn $31.00 per month and three meals each day. Some time ago Miss Carr gave permanent private employment to another NYA girl, Oma Gene Nelson, at the same salary. This youth is still working and Miss Carr states that she is very pleased with her services. The second youth to be employed, Geraldine Williams, will work during the vacation period at the hospital. If her work is satisfactory, she will be in line for the first permanent opening.

Miss Carr has taken a very personal interest in the girls who worked under her supervision on the NYA project, and her cooperation in giving these NYA girls private employment is very gratifying.

Sincerely,
Faith Smith
NYA Project Superintendent

Document 214
"I was union-minded"
[Interview by Glenn Scott with Olivia Rawlston, ca. 1977, People's History in Texas Archives, Special Collections, University of Texas at Arlington Libraries] [6]

World War II resulted in economic expansion and created new job opportunities for increasing numbers of black women in defense work as some were able to move into more desirable and better-paid jobs. Although the Texas garment industry provided better-paying jobs for women than most others, it hired few blacks until World War II. Olivia Rawlston's work with the ladies' auxiliary of the Brotherhood of Sleeping Car Porters was merely a prelude to her leadership of the segregated Dallas "B" local of the International Ladies Garment Workers Union (ILGWU).

Working conditions were terrible for them [Pullman porters]. They lived off of their tips before A. Philip Randolph was farsighted enough to see that if he could organize them that they would be able to make a living wage. He brought them from $15 a month up until my husband passed I think his salary was around $300 a month. . . . that was in '62.

Well, during the depression I can remember my husband made a trip and if his check was $10, we'd celebrate with a good dinner. . . . Really, the Pullman Company depended on the public paying their help. . . .

I became involved with the ladies auxiliary about 1935. . . . The ladies auxiliary in Dallas was organized in my home. We had about ten women for the first meeting. Then we went up to about twenty-five or thirty and we had a beautiful organization. . . .

[I got involved with] the International Ladies Garment Workers Union about '45. . . . I went to work at the shop [the Nardis Company] because J. Bernard Gold, he had in his mind that he could make operators out of [black women]—this was something entirely new. He was a Jew, he was a wonderful man, and I had a lot of respect for him. He's dead now. But he took the Negro woman out of the kitchen and put her on power machines in the city and it paid off for him. He lost a lot of business—this is history—because he had Negro women on the machines, and he made beautiful operators out of them. When I first started to work there, training, I made 35 cents an hour. . . . We made lovely money, and we used to have some beautiful affairs. There was some social life to that part of it. . . .

Mr. Gold himself was sympathetic toward unions. . . . Mr. Gold must have been a pretty smart man because he could see what the union could do for him, too. . . .

You see, our local was the branch local. During that time everything was segregated. But they [the white women] had their shop, they had their meetings, and we had ours. At Christmas time or something like that, we always had things together. Most of the officers in the union were broad-minded people. As a matter of fact, I think that even though it was segregated we had always worked together and we knew that it was in our interest to really pull together, and we did. . . .

I was union-minded in the beginning, and, of course, they [the factory workers] saw that I knew something about organized labor so, therefore, when we first set up, they made me their president. That's the way I got to be president, and was president there for thirteen years. . . .

We had 385 black women at one time working at Nardis. That would cover the presses and all of the employees there. And we had just about 98% of them union-minded and really working for the cause. . . . Most of the women that I know that worked in that shop was union-minded, and the whites, too. . . .

In our shop we did piece rate *for our work*, and we had one or two managers that felt that we would get too much. Whoever they'd make the time study on they took up too much time and said they could do better than that and then want to make more time studies, and of course, then I would say, "I don't think it's necessary to do that." . . . Naturally, we would pick out . . . a very good, steady girl to make studies on because that would be fair to the company and fair to the operator. Some girls would just go like lightning, but they don't do good work. And of course, that would be a handicap to us and to the manager, too. . . .

We made sport clothes in that shop. And of course, we made skirts, blouses, and waistcoats. . . . We had collar-setters, we had sleeve-makers . . . then we had girls to do the fronts and to do the backs and set the cuffs. . . . We had bundle girls, called them *floor* girls. . . . In our factory they were colored, but I'm sure in the other factory—you see, we had two factories—I'm sure they were white. We had all colored pressers. . . . They were collar-turners . . . button-hole girls. . . . Now at one time they had the black pressers up at the other shop, up at the other factory. . . . That's No. 1 and No. 2. We were No. 2. . . . White and black worked in the shipping department. . . .

Where Nardis was—where I took my training—the government had a sewing room there [during World War II]. That's before Nardis' taking over. A public work room for people that worked on garments, worked on *union-alls* and things for the soldiers. . . .

As a union representative if they [the white forewomen] got very nasty and we could catch them at it, we would file a complaint against them . . . then I would get the complaint, then I would turn the complaint over to the head chairlady in the factory, and then she would take it to [the ILGWU representative] and he would investigate it. . . .

I was fired for being, they said insubordinate because I didn't appreciate what the forewoman was doing, and I told her so, and I was called into the office. This particular manager was named James—I never forget it—and we had a heated argument. He took up a piece of iron—I guess it must have been something to hold the books down—and he threw it on the floor and cursed. I told him, "Now that doesn't excite me, just so you don't hit me with it that's all." So anyway, he fired me. I lost a day, and I was back to work the next day. I didn't want to go because I felt like he would be picking at me, always having trouble. But I can truthfully say whatever [the ILGWU local representative] told him, I had no more trouble out of him, and I was right back in my same position.

Document 215
Working on the Railroad
[Interview by Gene Brooks with Annie Cornell Campbell, June 10, 1989, Quarters Project Collection, South Texas Archives, John E. Conner Museum, Texas A & I University, Kingsville][7]

During World War II, as most able-bodied men went off to the armed services, a limited number of jobs in industry and war-related work became available to women. Annie Cornell Campbell was one of about ten African-American women employed by the Missouri Pacific Railroad at its shop in Kingsville.

I was born in Longview, Texas . . . on the 26th of August, 1917 and my parents name was John William, my fathers name. My mothers name was Alice William. And we lived on our own farm. My dad was one of the lucky ones. He had a . . . 288 acre farm. We had other peoples working for us. . . .

[Nineteen] forty-four I started into working for the railroad in the shop . . . and I worked in the afternoon and [after I'd] get my bath I'd go in[to their grocery] store . . . about 8 or 10 shop women was employed at that time . . . sweeping, picking up, some of the women was cleaning the engines, but I was one of the fortunate ones I was afeared and I just told the foreman I wasn't gettin on the engine and therefore I never got on the engine. And I carried mail, and I had to paint, I did a lot a hard work too, because after a long run when they start sending the men back from [the armed] service, they wanted to get rid of the womens out of the shop and they wasn't supposed to have put us on the main seniority roster and they went and place the womens right on the main seniority roster with the men and therefore we could buck anybody that we were older [had worked longer] than them. If a man had a job that I felt that I could do I could bump him which I did.

I'd exercise my seniority and so I start carrying mail. . . . My husband he was a great lover of the railroad and the CT of A [Colored Trainmen of America, a union]. They didn't have a meeting hall. They use to meet at the Masonic Hall. The CT of A had a ladies auxiliary, we stood 100% behind them. We worked and when they needed something we had money to give them to help do whatever they needed. We had paid for the [meeting] hall that way. . . . Well, we put on style shows, we used to have beautiful style shows. . . . And see they had to have lawyer fees and we would help em get it.

Document 216
In the Shipyards
[*Houston Informer*, September 23, 1944, p. 1]

Mrs. Inez Reynolds, discharged war worker in a local shipbuilding plant, has returned to work, according to union officials, after being fired for defending herself in an affray with a work supervisor of another craft who slapped her down after cursing her. According to reports she defended herself well. Union members protested her discharge from service in war production.

Document 217
"Women Urged to Push Bill Designed to Aid Them as Workers"
[*Houston Informer*, February 12, 1944, p. 6]

During World War II, there was a growing shortage of black domestics as women found other kinds of jobs. Black "kitchen mechanics" now commanded higher wages. The Social Security Act finally covered domestics in 1951. However, the federal minimum wage law was not extended to them until 1974.

Women, Attention: Write a postcard, letter, or send a wire to your congressman, urging his support of the Wagner-Murry-Dingell bill, for women workers have a lot to gain from this measure, designed to broaden the Social Security act to include domestics and farm laborers.

Document 218
"WAAC Officer . . . Says Service Is a Great Opportunity"
[*Houston Informer*, November 1943]

"The Woman's Army Auxiliary Corps offers a splendid opportunity for colored women to help achieve success in the war effort," Lt. Alice Marie Jones, native Texan, who was a member of the first class commissioned at Ft. Des Moines, Iowa, and presently stationed in Houston on recruiting duty, declared to *The Informer* in an exclusive interview Wednesday. A graduate of Prairie View State College, Lt. Jones has done well by her native state.

Document 219
"Houston Girl Returns from War Zone"
[*Houston Informer*, January 1, 1944, p. 1]

Home on leave for the Christmas holidays after ten months of active duty with our troops in the North African theatre of war, 2nd Lt. Leola Green related . . . the happy experience she had in being able to help her country in the war. . . .

Attired in her field uniform, with all the calm and coolness that one could expect of an army nurse in the war era, she was greatly impressed with the lack of discrimination. "An injured soldier ceases to be black or white in the fighting force," she said.

Document 220
"Private Lizzie Kelly Honored"
[*Waco Messenger*, November 10, 1944, p. 1]

World War II gave black women their first chance to serve in the military. A number from Texas were members of the Women's Army Auxiliary Corps (WAAC, later WAC). Lizzie Kelly, who had been a power sewing machine operator, joined the WAC and in 1945 was promoted to the rank of corporal.

A reception was given Saturday night, Nov. 4, by the J. M. M. of Toliver's Baptist Church in honor of Pvt. Lizzie Kelly who is now serving as a WAC in Walla, Walla, Wash. The Y.W.C.A. was beautifully decorated in red, white, and blue. Quite a number of young ladies were present also a good number of soldiers from the various camps.

Document 221
"I am going to become a lawyer"
[Veronica Salazar, "First Black Woman Lawyer Hits Her Stride," *Express-News* (San Antonio), March 25, 1984]

In the wake of World War II, more black women entered the professions of law and medicine. Hattie Briscoe became the first black person to graduate from St. Mary's University (a private school in San Antonio) in 1956. She may have been the first black woman to graduate from a law school in Texas.

For Hattie Elam Briscoe, success is getting up one more time after you have been knocked down. . . .

Briscoe, a former school teacher who spent more than 10 years in the classroom, switched careers at age 40 when she became San Antonio's first black woman lawyer. . . .

"It seemed like every time I achieved something special, some injustice would come along to knock me down. And seeing myself and my people constantly shoved aside, I knew I had to make some changes. I never could enter by the back door. . . ."

Her mother died when Hattie was nine but remained her daughter's strongest influence. . . .

A native of Smithville, Mabel White has been a successful Dallas businesswoman for over forty years. One of the city's first black licensed real estate brokers, she and her husband have provided low-cost rental dwellings in South and West Dallas. Operating under the name William White Enterprises, the couple's business interests also include commercial properties. She has been a member of the Good Street Baptist Church for over fifty years, is president of its Missionary Society, and has been active in district, state, and national Baptist conventions. Mabel White has also been a leader of the YWCA, the National Council of Negro Women, the National Association of Business and Professional Women's Clubs, the Dallas Black Chamber of Commerce, Church Women United, and the Dallas Museum of African American Life and Culture. (Courtesy Texas Black Women's Archives, African American Museum, Dallas)

Hattie's father moved his five children from Shreveport, La., to Marshall, Texas, where he remarried. Her stepmother was not too kind to her or the rest of the children.

"My stepmother would always talk against me and tried to convince my father to keep me from finishing college, so at the age of 16, I ran away from home," she says.

Briscoe worked her way through Wiley College by washing, ironing and cooking for a family of three. She obtained her bachelor of arts degree from Wiley in 1927 and moved to Wichita Falls, where she taught for four years[, married, and became a licensed cosmetology instructor].

In 1945, she returned to the classroom as instructor of cosmetology at Wheatly High School. She stayed there six years.

Then, in 1951, Briscoe says, she was inexplicably fired from her job the day after she received her master's degree in administration and supervision with a minor in industrial education from Prairie View A & M College. . . .

"I just couldn't understand what happened. I had worked so hard grooming my girls to strive for the best and without notice I was out." . . .

"When a doctor friend hit me with [the idea of] law school, I knew that was the answer." . . .

She recalls being told during the first semester at law school that women had no business being there. "I am a woman, I am in law school and I am going to become a lawyer," she answered. . . . She graduated No. 1 in her class.

Document 222

Black Female Professional Workers in Texas, 1900–1950

[William Joseph Brophy, "The Black Texan, 1900–1950: A Quantitative History," Ph.D. diss., Vanderbilt University, 1974, p. 113]

	1900	*1910*	*1920*	*1930*	*1940*	*1950*
Accountants, Auditors	N.A.	N.A.	0	N.A.	N.A.	9
Artists, Art Teachers	7	3	N.A.	6	8	27
Authors, Eds., Reporters	N.A.	N.A.	N.A.	3	5	10
Dietitians, Nutritionists	N.A.	N.A.	N.A.	N.A.	N.A.	55
Lawyers, Judges	N.A.	N.A.	N.A.	N.A.	1	2
Librarians	N.A.	N.A.	N.A.	13	36	104
Musicians, Music Teachers	69	150	130	188	175	316
Nurses, Professional [includes midwives]	676	64	84	158	228	440
Physicians, Surgeons	N.A.	N.A.	N.A.	N.A.	N.A.	9
Social, Welfare Workers	N.A.	N.A.	48	26	33	75
Teachers	1,097	1,846	2,909	4,284	4,928	6,186
Technicians, Med. & Dent.	N.A.	N.A.	N.A.	N.A.	N.A.	74
TOTAL	1,849	2,063	3,171	4,678	5,414	7,307

POLITICS AND PROTEST

Like their parents, twentieth-century blacks protested the humiliation, harassment, and brutality which they suffered because of their race. Discriminated against from the cradle to the grave, at the polls, in the criminal justice system, and in nearly every facet of their lives, black women fought back: they organized pressure groups, broke into new businesses and professions, picketed and sat-in during the civil rights movement, and assumed leadership roles in the National Association for the Advancement of Colored People (NAACP) and other organizations. Ultimately, they began winning election to public office in increasing numbers.

Document 223
Former Governor Opposes Votes for Women
[*Ennis News*, July 20, 1916]

"I am not for woman's suffrage," said [former governor] Mr. [Oscar B.] Colquitt. "Some men say, 'My wife can cast as intelligent a vote as the negro and mexican.' That is not the question. Probably she can cast a more intelligent vote than her husband who says it, but the point is that when you give the ballot to women, you give it to all women, regardless of color."

Document 224
Mrs. James B. Wells Opposes Woman Suffrage
["Women Don't Want Suffrage, Claim of Anti Leader Here; Asserts Best Will
Not Vote," *Fort Worth Star Telegram*, April 6, 1918, as cited in A. Elizabeth Taylor,

Barbara Jordan of Houston was the first black elected to the Texas Senate in the twentieth century (1966–1972) and the first black woman from the South ever to serve in the U.S. Congress (1973–1979). She went on to a successful career as a professor at the Lyndon Baines Johnson School of Public Affairs at the University of Texas at Austin. (University of Texas Institute of Texan Cultures)

Ruthe Winegarten, and Judith N. McArthur, eds., *Citizens at Last: The Woman Suffrage Movement in Texas* (Austin: Ellen C. Temple, 1987), p. 182]

There are two types of women who will vote. These are the Socialists and the negro women. The Socialists will vote because they are interested, the negroes because they enjoy it.

Document 225
Black Suffragists Request Membership
[Mrs. E. Sampson to "My Dear Mrs. Park," Folder 4, Box 3, McCallum Family Papers, I, Austin History Center, Austin Public Library, Austin (hereafter cited as MFP)]

In June 1918, Mrs. E. P. Sampson, the president of the El Paso Colored Woman's Club, sent a letter applying for membership in the national suffrage organization on behalf of her club. The National American Woman Suffrage Association had no individual club members. Membership was through state associations.

710 S. St. Uraire
El Paso, Texas.
June 1918

My dear Mrs. Park,-[Maud Wood Park, chairman of the National American Woman Suffrage Association's Congressional Committee, Washington, D.C.]

We would like to become an Auxiliary Branch of the National American Woman Suffrage Association.

Will you kindly send me the necessary information.

Yours truly
Mrs. E. Sampson

Document 226
"No colored women's leagues are members"
[Carrie Chatman Catt to Mrs. Edith Hinkle League, July 17, 1918, #19, Folder 4, Box 3, MFP, I]

The Texas Equal Suffrage Association sought advice about Edith Sampson's application from the National American Woman Suffrage Association. A response came from the national president, Carrie Chatman Catt.[1]

I will say that the question of auxiliaryship within the state is one for the state itself to decide. I presume that no colored women's leagues are members in southern states, although I do not know positively that this is true. There are a great many clubs in different northern states, individual colored women are direct members. Of course these women in the North are women with a good deal of white blood and are educated women, otherwise they would not be asking auxiliaryship.

Of late, however, there is a movement among the colored women and men everywhere to insist upon recognition and to get into all kinds of places that seem to have been closed to them before. This woman may desire to enter because she wishes to help the cause and she may merely be desirous of the recognition of her race. I am sure if I were a colored woman, I would do the same thing they are doing. . . . The constitution [of the National American Woman Suffrage Association] was amended last year, so that such a club as Mrs. Sampson's could not come into the National Association directly.

In some southern states it would be an impossibility to have a colored league without gravely upsetting the work and ruining the influences of the suffrage association. Whether this is true in Texas or not, I do not know, but I suggest that if you find it is so, you write Mrs. Sampson and tell her that you will be able to get the vote for women more easily if they do not embarrass you by asking for membership and that you are getting it for colored women as well as for white women and appeal to her interest in the matter to subside.

Cordially yours,
Carrie Chatman Catt, President

Document 227
"The negroes were not registered"
[Mrs. L. F. Beuckenstein to Minnie Fisher Cunningham, July 17–18, 1918, MFP, I]

Black women organized to protect their right to register to vote. There was no consistent policy followed by county officials. In Orange, the sheriff and tax collector apparently went back on an agreement to register the women.

The colored women of Orange were told at their church on Sunday that they would be registered. On Monday they proceeded to the Court house where our Sheriff & Tax Collector instead of being courteous in his refusal to register them was very insulting making our dusky population very indignant.

They then proceeded to employ an attorney to mandamus the sheriff and their attorney happened to be Geo Holland who at the time was and is chairman of the Men's Hobby Club of Orange Co. They went to Beaumont next day for trial and the Judge before whom the case came up was McDonald a great Ferguson supporter and admirer. The case was dismissed the negroes were not registered. . . . Hope nothing serious to the cause for which we are all laboring so hard for results from this affair in Orange.

Document 228
Registration in Travis County
[*Austin American-Statesman*, June 29, 1918]

Many colored women offered registration yesterday and were permitted to sign up. Collector Maud and other election officials told them the law provided only for the registration of white women to vote in the coming primary election and that no provision was made in it for colored women voting.

Document 229
"Six Negro women asked . . . to register"
[*Dallas Morning News*, July 11, 1918]

Fort Worth. Six Negro women asked to be allowed to register, but the Deputy Tax Collector said they were barred from [the] July primary in Tarrant county by action of the County Democratic Committee, but the colored suffragettes insisted they be allowed to register. They pointed to a white woman who was registering and asked why the ban on colored women. After some argument, they left without registering. All of them were well dressed and appeared intelligent representatives of their race. Some rode to the courthouse in automobiles.

Document 230
Women at the Polls
[Dorothy Robinson, "Interview with Christia Adair," April 25, 1977, in *The Black Women Oral History Project*, vol. 1, p. 60, with permission of K. G. Saur Verlag, a Reed Reference Publishing Company, and the Schlesinger Library, Radcliffe College]

In 1918, Texas women won the right to vote in the state Democratic primary. Although many black women registered, most were apparently turned away at the polls on election day, July 27. Christia Adair recalled her experience.

We dressed up and went to vote, and when we got down there, well, we couldn't vote. They gave us all different kinds of excuses. . . . So finally one woman, a Mrs. [Kitty] Simmons, said, "Are you saying that we can't vote because we're Negroes?" And he [the election official] said, "Yes, Negroes don't vote in [the Democratic] primary in Texas." So that just hurt our hearts real bad and we went on. There was nothing we could do about that but just take it as it was.

Document 231
"Mamma . . . was no white man's patsy"
[Lorece Williams of Caldwell County, quoted in Bertha McKee Dobie et al., eds., *Growing Up in Texas: Recollections of Childhood* (Austin: Encino Press, 1972), p. 113]

Mamma may not have been a one-woman revolutionary, but she was no white man's patsy either. There was power in her the day she confronted Mr. M—— at our front gate [ca. 1920s–1930s?] . . . a man who had a bad habit of riding his horse across our yards and flower beds. None of us ever said anything to him about it, because he was a white man. But one summer afternoon Mamma and us kids were rocking on the front porch when up rides Mr. M——. Mamma commenced to sing, softly, "Amazing Grace." By the time Mr. M—— reached our gate, Mamma had got the double-barreled shotgun and was holding it in her lap and rocking with a new determination. . . .

"Mr. M——," she went on, "you been riding across niggers' yards all these years. But I ain't going to stand for it. I'll shoot yo ass off sho as you bo'n." . . . "Ah, now, come on, Aunt Sarah, you don't mean that." "Oh yes I do. Don't you ride that horse 'cross this yard, 'cause if you do I'm gonna shoot the living s—— outta you. They's either gonna be a dead nigger, a dead horse, or a dead white man on this day." . . . He rode around our yard. He never came through it again.

Document 232
Christia Adair Becomes a Democrat
[Dorothy Robinson, "Interview with Christia Adair," April 25, 1977, in *The Black Women Oral History Project*, vol. 1, pp. 60–61, with permission of K. G. Saur Verlag, a Reed Reference Publishing Company, and the Schlesinger Library, Radcliffe College]

In 1920, Christia Adair took a group of public school students in Kingsville to greet the campaign train of Republican presidential candidate Warren G. Harding. She was so angry when he refused to shake their hands that she became a Democrat.

When Harding was running for President, the railroad company always sent special trains to bring special people down into that section. Because of my husband's seniority, he was always one of the brakemen that was on the train that would go to bring these home seekers and officials and things like that. And so my husband went on the train that went to bring Mr. Harding down.

Somewhere between Washington, or wherever they were coming from, to Kingsville, my husband observed that people were bringing school children to the train to shake hands with the candidate. And so he called me long distance and told me what was going on. I went over to the school and asked the teachers if they would take their children. And when they didn't have time, or didn't want to or something, I asked them, if the parents consented, could I take some of their children? And I did have 11 or 12 children, and I took them to the train. . . . I knew just about how the trains stopped and where the location of cars would be so I knew where to place my children to get the best attention. And when the train stopped, well, my husband was the rear brakeman, and he came out to open the observation gates so the candidate would get out to talk with the people. And so my children were right at the steps. And some white children were [brought] there by white teachers or parents, and he—Mr. Harding—reached over my children's heads to shake hands with the white children and never did pay any attention to my children. And I pulled my children out, hurt, disappointed and sorry for the children. But in my own heart, I said, "If that's what Republicans do, I cannot be a Republican. I'll have to change parties. From here on out I'll have to work for Democrat presidents."

Document 233
"Respectable black men and women had been beaten away from the polls"
[Dorothy Redus Robinson, *The Bell Rings at Four: A Black Teacher's Chronicle of Change* (Austin: Madrona Press, 1978), pp. 25–26]

When we came to Palestine [1930s], there was still fresh in the minds of the black population an incident in which respectable black men and women had been beaten away from the polls with ax handles and some had been placed in jail. Equally fresh in their memory were the horrors of a race riot in Slocum that had erupted a few years previously. These stories were related to us in hushed tones accompanied by a weird mixture of deep-seated bitterness, smoldering anger, and helpless surrender.

. . . There was the time when, in his capacity as county agent, Frank [her husband] was in a planning meeting for the Anderson County Fair, then known as the Texas Fruit Palace. None of the buildings on the fairgrounds was equipped with plumbing, and separate toilets were a legal fact. There was a toilet for white women, and when Frank requested similar accommodations for black women, the fair manager replied, "Let them go to the woods; that is what they are used to." . . .

Still vivid in my memory is the occasion when I was refused a ticket for a free drawing, even though the amount of my purchase qualified me for participation in the daily drawing that was being conducted by a local drugstore. When I requested the ticket, the owner told me quite emphatically yet not unkindly, "I'm sorry, but in this town, colored people do not participate in drawings." I replied with equal emphasis, "I'm sorry, but this will be the last purchase I'll make at this store." And it was, as long as he retained ownership. His attitude, however, was purely personal and did not represent any city-wide policy.

So in East Texas during the early 1930s, white was white and black was black and never the twain met on common ground, even though both groups experienced common sufferings, many of which were spawned by economic deprivation and by intellectual stagnation.

Document 234
"Desperate Conditions"
[Mrs. M. R. McKinney to Mary Church Terrell, founding president of the National Association of Colored Women, December 19, 1922, Container #6, Correspondence, September–December 1922 and undated 1922, Mary Church Terrell Papers, Library of Congress]

Corsicana, Texas. December 19-1922.

My dear Madame,

The accommodations and the conditions for the sick and old colored people are so poor and inadequate that in many cases they die for attention or suffer greatly. I am a colored registered nurse having been at one time on hire to care for the sick and Mexican patients but owing to that appalling situation I was forced to leave. While in the service I discovered many things concerning the affairs of the colored people here and I had always hope to be able to do something to better the situations as far as the sick people are concerned.

Why the place I had reference to was just a three room cottage with one bathroom and one little toilet to be used by male and female children and adults alike with absolutely no privacy. Only one general nurse to care for all patients. . . .

When there I considered the conditions thoroughly in a very quiet way. In a way that would be beneficial to the race and patients in this community. If I don't expose conditions it would be considered an insult to whites. *We are in a place where human bodies are burned anywhere and any time*. Nine have been burned or shot since last May only a short distance away. . . .

My plans are to build a modern hospital for colored people with a free clinic attached where the poor can be treated and cured free of charge. Thus I'm making general appeals for financial funds to persons that can help without making sacrifices. . . .

Will you listen in part to this sad case. It is just one of many. A very young man shot through the spine became paralyzed and [for] a time became an invalid. This young man's parents are very old and lived on a cotton farm owned by a white man. Many days the parents were forced to leave food and water at this invalid's side and go to work until nightfall. These white people advised the parents to send this boy to the county hospital—the above name place. They consented but the hospital officials always refused to take chronic cases so it was but a very few days before the parents were notified to come for their son. In the meantime the white farmer made the old parents say they were unable to care for him and were willing that he be turned over to the county as a pauper. Well their aim was all accomplished and young man sent to the county farm where criminals and outlaws are sent. Now you may ask why the county farm. I ask that same question myself. The answer is that there is no place for the people of color to go no provision have been made. So you have an idea of the desperate conditions of affairs.

Document 235
Mob Justice
[*Dallas Times Herald*, April 1, 1923]

From 1900 to 1910, 73 out of Texas's 254 counties experienced lynchings. By 1920, Texas led all states with the largest number of lynchings—eleven. Testimony before a congressional committee implicated Hiram Wesley Evans, a Ku Klux Klan leader, in the attack on a young black man, Alex Johnson. The Dallas County sheriff, Robert B. Seay, said he was satisfied with the treatment of Johnson. "He no doubt deserved it." [2]

Masked white men late Friday night carried Alex Johnson, negro bell boy, to a lonely spot on the Hutchins road a few miles south of Dallas, flogged him until blood flamed from his lacerated back and branded him on the forehead with the letters, "K.K.K." The men who took him from his home at 3500 Roseland avenue declared that the man had associated with a white woman in the hotel where he used to be employed. . . . Johnson under the threat of death to tell no one of the incident was returned to town and dumped in front of the hotel where the alleged liaison had taken place. [The assailants were] all well dressed and seemingly prosperous and took pieces of Johnson's clothing as souvenirs.

Document 236
"Texas Women Speak Out against Lynching"
[Monroe N. Work, *The Negro Year Book*, 1925–26 (includes the period 1922–1924) (Tuskegee, Ala.: Tuskegee Institute, 1925), pp. 27–28]

During the 1920s and 1930s, southern black and white women of goodwill recognized that cooperation was vital to making progress on racial problems. The Texas Commission on Inter-racial Cooperation (TCIC), founded in 1920, was composed of one hundred members, "half of whom shall be white divided equally between men and women, and half of whom shall be Negro divided equally between men and women." The Women's Division of the TCIC, organized as a separate entity in 1922, soon issued a strong statement condemning lynching. That same year Mrs. R. A. (Ethel) Ransom, a Fort Worth nurse and black club leader, was appointed Texas state director for the national Anti-Lynching Crusaders. [3]

We, the members of the women's section of the Texas state committee on Inter-racial Cooperation, find ourselves overwhelmed with the opportunity and the corresponding responsibility which we this day face in sharing the task of bringing about better conditions and relations in the South between the white and Negro races. . . . Lynching is the black spot on America's soul. . . . As women, as mothers of men, we protest. We condemn every violation of law in the taking of life, no matter what the crime.

Document 237

Interracial Cooperation among Women

[Minutes of the Texas Commission on Inter-racial Cooperation, Houston, Afternoon Session, November 5, 1926, Texas Commission on Inter-racial Cooperation Papers, Houston Metropolitan Research Center, Houston Public Library]

Mary E. V. Hunter summarized the philosophy of women's work in the TCIC at the group's 1926 convention.

The next speaker was Mrs. M. E. Hunter, Prairie View, whose subject was "Co-operation Between White and Negro Women on the State Commission." The following points were made by Mrs. Hunter:

1. A greater spirit of co-operation can be brought about between the white and colored people if members of each race defend those of the opposite race when criticism is brought against them.

2. The major factor to be utilized in bringing about social changes, as in any other realm of life, is education. Since this is true, the white and colored women of the community can work together for better school houses, equipment, longer terms, and better prepared and better paid teachers.

3. White and colored women can help each race better understand each other by making it possible for men and women of both groups who understand each side of the race problem to come before groups of the opposite race and tell of their intentions, desires, etc., of their race.

4. The local committees can use the Inter-racial Commission as a point of contact for each group to understand each other better. "I am thoroughly convinced that most of the short-comings of both races, when it comes to their attitude one toward the other, is the lack of understanding."

Document 238

Goals of the Texas Commission on Inter-racial Cooperation

[J. T. Clark to Members of the Commission on Inter-racial Cooperation, April 11, 1934, Texas Commission on Inter-racial Cooperation Papers, Houston Metropolitan Research Center, Houston Public Library]

Black and white women and men worked together in the Texas Commission on Inter-racial Cooperation. The organization's goals included the improvement of conditions in education, health, and economic and social justice.

1. To improve health and sanitary conditions among both whites and Negroes.

2. To promote educational advantages for Negroes.

3. To encourage in the daily press fair and impartial editorial and news policies where Negroes are concerned.

4. To promote economic and legal justice for Negroes.

5. To secure a state supported home for delinquent Negro girls.

6. To secure a state supported orphanage for Negro children.

7. To provide state supported hospitalization for Negro tubercular patients.

8. To create a spirit of goodwill, and replace traditional, inherited prejudices with intelligent appreciation and just recognition of merit.

Document 239
"There were places blacks could not go"
[Olive Banks, cited in *Bryan-College Station High School and Kemp High School, 1885–1985* (Bryan: Bethune Women's Club, 1985), unpaginated]

There were places blacks could not go [in the 1930s–1940s]. We could go to the Palace Theatre but we had to sit in the balcony and go around to the side doors. We couldn't sit on the main floor. There was the Downtown Cafe—we couldn't go in there to eat. . . . And the service stations had restrooms and when a black would want to go use the restroom they'd say it was out of order. In the dress stores, we couldn't go in the same dressing rooms. The whites had their own dressing rooms.

Document 240
National League of Republican Colored Women
[Daisy Lampkin to "Dear Fellow Republican," March 26, 1925, Container #7, Correspondence January–March 1925, Mary Church Terrell Papers, Library of Congress]

In 1925, Mrs. C. E. Adams of Beaumont was elected chaplain of the executive board of the National League of Republican Colored Women. The following report highlights the scope of the organization.[4]

The all day conference of the National League of Republican Colored Women held March 5th at Metropolitan A.M.E. Church, Washington, D.C. was a decided success.

Delegates attended, representing organizations in the following states:

Carlette Guidry-White, a track star for the University of Texas at Austin, was named Southwest Conference Athlete of the Year for 1990–1991. Female athletes have benefited greatly from the adoption of Title IX of the 1972 federal Educational Amendments to the Civil Rights Act of 1964 prohibiting discrimination by educational institutions receiving federal funds. Many universities have dramatically increased the percentage of their athletic budgets devoted to women's sports. (Photograph © Susan Allen Sigmon, University of Texas at Austin)

New York, New Jersey, Conneticutt [*sic*], Massachusetts, District of Columbia, Virginia, Maryland, Indiana, Illinois, Kansas, Kentucky, Texas, Georgia, Mississippi, Ohio and Pennsylvania. We now have enrolled over 400 organizations in 40 states.

At the meeting of the Executive Board, it was decided that the League would begin its program by working for the passage of a Federal Anti Lynching Law, Child Labor Law and elimination of discrimination in the Federal Government.

Document 241
"Home Economics Delegates Jim Crowed at Dallas Hotel"
[*Dallas Express*, October 27, 1933]

Dallas, Tex. Oct. 27, [1933]—Six representatives of the Negro colleges throughout the state of Texas were invited to attend the convention for home-economics instructors which was held at the Adolphus Hotel, Dallas, October 17–22. On their arrival at the hotel entrance they were ushered to a side entrance, through the basement to the freight elevator to the convention quarters, then segregated to themselves to discuss their problems.

After such experience they refused to make themselves content with such treatment and called the manager in question who told them their supervisor Miss May had not made any arrangement for their accommodation and assured them that their experience was not the hotel's fault.

After returning to the home of Mrs. H. D. Winn, 2700 Flora Street, where they stopped while in Dallas, they received a phone call from their supervisor Miss May who invited them to return to the convention, but they did not accept the invitation and departed for their respective institutions.

Document 242

Progressive Voters League

[Minnie A. Flanagan Papers, Dallas Historical Society, Hall of State, Fair Park, Dallas]

In 1937, Mrs. Minnie Flanagan and Mrs. Marzel Hill, as members of the Progressive Voters League of Dallas, increased membership and registered 7,000 voters by selling poll taxes through grass-roots organizing. Their successful tools included "Membership and Subscription Cards" and "Captain's Report Blanks."

Membership and Subscription Card

I hereby subscribe to the program of the Progressive Voters league which is as follows: Securing Better Parks, Schools, Jobs, Housing, Streets, Police, and other Political Benefits for the good of Negro people.

CAPTAIN'S REPORT BLANK

NAME OF CAPTAIN ⎯⎯⎯⎯⎯⎯⎯⎯⎯⎯⎯⎯⎯ PRECINCT NO. ⎯⎯⎯

NOTE: As captain you are expected to know the boundary lines of your precinct, assign workers to each block therein and make a daily or biweekly check on the block workers to see that they are following the instructions described in the precinct set-up. The success of any political campaign depends upon the strength of the precinct organization. This captain's report should cover only the results that obtain in the precinct activity of the block workers. See to it that every person in your precinct is contacted and urged to pay his poll tax *before January 31. We must reach our goal of 10,000 registered voters!!!*

NAME OF BLOCK WORKERS	CONTACT TOTALS	TAX RECEIPT TOTALS	EXEMPTION TOTAL

Document 243
Juanita Craft

[Dorothy Robinson, "Interview with Juanita Craft," January 20, 1977, in *The Black Women Oral History Project*, vol. 3, p. 15, with permission of K. G. Saur Verlag, a Reed Reference Publishing Company, and the Schlesinger Library, Radcliffe College]

Juanita Craft joined the NAACP in Dallas in 1935 and over the next fifty years rose to state and national leadership in the fight for civil rights.

In 1938 when we were fighting for the right to serve on a jury in Dallas, Texas, a man by the name of G. F. Porter [an educator] who answered a [jury] summons was thrown from the courthouse. His head struck the pavement; he became blind and walked the streets of Dallas blind for eleven years prior to his death. I said to everybody, "When you receive a summons—go and serve, the price has been paid." . . . I want these rights and I accept the responsibilities.

Document 244
The Fight for Pay Equalization

[Helen Spencer, "Along the Road to Civil Rights: Four Dallas Women," paper presented at the Texas State Historical Association Annual Meeting, Austin, February 27, 1992]

In Dallas, black women played prominent roles in the fight for equal rights beginning with Thelma Paige Richardson, the plaintiff in the suit against the Dallas School District in 1942 for equal pay for black and white teachers. . . .

Thelma Paige Richardson was catapulted into prominence when she became the plaintiff in a suit which demanded equal pay for black and white teachers in Dallas. Little did she know that when the Texas Council of Negro Organizations was formed in 1942 with the idea that it would be "a potent force" in any effort to realize for African-Americans a fuller share of the fruits of citizenship in this country that she would be the one to help them realize that dream. . . .

Council members announced that they would file suit for any local group of teachers or citizens who wanted to address the issue of the inequity in teachers' salaries. . . .

African-American teachers in Dallas, through the Dallas Negro Teacher's Alliance, decided to file the suit. The Alliance granted authority to the Council [of Negro Organizations] to handle the suit and conduct the fight. . . .

Perhaps, the most difficult task in the 1940s in filing a discrimination suit was the selection of a plaintiff. . . . few Blacks were willing to have their lives disrupted by an endless succession of meetings and court appearances. The racial hostility that one routinely encountered intensified once he/she became a plaintiff. As such, his/her job was placed in jeopardy and the family subjected to harassment by whites who regarded him/her as a troublemaker and a symbol of racial agitation. The plaintiff would become a target for pranksters and extremists. . . .

Thelma Paige Richardson was the best candidate. . . . She had no immediate relatives in the Dallas area; therefore, few people close to her could receive a negative impact from her actions. . . . she knew the risk she was taking by being named as the plaintiff, but she knew what the "decision meant to her race, her fellow workers, herself. . . . She was motivated not by love of publicity, not by dramatic heroism, but by civic pride and by the worth of the cause." [5]

The original petition (filed in May 1942) against the Dallas Board of Education and Superintendent Julius Dorsey showed that after graduating from Colorado State Teachers College and teaching in the district nine years, Mrs. Richardson's salary was only $1260 a year while the salary of a white teacher with the same qualifications for the same work was $1800 a year, and while African-American principals with high school permanent certificates had a salary of $2300 to $2700 a year, their white counterparts earned a salary of $5000. The arguments presented on behalf of Mrs. Richardson advanced the notion that for a long period of time the district maintained the policy for paying African-American teachers lower salaries than those paid to their white counterparts solely on the basis of color. No other difference existed. State and local criteria for teaching as well as teaching load and conditions were the same for both groups— blacks and whites. Further, Richardson was a taxpayer in Dallas; the same valuation and schedule were used on her property as other citizens when state and local taxes were collected. However, she was denied equal benefit from those taxes through discriminatory practice in the payment of taxes in the school system. Teachers' salaries were paid from public school funds raised from state and local taxes.

The arguments were sound, indeed. And the fight for equal pay which began in January 1942 ended in March of 1943 with the plaintiff winning. For the first time, in March of 1943, African-American teachers and principals in the Dallas School District receive the same salary as their white counterparts.

Document 245
Robinson Excluded from Dining Car
[Dorothy Redus Robinson, *The Bell Rings at Four: A Black Teacher's Chronicle of Change* (Austin: Madrona Press, 1978), p. 67]

White prisoners-of-war (Germans I suppose) were marched under guard through my coach to enjoy a meal in the dining car to which I had been denied admittance. On that day [in 1944], while the train stood at the station of a small town, I munched on a dry sandwich purchased from a street vendor, and wondered how Americans, especially black Americans, could sing of the "land of the free." I cursed the democracy that would demand the supreme sacrifice of my brothers who were then on active duty, and deny me the privilege of eating a meal simply because I was black.

Document 246
"I really want to do a good job"
[Lulu B. White to (A.) Maceo (Smith), October 25, 1949, Lulu B. White file, Papers of the National Association for the Advancement of Colored People, Manuscript Division, Library of Congress, Washington, D.C.]

Lulu B. White has been called the driving force behind the Houston branch of the National Association for the Advancement of Colored People, the "matriarch of the civil rights movement" by Texas historian Merline Pitre, and a "rebel with a cause." She was the full-time salaried executive secretary of the Houston branch of the NAACP from 1943 until 1949, the first black woman in the South to hold such a position. Under her leadership, the chapter grew to 5,679 members by 1943, then doubled to 12,000 by 1945, the second highest in the United States and the largest in the South. In 1950, she became a national fieldworker, organizing in such states as Missouri and Arkansas.

Tuesday, Oct. 25, 1949

Dear [A.] Maceo [Smith, a Dallas NAACP leader]:

I really want to do a job, a good job, as Director of Branches. Along with our Freedom Bond Drive, I have a feeling that we should have a Conference, or an Educational Clinic, at which time there would be no official business done as such, such as reports, etc., but a day spent in really teaching and learning. I think also in sponsoring such a conference, we should seek the cooperation of the Council of Negro Organizations, and other organizations that are not members of the Council—all the lodges, secret societies, fraternities, sororities and what have you, in sponsoring such a conference. . . .

A one day Clinic, or Conference could be had, with an outstanding speaker for the night meeting, which would mean lots to us at this time. Money could be raised also; therein much good would be done.

We would not crowd the day with too much. Concentrate on about three things. Participating in the affairs of our government by voting, could be a lesson. Why we should be prepared to run for and hold office in government, etc.

The Poll-Tax will be repealed, then there is the struggle to get our folks to register or meet the requirements of voting. We must recognize also, that there will be legislation attempted, designed to keep the Negro from the Polls, as has been done in other states like Louisiana, and we must be in a position to do something about it. So we could have a panel on legislation. How and where to get a copy of a bill is an important thing. Recognizing a good bill from one which does not include the good for all the people (us).

Certainly, there is the problem of housing that needs to be kept before our people all the time. Each of us should strive to be homeowners, or live in a decent house. In other words, we should be doing something to get our people ready for a new life that we are fighting for. We could not hold such a conference without having a panel on the Educational front. There are many things around which a Clinic could be held.

In talking with Dr. Rhodes, he said he already had such a conference in mind and had done some work towards the planning of it, but he would be glad to cooperate with us. Since he is our State Educational Chairman, it would be a fine thing if he would issue the call for the conference. Those who have attended such a conference would go back into their communities and I could hold the same type of conference in their zones, with the assistance of Don and Tate. In this way, we can soon get Texas saturated with the work of the NAACP, and to set in motion our Five Year Plan.

Enclosed is a letter I have sent to a few of our NAACP leaders, as a "feeler," to see if such a conference is wanted. In my mind, I have the whole thing tied with our Freedom Bond Drive. The date of the Conference could be the launching of our Drive. Then we could call it a Conference for Freedom, or some such thing.

I will be glad to get your thoughts on this and if you think well enough of it, why don't we go to Marshall and talk it over with Dr. Rhodes? After then, I could officially present it to the Board for approval: Or do you think that I should present it to the Board first? If you do, then I hereby submit it to the Board for approval. The Board and other leaders of the state must help me do a good job. Please approve, and let's do a job that we can feel good when we don't have to fight any more.

Sincerely,

Lulu

Document 247

"If we can work together just a little harder"

[Lulu B. White to "Dear Friend," October 22, 1949, Lulu B. White File, Papers of the National Association for the Advancement of Colored People, Manuscript Division, Library of Congress, Washington, D.C.]

DIRECTOR OF STATE BRANCHES
NATIONAL ASSOCIATION FOR THE
ADVANCEMENT OF COLORED PEOPLE
2620 TUAM STREET
HOUSTON 4, TEXAS
October 22, 1949

Dear Friend:

My first endeavor as State Director of Branches for the National Association for the Advancement of Colored People of Texas is to seek the co-operation of all our leadership, so as to unite the broadest section of our people in the defense and extension of our Civil Rights. If we can work together just a little harder—all our aims and objectives will be reached. Therefore, we can no longer content ourselves with sporadic work in our local communities, meeting issues as they confront us here and there, for we now know what effects [*sic*] one—effects all.

The enemies of democracy are concentrating their efforts to destroy our most effective Civil Rights—the right to vote and to be candidates for office—the right to jobs at equal pay—and the equal right to education. Only a united effort can meet this attack.

Today, with the possibility of a Poll Tax Repeal, a great forward advance can be made if we are united and prepared. If we are not, a deluge of restrictive legislation, aimed at excluding Negroes from the polls, may confront us, as it has in other southern states. For these reasons, I am asking you to consider with me and leaders of other organizations the need for a statewide conference that will formulate a common program of action which will give us an educational background for our five year plan of action.

The success or failure of such a conference depends upon the response and hard work of leaders in every community and organization. That is why I am writing to you and asking for an immediate reply. It would be of great service to me to have a letter from you telling me that you will support this effort, giving me any suggestions you might have. If you can and will serve with me on a state committee for this and other activities for this fiscal year, please answer at once, so that our plans to be presented to the Executive Board might be completed as soon as possible. Please write today.

Yours truly,
Lulu B. White
State Director of Branches
National Association for the
Advancement of Colored People

Document 248
"You guys can give me some really 'Tuff' assignments"
[Lulu B. White to "Dear Gloster [B. Current]," September 16, 1950, Lulu B. White file, Papers of the National Association for the Advancement of Colored People, Manuscript Division, Library of Congress, Washington, D.C.]

Little Rock, Ark.
September 16, 1950

Dear Gloster:

Boy! Oh Boy! You guys can give me some really "Tuff" assignments. I thought St. Louis was tough enough, but it is as sweet as a lamb. Let me tell you what this is like.

Every Negro here is in a different class and he does not want to work with another one not in his class. But when I get through with them they will at least know that there is one organization in Arkansas in which they all may take part and not lose their social status. When they even have what they call the FFA's [First Families of Arkansas] Ha. Ha.

Enclosed is a letter I have sent to all Branches. To Presidents and Secretaries. Also one to people who are not members of the Association but who have money and influence. I sent out one hundred of those. I had previously written them for dates with their Branches. I find that there are a lot of well off people here, but have not been able to get a big contribution yet. I will, however. I have several spotted.

Enclosed is a copy of a letter I wrote to the Rev. Mr. Simpson and the Houston Executive Board. I think what I will do is to ask the National office to pay the bill and then they can hold the Houston Branch responsible to them. (Smile) I do hope the National will help me collect. Under other circumstances I would give it all to them, but not now. Of course it looks like I have given it all to them anyway.

We will close our drive here on the 29th of October. I will not be here all the time, but will be working with them. This closing meeting will be a statewide Mass meeting, held here in Little Rock. I am getting a booklet which will contain all the Branches, Businesses, etc. in Arkansas. It will net us around 2,000 but write to me, and send me some literature. These people in these small places have not heard of the NAACP. Please send all the cuts of the National officers. Send a picture of the National Board. This is for the booklet.

Hello to everybody. Kindest personal regards to you and yours.

Lulu

P.S. Send me a sample of a good letter to be sent teachers of Ark. A real good one, asking for a contribution.

Document 249
Christia Adair Defies the Attorney General
[Dorothy Robinson, "Interview with Christia Adair," April 25, 1977, in *The Black Women Oral History Project*, vol. 1, pp. 63–65, with permission of K. G. Saur Verlag, a Reed Reference Publishing Company, and the Schlesinger Library, Radcliffe College]

In 1956, Texas Attorney General John Ben Sheppard vowed to run the NAACP out of Texas by filing barratry charges against it and intimidating its leaders. He put Christia Adair, executive director of the Houston NAACP, on the witness stand in Tyler for seventeen days, but she divulged not one single name.

. . . I was on the job when we entered the school segregation cases. Our office was one of the offices where they [the state attorney general] sent an auditor. . . . They just went through our office like storm, they tore our drawers. All our files, they emptied them. They rented photostatic copying machines and set them up in our office. They took photostatic copies of every scrap of paper, everything they wanted. They just left our offices like the Wreck of the Hesperus. If I knew anything at all, I knew how to file and our office was in perfect order. . . . they still padlocked our office and put us out of business.

Well, the case was set in Texas. . . . and what they were trying to make me deliver was my membership roll. Well, in this town, this county [Houston, Harris County], maybe I should say, if a man worked at any of the industries, steel or oil, any of those places, and it became known that he was a NAACP card-carrying member, he would be fired. . . .

So I didn't have any business with the membership roll and they couldn't understand why I didn't have one. But I didn't have one. And I'd say, "I don't need a membership roll." I would show them the envelope that we got membership money in. I said, "This envelope has the name and addresses and amounts of money for membership, and they turn it in to me. I don't do anything but take the money out of them. I don't need it because the money goes to the national [office], and they are the ones that have to have the names of these people who pay." So they said, "Where is that?" Well I said, "I don't have that. I send that to the NAACP in New York. . . ."

I had had communication with the executive offices [of the NAACP] in New York. I knew what to do and what to say and how to do it. . . . One of the main things was that they [Texas Attorney General's office] were after membership rolls anywhere they could get them.

So they subpoenaed me to come to court and I went to Tyler. . . . [The] trial seems to have lasted about six weeks or maybe two months. . . . I was put on the stand to question and test out for five hours. . . . and they asked me, "Do you belong to anything else besides NAACP?" And I did. And I started out. They asked me the name of them and I started out naming them, and started with the Methodist Church and the Eastern Star and it went on through. And I said, "And I belong to the Harris County Democrats," and they said, "Well, what is that?" . . . And I said, "Are you asking me what the Harris County Democrat does or are you asking me what the NAACP does?" "What the Harris County Democrat does." And I said, "Well, I didn't know they were on trial today."

. . . But anyway, they showed themselves up a lot and we won the case. After ten months, we were able to open our office and go back, which meant I went back over the whole restoration period of restoring the organization, getting members and getting money and was pretty well whipped out.

Document 250

"A bomb was thrown on my premises"

[Mrs. Birdie Mae Sharpe, August 9, 1951, Juanita Craft Papers, 3N 321, F-1, Center for American History, University of Texas at Austin]

This is to certify that I, Mrs. Birdie Mae Sharpe am the owner of the property at 4527 Crozier St. [Dallas] On the night of July 12, 1951, at 10:10 PM a bomb was thrown on my premises. I was seated in such a position that I saw the missile as it soared over the fence, and shot at a fleeing car. I hailed a police car, and the officers arrived in time to cut the fuse before the bomb exploded.

Document 251
Althea Simmons Sits In at Dallas Lunch Counters
[Althea T. L. Simmons, in Brian Lanker, *I Dream a World: Portraits of Black Women Who Changed America* (New York: Stewart, Tabori, and Chang, 1989), p. 35]

Althea Simmons began fighting for civil rights in the late 1950s. She went on to become executive secretary of the Texas State Conference of Branches of the National Association for the Advancement of Colored People and chief congressional lobbyist for the organization in Washington, D.C.

The most dehumanizing incident of my life occurred in the late 1950s while we were trying to desegregate the eating facilities in Dallas. My sister, who was one of the first black students in law school at SMU [Southern Methodist University], and a white male law student and I sat at the lunch counter at the bus station downtown. Nobody shouted at us, nobody said anything to us, nobody wiped the counter in front of us. They just ignored us. We sat there for about five or six hours. Nobody made any kind of gesture that could be perceived as being hostile. We just didn't exist. Even now it's painful because I am a person and for all practical purposes I did not exist.

Document 252
"Sitdown Group Gets Service at [Houston] City Hall"
[*Houston Post*, March 26, 1960, Negro Scrapbook, p. 104, Houston Metropolitan Research Center, Houston Public Library]

About 25 young Negroes were served coffee, soft drinks and cheese crackers Friday afternoon in the City Hall cafeteria.

They sought—and were served—refreshments after picketing the City Hall for about 30 minutes along with a half dozen young white sympathizers.

It was the first crack in a pattern of closed lunch counters which the young Negroes had encountered since they began their anti-segregation sitdowns in Houston on March 4.

The first two of the pickets, a boy and a girl, entered the basement cafeteria and sat down at counter stools about 2:40 PM.

"This is cafeteria style—you'll have to go through the line," they were told by Mrs. Elenora Russell, the cafeteria manager.

They did, with the girl buying a Coke and the boy coffee, and returned to their seats.

As the word spread outside, more and more of the 35 Negro pickets entered and were served, along with several of the white pickets. . . .

Mrs Russell said she and her brother-in-law, Frank Russell, the cafeteria operator, had discussed a possible sitdown earlier and decided on their course of action.

"I'm not in the same position as a private operator," Russell told reporters. "This is public property. The City Hall is a tax-supported institution. . . . I didn't want to do anything unconstitutional or illegal."

While the pickets were being served, Mayor Lewis Cutrer was welcoming visiting Argentine Ambassador Emilio Donato del Carril and about 20 members of the Houston consular corps.

They were having coffee and cake in the mayor's private dining room, just across the hallway from the cafeteria.

The Ambassador and the consular officials had arrived amid shrieking motorcycle sirens only about 10 minutes after the picketing began.

Looking slightly bewildered, Ambassador del Carril walked into the City Hall between a picket sign reading "We Want a Freedom Sandwich" and another one inscribed "White-Colored Americans" with the "White-Colored" crossed out.

One of the white pickets identified himself as a Rice Institute graduate student, but declined to give his name.

The City Hall cafeteria, operated under a concession by Russell, is primarily for city employees. But it is open to the public.

Commenting later on the cafeteria happenings, Mayor Cutrer said they were "a complete surprise—a bolt from the blue."

"Mr. Russell has the cafeteria leased from the city," the mayor said. "He's operating it, it's his business."

Mayor Cutrer also reiterated his statement Thursday that he would not appoint a bi-racial citizens committee to study the situation as long as the demonstrations continued.

The first demonstrators to be served were silent and appeared nervous. As more collected, they talked quietly among themselves and sometimes smiled.

Outside the cafeteria in a hallway, groups of city employees—up to 20 at times—gathered to watch. Only one or two entered.

While the Negroes were being served, Councilmen Louie Welch, W. H. Jones and Bill Swanson visited the cafeteria.

A bomb scare was telephoned to the City Hall switchboard at 3:15 PM, and about 20 police officers and the mayor searched waste baskets and other possible hiding places. Nothing was found.

Asked if the cafeteria would continue to serve Negroes, Mrs. Russell replied as long as people are orderly and behave themselves, they should be served.

Mayor Cutrer, asked the same question, said, "That's a decision that will have to be made."

One of the demonstrators identified himself as a Texas Southern University student from Haiti. His opinion of the cafeteria service:

"This was our first home run."

Document 253

Hattie Mae White Gets Elected

[Barbara Karkabi, "Hattie Mae and Mary's Friendship Brought People Together," *Houston Chronicle*, September 17, 1989, reprinted with permission of the *Houston Chronicle*]

Hattie Mae White was the first black Texan to be elected to public office since the late 1890s, serving on the Houston school board from 1958 to 1967.

[Hattie Mae] White's election shocked the city's conservative political establishment. After her victory, the windshield of her car was splintered by air rifle pellets, and a gasoline-soaked cross was set ablaze in her front yard.

"I believe it was the first time that blacks and whites had ever worked together on an organized campaign," said White, holding herself straight and proud in the un-air-conditioned living room of her home. . . .

White, a former teacher and a mother of five, said she decided to run for the school board after a fellow parent announced during a meeting that it was not time yet for a black to hold that [post]. "I didn't think anyone could determine when the time was for a black to run."

White had been a member of the Parent Council for several years. When she made a speech documenting the injustices of segregation for blacks in the schools, friends and supporters urged White to run. It took several years for White to make her decision.

"It was not an easy thing to do," White said. "But I remember my husband Charles (an optometrist), took me on his knee and told me that if I did win, it would be a wonderful heritage for the children."

Document 254
To the Editor of the *Houston Post*
[Mrs. B. J. Covington, "A Travesty on Justice," *Houston Post* (late 1950s?), author's collection]

After reading with deep concern the pro-segregation bills, now before the [Texas] House State Affairs Committee, I will say that these bills are a travesty on justice, conceived in iniquity and designed to crush and subdue the spirit of the Negro. I do not believe that anyone with the least sense of justice could place his hand of approval on any one of these bills.

Document 255
A Victory in the State Capital
[Ada C. Anderson, "From the Ice Palace to the Austin Human Relations Commission," paper presented at the Texas State Historical Association Annual Meeting, February 27, 1992, pp. 1–3]

The first overt attempt by adult citizens to push integration [in Austin] was organized by a group of African-American mothers of the Austin chapter of Jack and Jill of America, Inc. The year was 1962. Against this backdrop, picture the mothers of Jack and Jill planning their children's activities for the year. With the announcement that an ice-skating rink was to open under the name of "The Ice Palace," ice skating lessons were added to the list of planned activities. The fact that the location was . . . near the black community . . . led us to expect The Ice Palace to be open to our children. . . .

Two days before the grand opening, we received word that this facility was for "whites only." We called a meeting: out of Jack and Jill we organized the Mothers Action Council—MAC. We made picket signs, just in case. I was elected chair of the committee, partly because I was not dependent on the white community for livelihood. On the evening before the grand opening, I went alone to The Ice Palace and toured the facility while the staff was feverishly readying the premise for the big celebration. "May I help *you*?"; "Yes?" demanded the employees, with scowling faces. Then it came: "We don't have accommodations for blacks."

On opening morning the members of the Mothers Action Council arrived with their children and proceeded to the ticket line. When refused, they returned to their parked cars for the picket signs which had been prepared the evening before. Picketing began within approximately 10 to 15 minutes after the first admission ticket was sold and continued every weekday evening and all day Saturday and Sunday—through rain, sleet, and snow until the owners dropped the racial barriers approximately a year later.

Document 256
A Challenge to the City Council
["Mayor Holds Austin Opposed to Human Relations Ordinance," *Daily Texan*, October 23, 1963]

In a public hearing on a proposed human relations ordinance, one Austin woman minced no words in confronting the white majority.

A frustrated Negro maid said angrily, "You let me work in your homes. I stay with your children weeks at a time, sometimes they know me better than their own mother. I even sleep in your house. You know that my color doesn't rub off on your sheets. And I can't eat in your restaurants. Why? What are you afraid of? What are you afraid of?"

Document 257
Welfare Rights
[Velma Roberts with Ruby Williams, "Welfare Is a Right," in Daryl Janes, ed., *No Apologies: Texas Radicals Celebrate the '60s* (Austin: Eakin Press, 1992), pp. 113, 115, 119]

Velma Roberts was an organizer and the first and only president of Austin Welfare Rights Organization, which lasted from 1968 to 1975.

Even though at the time I didn't consider myself to be political, I had the personality needed to be an activist. I didn't take nothing off of nobody, Black or White. I understood what little rights I had and didn't believe in letting anybody put me down. . . .

For others to understand the uniqueness of an organization such as WRO, they need to know something about what being on welfare was like. AFDC was only for children. Those children had to be living with only one parent; most of the time it was the mother. A welfare caseworker had the legal right to come into a mother's home at any time of the day or night. If a man was present, they would more than likely cut her from the rolls. You couldn't have any luxuries, such as TV, radio, and nothing new, like curtains, without having to explain how you came about it. If your mother bought you anything that they could put a dollar value to, they did and then subtracted that amount from your check.

The welfare system made people feel like less than dirt. It was their fault that they were on welfare and if they weren't so lazy, they would get a job. But the minute a woman went out and made any money, that money also was subtracted from her AFDC check. The AFDC check was only 75 percent of budgeted need (not real need) as calculated by the Welfare Department.

The first issue the Austin Welfare Rights group chose to address was the free or reduced lunch program in the elementary schools. By federal law all children on AFDC qualified for free or reduced school lunches. Very few mothers knew about the program because it was not advertised, even though the law stated that school districts were to notify the public of the program. Secondly, the reduced amount was still too much for the working poor.

. . . Welfare Rights and Community United Front fed children hot breakfasts before they went to school, and at the same time lobbied the school board to institute a pilot breakfast program, which they did in all Title I (disadvantaged-poor) schools. After one year the program received high marks from both the kids and the teachers.

. . . As long as there is injustice in the world, I'll find something to fight about.

Document 258
"AFDC changes are especially unfair"
["Reagan's Welfare Cuts Create More Poverty," flyer produced by the Houston Welfare Rights Organization, November 13, 1981, African American Miscellaneous File, Box 1, File 17, Houston Metropolitan Research Center, Houston Public Library]

The National Welfare Rights Organization was formed in 1967 to educate potentially eligible recipients about benefits and to win additional funds and services. Women in cities across the country, including Texas, began organizing. In Austin, the local chapter raised funds and organized under the leadership of Velma Roberts. In Houston, women condemned cuts to the program by the Reagan administration.

REAGAN'S WELFARE CUTS CREATE MORE POVERTY
by the Houston Welfare Rights Organization
429 Neyland St., Houston, TX 77022 (Nov. 13, 1981)

President Reagan has cut the aid of families with dependent children (AFDC) program by $2 billion, removing 40,000 Texas children from the rolls. He has also cut $1 billion from food stamps dropping 70,000 Texans. Many other people have found their benefits reduced and any cost of living adjustments delayed. For example, the food stamps adjustment is now a year and a half behind. These cuts create more poverty, by helping fewer people.

AFDC changes are especially unfair because they cut off groups of people, rather than those with more income or more resources. Since AFDC does not have national minimum benefits, Texas which has the lowest payment in the country, about $32 per month per child, has had to deny much poorer people than the states on the east and west coasts.

We also oppose block grants because they hurt our friends and day care centers. The block grants could be used for almost anything. Before those programs helped only the poor. For example, now Texas could spend it all on highways or water projects.

Our experts tell us that balancing the budget does less to fight inflation compared to the harm to poor children. We need an inflation program that reduces the price of necessities like housing, utilities, food and health care, rather than interest on loans, cars, major appliances and luxuries.

We also urge you to oppose the other cuts in food programs, social security and social security disability, legal services, community services programs, Title I day care, public housing and section eight, health care, rehabilitation and jobs programs like CETA.

Also vote for the welfare ceiling referendum in November 1982 to replace the $80 million biennial ceiling with one percent of the state budget and allow an AFDC grant increase for the first time in 14 years. Contact Impact, AFDC campaign, 2704 Rio Grande, Apt. 9, Austin, TX 78705, (512) 472-3903.

We invite you to ask us to participate in your coalitions and to come to our regular monthly meeting, Monday, November 30, 1981, annex to St. Anne de Beaupre Catholic Church, 8910 Link Road, N. Loop West & Princeton Streets.

Document 259
Testimony of Representative Barbara Jordan before the House Judiciary Committee, July 25, 1974
[Reprinted in Ira B. Bryant, *Barbara Charline Jordan: From the Ghetto to the Capitol* (Houston: D. Armstrong Co., 1977), pp. 51, 54–55]

Barbara Jordan was elected to the U.S. Congress from Harris County in 1972, becoming the first black congressperson from Texas. She gained national fame for telling the U.S. public why President Richard Nixon ought to be impeached.

Earlier today, we heard the beginning of the Preamble to the Constitution of the United States. "We the people." It is a very eloquent beginning. But, when that document was completed on the 17th of September in 1787, I was not included in that "We, the people." I felt somehow for many years that George Washington and Alexander Hamilton just left me out by mistake. But, through the process of amendment, interpretation and court decision, I have finally been included in "We, the people."

Today, I am an inquisitor. I believe hyperbole would not be fictional and would not overstate the solemnness that I feel right now. My faith in the Constitution is whole, it is complete, it is total. I am not going to sit here and be an idle spectator to the diminution, the subversion, the destruction of the Constitution. . . .

If the impeachment provision in the Constitution of the United States will not reach the offenses charged here, then perhaps that 18th Century Constitution should be abandoned to a 20th Century paper shredder. Has the President committed offenses and planned and directed and acquiesced in a course of conduct which the Constitution will not tolerate? That is the question. We know that. We know the question. We should now forthwith proceed to answer the question. It is reason, not passion, which must guide our deliberations, guide our debate, and guide our decision.

Document 260
Barbara Jordan on the Equal Rights Amendment
[Speech by Barbara Jordan at a conference during International Women's Year, November 10, 1975, Lyndon Baines Johnson School of Public Affairs, Austin, reprinted in Barbara Jordan and Shelby Hearon, *Barbara Jordan: A Self-Portrait* (Garden City, N.Y.: Doubleday and Co., 1979), pp. 214–220]

As a member of the House of Representatives Judiciary Committee, Barbara Jordan fought for the extension of the ratification process for the Equal Rights Amendment for a second seven years. She said, "I regret that fourteen years is repugnant as a time frame for ratification for some members of this committee. Fourteen years is not repugnant to me. A generation is not repugnant to me. Who am I to say let's short circuit the time during which I may seek to protect and guarantee my personhood in the community of humankind. I can't restrict that and certainly no constitutional scholar can restrict that."

. . . In 1975, International Women's Year, it is very easy for all of us to be optimistic about the advances of women. We can talk about social advancement, educational advances, economic justice coming to women. But we know that the government of the United States of America remains so sharply focused on problems of inflation and recession and depression and unemployment that it is unlikely that issues related to women will receive any primacy of attention.

. . . In this country, we have climbed over some of the legal obstacles which affect women. We have gotten around some of these social and educational obstacles, barriers, and moved ahead to opportunity in those areas. But there can be no letup. There can be no slackening of effort, because we still must keep a momentum building, growing, sustained.

The progress of the Equal Rights Amendment is good. But we are still four states short . . . The amendment is so simple, . . . "Equality of rights under the law shall not be denied or abridged by the United States or by any other state on account of sex."

Now, to me, that is stated in plain, simple, ordinary English. Yet there are those who have great difficulty understanding what those words mean.

. . . In Maryland, for example, there was a minister testifying against the amendment and he said that the "supporters of the amendment are products of unhappy homes, unhappy marriages, unhappy parents, and they are to be pitied." . . .

And in Virginia a woman told the legislature . . . : "Please don't make us stoop to equality; we love being treated with superiority."

In Georgia, a state representative called the amendment "so stinking of Communism, it's just pitiful to think of doing something like that to America. He said, . . . "That amendment would lower our ladies to the level of men."

Now, I don't know how those words of the proposed amendment can be so misconstrued, but they can be. The problem remains . . . that we have difficulty defining ourselves. The problem remains that we fail to define ourselves in terms of whole human beings, full human beings.

. . . I don't care which country you would like to view—Britain, Sweden, Finland, Denmark—look at them. The problem is the same: the women at the bottom, the men at the top.

So what are women going to do about it? What are we going to do about it? How are we going to change all that? How are we going to somehow reverse the trend that has women at the bottom of whatever profession we are talking about—a scientist or a physician or a scullery maid?

It is going to take long, hard, slow, tedious work. And we begin with ourselves. We begin with our own self-concept. We begin to try to internalize how we really feel about ourselves and proceed to actualize the thinking that we finally evolve from the look inward and the projection outward.

. . . The women of this world—as the women of Texas, and the women of the United States of America—must exercise a leadership quality, a dedication, a concern, and a commitment which is not going to be shattered by inanities and ignorance and idiots, who would view our cause as one which is violative of the American dream of equal rights for everyone.

Eddie Bernice Johnson, a native of Waco, has had a distinguished career as a successful business-woman, professional nurse, health care administrator, and lawmaker. She was educated at St. Mary's College, University of Notre Dame and received a bachelor's degree in nursing from Texas Christian University and a master's in public admin-istration from Southern Meth-odist University. In 1972 she won a landslide victory to the Texas House of Representatives, representing Dallas County, becoming the first black woman to serve that area. While there, she was a strong advocate of leg-islation benefiting women and minorities. In her second term, she became the first woman in Texas history to chair a major House committee—Labor. She resigned during her third term when appointed by President Jimmy Carter as Regional Director of the Department of Health, Education and Welfare (1977 to 1979). She was elected to the Texas Senate in 1986, the first woman and first black to represent the Dallas area there. As chair of the state Senate Subcom-mittee on Congressional Redistricting, she was instrumental in creating a new House district (#30), which she then won in 1992, with 74 percent of the vote, the second black woman from Texas to serve in Congress. (The first was Barbara Jordan.) Johnson was elected Whip of the Congressional Black Caucus, and was appointed to the Public Works and Transportation and Science, Space and Tech-nology committees. Her legislative priorities have been the economy, accessible health care, education, jobs, the environment, and expanding workplace oppor-tunities for minorities. She was re-elected to a second term in 1994. (Courtesy Congresswoman Eddie Bernice Johnson)

. . . We only want, we only ask, when we stand up and talk about one nation under God, liberty, justice for everybody, we only want to be able to look at the flag, put our right hand over our hearts, repeat those words, and know that they are true.

Document 261

"I have a long history of . . . commitment to women"

["Candidate [Eddie Bernice Johnson], Women's Political Caucus at Odds," *Texas Woman's News* (Dallas), July 1986, p. 2]

Attorney Sheila Jackson Lee was elected to the United States House of Representatives in 1994 to represent the 18th Congressional District in Harris County (Houston). Upon arriving in Washington, she was elected president of the Democratic Freshman Class and was appointed to serve as the freshman member of the House Democratic Steering and Policy Committee. She serves on the Committee on the Judiciary and is a member of the Human Rights Caucus and the House Democratic Caucus Task Force on Hunger. She was previously the first African-American female at-large member of Houston's City Council and served as an Associate Municipal Court Judge there. A graduate of the University of Virginia School of Law, she is one of only three black women to have served as Director of the State Bar of Texas. (Courtesy Congresswoman Sheila Jackson Lee)

In 1986, former state representative Eddie Bernice Johnson made a run for the Texas Senate. She had a bitter moment when the Dallas Area Women's Political Caucus (DAWPC) endorsed one of her male opponents in the Democratic Primary. She wrote to the **Texas Woman's News** *describing her feminist record and saying that women must be elected to office for women's equality to be adequately addressed. DAWPC and the Texas Women's Political Caucus both endorsed her in the general election, which she won by 3 to 1, becoming the first black to represent Dallas in the state Senate. In 1992, Johnson was elected to the U.S. Congress with 74 percent of the vote.*

Ms. Janetta S. Walls, Chair
Dallas Area Women's Political Caucus
P.O. Box 141141
Dallas, Texas 75214

Dear Ms. Walls:

Thank you for your letter of June 12 regarding my victory in the Democratic Runoff for State Senate.

After the February general meeting of the Dallas Area Women's Political

Caucus I received a letter from Charlotte Taft, the screening committee chair. She informed me that your organization had voted to endorse one of my opponents, who is male, in our race for State Senator from District 23. I sent a letter to Ms. Taft at that time, but apparently she did not forward it to you. In the letter I expressed my serious reservations about the Caucus and I want to reiterate them and expanded upon them to you now.

I have a long history of activity and commitment to women. I was a charter member of the Texas Women's Political Caucus in the 1970s and served on the State Executive Committee. I was also a founding member of the original Dallas Women's Political Caucus. I have been a member of both organizations most of the time since.

When I joined the WPC, I was committed to the goals of the organization and spent many hours working for and with the Caucus. I was a member of the DAWPC Advisory Board at the time of your February meeting.

As the Caucus has known over the years, and as you may know, I was the first black woman to represent Dallas County in the Texas legislature, elected in 1972. My services to women began, however, years before. I was the founding president of the National Council of Negro Women in the late 1950s. I later was on the state board of the Women's Equity Action League and a founding board member of Women for Change, which established the Women's Center of Dallas.

During my three terms in the Texas Legislature I sponsored many pieces of legislation benefitting women and children. Among them were the Credit Act, which eliminated discrimination against women in obtaining credit or loans; the Maternity Leave Bill for teachers; and the Breakfast Bill for school children. I also spoke and worked for Rep. Sarah Weddington's bills making abortion and amniotic testing more available, and I sponsored child care legislation.

I was extremely supportive of the Equal Rights Amendment and worked to prevent Texas from rescinding it. In 1975, when rescission was attempted, I served on the Constitutional Amendments Committee which heard state-wide testimony for and against rescission. It was my motion to table that legislation that killed the recision attempt and kept Texas in the ranks of states that passed the ERA.

When I was in Austin I filed a suit against seven state agencies for discrimination against women, and won.

In 1978 I was among the first women to receive Women Helping Women awards for my contribution to women and the women's movement. I am currently a member of the Women's Issues Network Board and am its immediate past vice president.

The National Women's Political Caucus was founded to represent women in the political process because no other organization was defending women from that kind of discrimination. In the early years of the Dallas Women's Political Caucus we took great care to endorse the woman in any political race unless she was opposed to equality and progress for women. In the event the male in the race also had made courageous stands on behalf of women we also made dual endorsements. But the Caucus' main objective was to find good women, run them for office, support them and elect them. The conclusion that led to forming the Women's Political Caucus in the first place was that until women are actually elected to serve on our city councils and county courts, in our legislatures and our statewide offices, as governors, in Congress, in the Senate and, yes, as President of our country, women's equality is not going to be adequately listened to, addressed, nor realized.

This is the kind of women's political organization to which I want to belong and by which I want to be supported.

In the DAWPC's February meeting your membership voted to endorse a man with a three year record of legislative action even though your screening committee recommended a dual endorsement, supporting me also. When the DAWPC membership fails to endorse a woman with my record, I feel we no longer have anything in common.

Reluctantly, therefore, I have decided to request that my name be removed from both the membership and the advisory board of the Dallas Area Women's Political Caucus, and that the remainder of the money from my membership be considered a contribution.

I wish to disassociate myself from the local organization and from the Texas Women's Political Caucus which, through an illegal voting maneuver, also declined to endorse my candidacy. I respectfully request that my name not be included on any of the Caucus endorsement lists or cards.

Somewhere along the way the Dallas Area Women's Political Caucus and the Texas WPC have lost their primary purpose. You have veered onto the wrong path. You have some serious problems and they need to be corrected.

You must not continue to mislead women into believing that the Women's Political Caucus is a woman's organization that promotes women.

I look forward to rejoining the Caucus in the future when it returns to abiding by its stated goals.

Sincerely,
Eddie Bernice Johnson

Document 262

Wilhelmina Delco Faces New Frontiers

[A. Phillips Brooks, "Delco looks ahead to new frontier: retirement in '95," *Austin American-Statesman*, November 3, 1993, pp. A1, 23]

Wilhelmina Delco, the first African American elected to the Texas House of Representatives from Travis County, is accustomed to crashing barriers and blazing trails.

At a news conference Tuesday, the former school trustee, community college pioneer and state legislator confirmed she is facing a new frontier: retirement from elective politics. Delco said she would not seek an 11th term in her District 50 seat in the Texas Legislature. Her term expired in January 1995.

Despite a string of firsts, Delco, 64, is leaving with some regrets.

"I came to the Legislature 20 years ago with the firm intent of solving the school finance crisis," a teary-eyed Delco said. "One of my disappointments is that we're no closer to solving it now than we were then.

"It's time for a fresh face from District 50, and the groundwork has been laid for a successor."

District 50 includes Northeast Austin and northeast Travis County.

Delco rose from housewife to the No. 2 position in the Texas House during a public service career that spanned more than 25 years. In 1991, she was appointed speaker pro tem of the House, becoming the first woman and the second African American to hold that position.

Before that historic appointment and her election to the House in 1974, Delco had accumulated a string of firsts, forging opportunities for women, children and minorities despite formidable racial and gender barriers.

It started with her involvement in the Parent Teacher Association, her daughter Loretta Edelen said.

"The real catalyst for her involvement was her children, starting with Girl Scouts and PTA," . . . but found the real decisions affecting children were made by the school board.

So in 1968, at a time when Austin schools were segregated, Delco launched a bid for the Austin school board and became the first black to be elected trustee. Ever since, blacks have served on the board.

Some say Delco's campaign was helped by the assassination of the Rev. Martin Luther King Jr., who was killed two days before the election. Even so, they said Delco's powerful oratory and inclusive leadership style appealed to West Austin business and community leaders.

"People expressed their sorrow for Martin Luther King, then said they were going right out to vote for Wilhelmina Delco," said Ada Anderson, an Austin businesswoman. "King's assassination pointed out the need for broader representation from across neighborhoods and racial lines, but it was Wilhelmina who sold them."

Delco pioneered educational opportunities for minorities and poor people, including helping to found Austin Community College in 1973 and serving on the first ACC board of trustees. Delco said the college offered students with limited financial and educational opportunities the chance to "lift themselves up and seize careers and education."

"It was a bridge for women, working people and students who lacked resources," she said.

"Community college made access to higher education available for many that would not otherwise have had it. Also, women and working people needed flexible education, technical training and other skills that weren't offered at our other fine colleges and universities."

Serving on boards was fine, but Delco soon learned that she could have the greatest influence on educational decisions at the state Capitol. So in 1974, Delco campaigned for and won a seat in the House.

There she chaired the Higher Education Committee for a dozen years and achieved one of her greatest milestones, forcing state leaders to share the Permanent University Fund, a $5 billion state endowment whose interest and earnings were set aside exclusively for the University of Texas and Texas A & M University.

After a six-year struggle, historically black Prairie View A & M was given a share of the permanent fund, and the Higher Education Assistance Fund was created for all other public universities, such as Southwest Texas State, that didn't share in permanent fund dollars.

Though she is credited most with advancing higher education for women and minorities, her colleagues said Delco never was far from public education issues facing the state.

"I had the privilege of working with her on public education," Rep. Libby Linebarger, D-Manchaca, said. "She is a strong, outspoken advocate on public education and was instrumental in forging compromises on school finance."

. . . Delco, a native of Chicago, graduated from Fisk University in Nashville, Tenn. She is married to Exalton Delco, who recently retired from ACC. They have four children and eight grandchildren.

Delco said she wants to make way for younger African American leaders who can bring new strategies to problems facing minorities, children and others. But she warned that she won't be far from public service and might seek the political limelight again.

"There are a lot of things I want to do to help children and the cause of

Ana Sisnett, known as TECHNO-MAMA, is on the staff of the Foundation for a Compassionate Society. Since the mid-1980s, she has led computer training for women in Austin and at national and international conferences, focusing on women of color. (Photograph copyright © 1993 by Danna Byrom)

education in Texas. I'm going to be very involved in one way or another. I'm not sure where yet," Delco said.

Document 263
TECHNOMAMA: ANA SISNETT
[Ana Sisnett, excerpts from "Report on International Activities for the Foundation for a Compassionate Society, 1992–1993," Austin, unpublished, 1994; revised June 23, 1995]

Ana Sisnett, known as TECHNOMAMA, is responsible for the computer networking project of the Foundation for a Compassionate Society, a private, nonprofit organization based in Austin. Sisnett does computer training for women both at the foundation's facility in Austin and at national and international conferences, particularly for women of color. Her work facilitates and encourages the use of electronic mail and other media, powerful tools for activism among women's groups around the world.

First Afro-Latin and Afro-Caribbean Women's Conference
Santo Domingo, Dominican Republic, June–July 1992
My international work with the Foundation began after I returned to my birthplace, Panama, for the first time in twenty-seven years, after an absence of thirteen years. A week later I was in Santo Domingo at the *Afro-Latin American and Afro-Caribbean Women's Conference*, hosted by El Mo-

vimiento por la Identidad de la Mujer Negra (IDENTIDAD) and other women's groups who worked in solidarity with Black women's leadership. This week-long gathering was attended by three hundred Black women from 32 countries. . . . The network welcomes women living elsewhere who were born in or who have roots in Latin America and the Caribbean.

African Women in Europe: "Strengthening Our Links"
London, England, October 1992
In October 1992, a delegation of six women of color living in North and South America went to London for *African Women in Europe: Strengthening our Links,* . . . attended by three hundred women. . . . The network of African women has already led to increased representation of African women in women's organizations in Europe and in international fora.

Refugee and Migrant Women's Study Tour
The Netherlands, Germany, Switzerland, Italy, November 1992
From November 1–15, 1992, five of the women who went to London traveled through Holland, Germany, Switzerland, and Italy. We met groups working with refugee and migrant women, particularly on the issues of trafficking of women. Unfortunately, the women are often tricked, coerced or otherwise forced to: work as domestic workers, arrive as mail order brides, prostitutes, drug couriers at the mercy of changing immigration and asylum laws and abusive employers or spouses. . . .

Strategy Meeting of the "Women's Rights as Human Rights" campaign
in preparation for the UN World Conference on Human Rights Center
for Women's Global Leadership, Rutgers, NJ, February 1993
Gisèle-Audrey Mills (a computer networking consultant to the Foundation) and I did computer networking demonstrations and training at the Center for Women's Global Leadership. Women from around the world developed media strategies and plans for the Women's Tribunal, . . . part of the worldwide campaign ["Women's Rights as Human Rights"] . . . to ensure recognition of women's rights during the UN Human Rights Conference in Vienna, Austria (1993).

First International Interdisciplinary Congress on Women
San José, Costa Rica, February 1993
This Congress at the Universidad de Costa Rica furthered our work on computer networking as a tool for activism among women internationally. . . . Major panels included issues affecting women's human rights. Black women visited retired dock and railyard workers and their families

in Puerto Limón, a Black community on the Atlantic coast of Costa Rica and the EARTH school, an agricultural college. We conducted interviews of 12 Black women as part of Radio FIRE's [Feminist International Radio Endeavor—a shortwave radio program] coverage live from the plaza of the UCR campus. We also visited Radio for Peace International / Radio FIRE studios on a tour of the University for Peace in Santa Ana (just outside of San José).

UN World Conference on Human Rights/NGO Forum
Vienna, Austria, June 1993
The Foundation [for a Compassionate Society] sponsored a delegation of fourteen women to attend the *UN World Conference on Human Rights*. This multinational, multicultural delegation was organized to focus attention on the local, national and international connections between sexual violence against women and girls in the former Yugoslavia. In Vienna, delegates spoke about women's issues in their countries and networked with others who work on domestic violence, sexual assault and women's health. Some delegates traveled to Zagreb to meet survivors and others working in solidarity with all sides of the conflict in the former Yugoslavia to develop long- and short-term strategies. . . .

The struggles of the families of anencephalic babies born in the border area of Texas, Filipina migrant women in Italy, North American Indigenous and Latina women were included in the discussions. . . .

. . . Delegates attended the Women's Tribunal, a day-long hearing led by a panel of six male and female judges, on experiences of gender-based abuses such as date rape, incest, domestic violence, burning, female genital mutilation and violence against lesbians.

. . . As a direct result of the delegation, we will be participating in developing leadership among women of color from the US for the UN Population and Development conference in Cairo, Egypt (1994) and in Beijing, China (1995).

The Sixth Cross-Cultural Black Women's Summer Institute
Caracas, Venezuela, August 1993
The two-week Institute takes place every two years. . . . This year's focus, *Five Centuries of Resistance and Cultural Affirmation in the Americas*, brought together two hundred women from Black, Indigenous and minority populations around the world including India, Africa, Europe, the Pacific, and the Americas. The collective efforts of participants and organizers included visits to women's organizations, cultural events, workshops, plenaries and

a couple of parties (!). Foundation staff provided translation and technical assistance throughout the Institute.

As a woman of color doing this work it has been both inspiring and frustrating. Inspiring because I have met great women from around the world: Frustrating because I have been able to see more clearly that Black women have a long history of activism internationally of which we are all tremendously ignorant. . . . There is a need for a more integrated analysis where race, class, gender and other factors are seen to be interconnected everywhere.

Document 264
"wo'mn of colour contemplates war"
[Sharon Bridgforth, *Voices in the Dark* (Austin: Geecheee'd Out Press, 1992), pp. 32–35]

Sharon Bridgforth, an Austin poet and playwright, makes connections between the Persian Gulf War of 1991 and violence in American cities.

> they say there was war
> I say what's new
> they say our country
> set out to annihilate millions of
> wy'mn & children of colour
> I say what is new
>
> they say the president of
> the united states and his
> hand fulla
> white men / wealthy advisors
> declared war on a
> nation that could not properly
> feed itself
> i say tell me something i don't know
>
> they say the bombing began february 16, 1991
> i say
> obviously
> they ain't never seen
> my neighborhood
> half burned structures
> of usta be buildings
> stand uninhabitable

with jagged /glass-etched windows
that frame the faces
of children / looking
for a place to hide /a
refuge from the streets / where
rage is a weapon.
fueled by the insatiable
hunger that poverty
creates / we are all
prisoners where i
live.
detained within a 5 mile radius
we
become each other's
targets.
. . . .
i regret
to say/somebody's
gone have
to pay
so my babies
can eat in peace

they say there is war
i say lets ban together
and stop the war now!

Document 265
"A Shared Vision"
[Unpublished speech by Dr. Dorcas Bowles, Dean, School of Social Work, University of Texas at Arlington, December 13, 1993, author's collection]

On December 13, 1993, Dr. Dorcas Bowles was inaugurated as dean of the School of Social Work at the University of Texas at Arlington. She was formerly a professor of social work at Louisiana State University, acting dean and professor of social work at Smith College, dean and professor of social work at Atlanta University, and interim president of Atlanta University.

As the newly appointed Dean of the School of Social Work . . . I would like to take this occasion to share with you some of my thoughts about the School and its future. . . . the past ten years have been years of dramatic change in our world, our nation and our state. We were witnesses to the handshake of peace between the Palestinian Liberation Organization Chairman Yasser Arafat and Prime Minister Yitzhak Rabin of Israel; we saw Nelson Mandela and F. W. DeKlerk become Nobel Peace Prize laureates with the hope that the tenuous peace brought about in South Africa will endure and eradicate the vestiges of apartheid. We have seen the winds of change sweeping through Eastern Europe. . . . We have seen in our country unparalleled prosperity countered by the development of an economic underclass that is clearly visible in the faces of those who are homeless. We are witnesses to an intensification of the competitive challenge to our nation's stature as the world's economic leader. Among the images burned into our memories are the return of the hostages from Iran, the exploding Challenger, the Persian Gulf War, the tragedy of Somalia, and the massive flooding suffered in 9 midwestern states during the spring and summer of 1993. . . .

"Change" . . . [is] a critical word now being used in the world of higher education, as colleges and universities struggle to meet the needs of a new breed of student, and find creative ways to deal with fiscal uncertainties of the 1990s while enhancing their service commitments through community and business alliances. . . .

The following areas reflect future challenges requiring our attention. First, issues of professional identity are important. Our history is not devoid of conflicting viewpoints. Since the beginning professionalization of social work to the present, there has been tension and disagreement between those who believe in individual internal pain as the major cause of distress and those who believe that environmental forces are primary. . . .

We must refine and capitalize on our uniqueness. We can do so by concentrating our research activities on selected, core problems—violence, child abuse, the elderly, child welfare including permanency planning, drug and alcohol addiction, homelessness, teenage pregnancy, gender and ethnicity, to name a few. . . .

We must work collaboratively with other disciplines. . . . This decade will see an ever increasing collaborative involvement of psychologists, sociologists, urban planners, medical professionals, anthropologists, economists, educational specialists, and teachers, to name a few. . . . Initiatives by the Community Service Clinic and The Center for International Studies on Ethnicity and Gender with the Arlington Independent School District reflect possibilities of what we can achieve through such collaboration. . . .

The ethnic composition of the U. S. is changing. . . . we are seeing not only the "greying" of America, but as well, the "browning" of America. . . . Texas, like other parts of the country, is experiencing diversity in the people who comprise it. This diversity is reflected in language, cultural practices, and a range of beliefs with respect to illness and health; in differences in birth rates; and in differences in social service needs and duration of care required. Our School must continue to vigorously build an environment that values diversity and is conducive to attracting and retaining a diverse student, faculty and staff population. . . . the School must place increased attention on the inclusion of content regarding differences in the curriculum. This must include an increased emphasis on family theory to include ethnically diverse families and the range of family structures that currently exist—married, single parent, reconstituted or blended, separated or divorced, extended, lesbian and gay. . . .

As a School, we must renew our commitment to educate students for public service. . . . The return of continuing education to the School will allow us to promote ongoing learning to members of the profession. . . . We must prepare our students to adapt to a life dominated by technology. . . . We must continue to focus on broadening the international thrust of our curriculum. . . .

The women's movement has already catapulted us into some needed re-evaluation and revision of our theories about development as it relates to gender. We can no longer use research on men's development and extrapolate its effect on women. A second change will entail teaching our students to competently deliver services in an increasingly health care dominant environment . . . the need for increased content on AIDS and how to work with AIDS persons, families and especially the conservative estimated number of 150,000 children, who will not be infected with the AIDS virus, but who will be left as orphans. Rehabilitation and counseling for drug and alcohol users, many of whom engage in violent activities, will require our best theoretical, research and practice skills. Additionally, as poverty in this country becomes more pronounced, we will need to focus on community development. . . .

I believe that a School of Social Work must play an active role in being the social conscience of the University. . . . by taking a leadership role in the initiation and address of critical issues related to diversity, gender and the creation of an environment that is supportive to all of its members. . . .

The opportunity to serve as Dean of the School of Social Work at the University of Texas at Arlington—to leave one's mark and make a contribution—is a privilege. I accept it with deep humility and great confidence in what this School can become.

Document 266
"I am a citizen of the world!"
[Rosalee Ruth Martin, "New Self Definition," *Nokoa* (Austin), September 4–10, 1992, p. 2]

Dr. Rosalee Ruth Martin is chair of the Social Science Division of Huston-Tillotson College in Austin.

NEW SELF DEFINITION

I have had the great fortune of visiting several countries around the world. Everywhere I went I saw myself, a person of African descent. I saw myself on Egypt's Nile river: I am the ancient Nubian. I saw myself on Senegal's Goree Island, being placed on the "Slaver" to be shipped throughout the world. I blend within the millions of people in Salvador, Bahia, Brazil. . . . I am they and they are me!

I am everywhere! There are more of me than [any] other group. I am a person of color. I am in the majority in this world. I am a citizen of this world! No longer will I define myself as a minority! No longer will I allow persons to put me in a position of powerlessness! No longer will I cooperate in my own oppression! I am in the majority and that gives me a position of power.

I am a citizen of the world! I am in the majority. . . . That gives me Power . . . that gives me HOPE.

And Now Goodnight

I have told you tuneful tales,
Gathered from the hills and vales,
Wheresoever mine own people chanced to dwell.
If the tales have brought you mirth,
Brought more laughter to the earth,
    It is well.

For I vowed in you I could.
And I promised that I would
Sing a little lay of laughter that would rid
Thine own heart of cares awhile,
Leave upon thy face a smile,
    And I did!

—Bernice Love Wiggins, *Tuneful Tales* (El Paso: by the author, 1925), p. 174

Chapter 1. Free Women of Color

1. Randolph B. Campbell, *An Empire for Slavery: The Peculiar Institution in Texas, 1821–1865* (Baton Rouge: Louisiana State University Press, 1989), pp. 16–17.

2. Robert B. Davis., ed., *The Diary of William B. Travis* (Waco: Texian Press, 1966), pp. 95–96. Original spellings and punctuation have been retained in this document and in all other documents.

3. Campbell, *An Empire for Slavery*, pp. 205–206.

4. The myth of the Yellow Rose of Texas apparently originated with a diary entry of William Bollaert on July 7, 1842, in which he noted that the "Battle of San Jacinto was probably lost to the Mexicans, owing to the influence of a Mulatto Girl [Emily] belonging to Colonel Morgan [incorrect], who was closeted in the tent with General Santana [Santa Anna] . . . and detained Santana so long that order could not be restored readily again" (in W. Eugene Holland and Ruth Lapham Butler, eds., *William Bollaert's Texas* [Norman: University of Oklahoma Press, 1956], p. 108 *n*24). Historian Margaret S. Henson questions the entire myth in her articles "She's the Real Thing," *Texas Highways* 33 (April 1986): 60–61, and "Emily D. West, a.k.a. Emily Morgan," unpublished biographical note, May 15, 1984.

5. Campbell, *An Empire for Slavery*, p. 205.

6. Andrew Forest Muir, "The Free Negro in Harris County, Texas," *Southwestern Historical Quarterly* 46, no. 3 (January 1943): 219.

7. Harold Schoen, "The Free Negro in the Republic of Texas," *Southwestern Historical Quarterly* 40, no. 4 (April 1937): 281.

Chapter 2. Slavery

1. Randolph B. Campbell, *An Empire for Slavery: The Peculiar Institution in Texas, 1821–1865* (Baton Rouge: Louisiana State University Press, 1989), pp. 144–145.

2. John Rogers, *Lusty Texans of Dallas* (New York: Dutton, 1951), p. 92. The hanging was first reported on May 17, 1853. See William Farmer, "The Dallas Fire of 1860," ca. 1897, quoting W. H. Beeman in 1892 (unpublished manuscript submitted to the Dallas County Historical Commission, March 1988); Frederick Law Olmsted, *Journey through Texas* (1857; reprint, Austin: University of Texas Press, 1978), pp. 120–121.

3. *Galveston Weekly News*, March 30, 1858; *Houston Daily Telegraph*, April 7, 1858.

4. Paul Dean Lack, "Urban Slavery in the Southwest," Ph.D. dissertation, Texas Tech University, 1973, p. 263; Ben C. Stuart, handwritten manuscript, "History of Galveston," Chapter 18, Rosenberg Library, Galveston.

5. For material on Melinda Rankin, another woman living in Texas who opposed slavery, see William Stuart Red, *A History of the Presbyterian Church in Texas* (Austin: Steck Company, 1936), pp. 329–331.

6. Ronnie C. Tyler and Lawrence Murphy, eds., *The Slave Narratives of Texas* (Austin: Encino Press, 1974), p. 111, quoting Millie Forward.

7. Randolph B. Campbell, *A Southern Community in Crisis: Harrison County, Texas, 1850–1880* (Austin: Texas State Historical Association, 1983), pp. 233, 236–237.

Chapter 3. Reconstruction and Beyond

1. Cited in Michael R. Heintze, *Private Black Colleges in Texas, 1865–1954* (College Station: Texas A & M University Press, 1985), p. 16.

2. Reel 32, Letter of William Sinclair to J. T. Kirman, February 26, 1867, Record Group 105, Bureau of Refugees, Freedmen, and Abandoned Lands, Texas, National Archives; Jane Howe Gregory, "Persistence and Irony in the Incarceration of Women in the Texas Penitentiary, 1907–1910," master's thesis, Rice University, 1994, pp. 9, 13, 18–19, 26, 30, 34–51, 93.

Chapter 5. The Arts

1. The interviewer's questions have been omitted.

Chapter 6. Churches, Clubs, and Community Building

1. Dorothy Salem, *To Better Our World: Black Women in Organized Reform, 1890–1920* (Brooklyn, N.Y.: Carlson Pub., 1990), p. 42.

Chapter 7. Earning a Living

1. Eighteen of the fifty-four restaurant owners listed were women.

2. Sarah Stages, *Complaints: Lydia Pinkham and the Business of Women's Medicine* (New York: W. W. Norton, 1979), pp. 11, 121.

3. Ada Simond, "Midwife Was Key to Community," in *Looking Back 1983* (Austin: Austin Independent School District, 1985).

4. He is referring to the University of Texas Medical Branch at Galveston, which was segregated at the time. The first black woman who graduated from UTMB was Virginia Stull—in 1966.

5. Neil Sapper, "A Survey of the History of the Black People in Texas, 1930–1954," Ph.D. diss., Texas Tech University, 1970, p. 227.

6. The interviewer's questions have been omitted. Ellipses refer to deletions of Rawlston's comments.

7. The interviewer's questions have been omitted.

Chapter 8. Politics and Protest

1. Ruth White, congressional secretary, National American Woman Suffrage Association, to Mrs. Edith Hinkle League, Texas Equal Suffrage Association, Galveston, Texas, July 12, 1918, Washington, D.C., McCallum Family Papers, #17, Folder 4, Box 3, I, Austin History Center, Austin Public Library.

2. Alwyn Barr, *Black Texans: A History of Negroes in Texas, 1528–1971* (Austin: Jenkins Publishing Company, 1973), pp. 136–140.

3. Report of the Annual Conference, Texas Commission on Inter-racial Cooperation (TCIC), Dallas, November 4, 1927, with reports from Special and Standing Committees and the Executive Committee Meeting, Houston, November 19, 1927; "General Rules," TCIC, November 6, 1925; both from TCIC Papers, Houston Metropolitan Research Center, Houston Public Library; Mary Talbert to "My dear Mrs. Terrell," February 16, 1923, Container #6, Correspondence January–February 1923, Mary Church Terrell Papers, Library of Congress.

4. Nannie H. Burroughs to Mary Church Terrell, January 7, 1925, Mary Church Terrell Papers, Container #7, Correspondence, January–March 1925, Library of Congress.

5. *Dallas Express*, March 6, 1943.

BIOGRAPHIES

Adair, Christia Daniels (1893–1989)

Christia Adair spent her life in relentless pursuit of civil rights. Born in Edna, she was the superintendent of her Methodist Sunday School at age sixteen. She attended high school in Austin and college at Prairie View State Normal and Industrial College (now Prairie View A & M), graduating in 1915. She taught school until her marriage in 1918 to Elbert Adair, a railroad brakeman, when she moved to Kingsville. Along with other black and white women, she organized a Mothers Club which succeeded in closing down illegal gambling houses catering to teenagers. Adair and other black women worked with the local white women's suffragist group in gathering petitions for the right of women to vote in the Democratic Party primary of 1918. On election day, she and her friends were shocked when they were not allowed to vote. Adair became an activist for equal rights and a Democrat when she took black schoolchildren to see Republican presidential candidate Warren G. Harding in 1920 in Kingsville and he reached over their heads to shake hands with white schoolchildren. The Adairs moved to Houston in 1925. She became involved in the city's NAACP, serving as executive secretary from 1949 to 1959. Among the group's accomplishments during her tenure were the removal of "whites only" signs at the airport and the integration of many public facilities, including the library and department store fitting rooms. In her later years she was among the first black precinct election judges. The National Organization for Women gave Adair an award for her work for suffrage. In 1977, a city park was named in her honor, and she was inducted into the first Texas Women's Hall of Fame in 1984. (*Houston Chronicle*, January 8, 1990; Dorothy Robinson, "Interview with Christia Adair," April 25, 1977, in *The Black Women Oral History Project*, vol. 1, pp. 41–99, with permission of K. G. Saur Verlag, a Reed Reference Publishing Company, and the Schlesinger Library, Radcliffe College)

Anderson, Pearl Carina Bowden (1898–1990)

Dallas philanthropist Pearl C. Anderson was a native of Louisiana, born of mixed parentage. Her sporadic schooling included time in a one-room Rosenwald school and at Coleman College in Arcadia, Louisiana. This sufficed to get her a teaching job. In 1918 she moved to Dallas, hoping to earn a living. She sold ice, then convinced a lumber company to extend her credit to build a grocery store on land she had purchased; she ran this enterprise for several years. By chance she met and became a nurse in the practice of Dr. J. W. Anderson, Dallas's first black physician. They married in 1929; he was twenty-eight years her senior. The Andersons traveled extensively until his death in 1947. Their real estate in downtown Dallas, valued at $350,000 in 1955, was the basis of her generosity. She donated it to the Dallas County Community Chest Trust Fund (now United Way) to benefit people of all races. Mrs. Anderson gave both time and money to the American Red Cross, Terrell State Hospital, the Lighthouse for the Blind, and Bishop College. An auditorium at Meharry College (her husband's alma mater), a school, and a day care center in Dallas are named in her honor. Bishop College awarded her an honorary doctor of law degree in 1968. (Vivian Anderson Castleberry, *Daughters of Dallas* [Dallas: Odenwald Press, 1994], pp. 272–273)

Barnett, Marguerite Ross (1942–1992)

Educator Marguerite Ross Barnett moved to Texas when she accepted the presidency of the University of Houston in 1990, one of the first black women to head a major university. A Virginia native, Barnett earned her bachelor's degree from Antioch College and her master's and doctoral degrees from the University of Chicago. She taught political science at the University of Chicago, Princeton, Howard, and Columbia before becoming an administrator. She held positions as vice-chancellor for academic affairs at the City University of New York and chancellor at the University of Missouri–St. Louis before coming to Houston. Author of numerous books and articles, particularly on South Asia, Barnett's work on the Tamils won a 1981 American Political Science Association award. (*Houston Chronicle*, May 2, 1990, pp. 1-A, 6-A, February 27, 1991, p. 1-A; *New York Times*, February 27, 1992, p. C20)

Bellinger, Josephine Crawford (1910–1993)

Josephine Bellinger was a pioneer in black journalism as publisher with her husband, Valmo C. Bellinger, of the *San Antonio Register*. She was born in Dallas and spent much of her childhood in Waxahachie, where she graduated from Oak Lawn High School. She went on to Western University in Kansas City, Kansas, where she studied business education. After graduating, Bellinger accepted a position on the *San Antonio Inquirer*. She worked briefly in Houston before returning to San Antonio around 1933 to work for Valmo Bellinger on the *Register*, which he had founded in 1931. The couple married several years later. Mr. Bellinger devoted much of his time to political activities, while Josephine Bellinger ran the newspaper. She filled a variety of roles for the newspaper—from photo engraver to layout person, managing editor to headline writer—and served as society editor with her popular column "Jo's Jottings." Her work for the weekly continued until its sale around 1979. The Bellingers also owned a large cattle ranch in Kendall County. Mrs. Bellinger was active in St. Philips Episcopal Church and the Negro Little Theatre at the Second Baptist

Church. She was a charter member of the San Antonio chapter of the Links, Inc., belonged to Iota Phi Lambda Sorority, Inc., and was inducted into the Texas Black Women's Hall of Fame. (Author's interview with Josephine Bellinger, September 27, 1991; funeral program, February 20, 1993, author's collection)

Bowden, Artemisia (1879–1969)

Educator Artemisia Bowden's fifty-two years at St. Philip's College in San Antonio carried the school from its humble origins to financial security. Bowden was born in Albany, Georgia, and attended schools in North Carolina. She received her teacher's education at St. Joseph's Parochial School in Fayetteville. After one year teaching at High Point (North Carolina) Normal and Industrial School (1901–1902), she was named head of St. Philip's School by Episcopal Bishop James Steptoe Johnston. In the early years, she performed many roles, including teacher, principal, business manager, and spokesperson. But it was her activities as chief fund-raiser that ensured the school's survival. In 1927, it became St. Philip's Junior College, of which she was president, the first woman to head a Texas college. In 1942, St. Philip's was incorporated into the San Antonio public school system and later became a community college. From 1942 until her retirement in 1954, Bowden was dean of the college. She was active in many civic groups, including the Texas Commission on Inter-racial Cooperation, the San Antonio Metropolitan Council of Negro Women, and a number of educational associations. She was also a founding president of the Negro Business and Professional Women's Clubs. Bowden was awarded honorary degrees from Wiley and Tillotson colleges. (Jo Eckerman, "Artemisia Bowden: Dedicated Dreamer," *Texas Passages* 2, no. 1 [Winter 1987]: 1–2, 10; files of the Institute of Texan Cultures, University of Texas at San Antonio)

Branch, Mary Elizabeth (1881–1944)

As president of Tillotson College in Austin, Virginia-born Mary Elizabeth Branch rescued the school from ruin and groomed it into one earning an "A" rating and accreditation from the Southern Association of Colleges and Secondary Schools. The daughter of a former slave, Branch attended the normal department of Virginia State College in Petersburg, where she later taught for twenty years. She did her undergraduate work at the University of Pennsylvania, Columbia, and the University of Chicago, from which she received her bachelor's degree in 1922 and her master's degree in 1925. Branch then accepted a position as dean of girls at Vashon High

School in St. Louis, at that time the largest school for black women in the United States. She served as president of Tillotson from 1930 until her death and was the first woman to head an accredited Texas institution of higher learning. When Branch took over the reins, the school suffered from a small enrollment, dilapidated buildings, and an inadequate library, all of which she remedied within her first five years. Branch was a member of the Negro Advisory Board of the Texas division of the National Youth Administration (beginning in 1935), Alpha Kappa Alpha sorority, and the National Association for the Advancement of Colored People, serving as a chapter president in 1943. Under her leadership, Tillotson was among the first schools to join the United Negro College Fund. Virginia State College and Howard University each granted her honorary doctorate degrees. (Olive D. Brown and Michael R. Heintze, "Mary Branch: Private College Educator," in Alwyn Barr and Robert A. Calvert, eds., *Black Leaders: Texans for their Times* [Austin: Texas State Historical Association, 1981], pp. 113–128)

Brooks, Carrie Jane Sutton (1903–1964)

Carrie Jane Sutton Brooks was born into the prominent Sutton family of San Antonio. Her parents, S. J. and Lillian Viola Sutton, were leaders of the Second Baptist Church there and pioneers in the field of education. Carrie Jane Sutton graduated from that city's Riverside High School as valedictorian and attended Howard University. While at Howard she served a term as president of Alpha chapter of Delta Sigma Theta sorority. She received her medical degree from Howard in the 1920s and was among the first black interns at Freedmen's Hospital in Washington, D.C. She practiced for a few years in San Antonio, specializing in women's and children's health. Dr. Brooks helped found the Pine Street Branch YWCA for blacks. In 1924, she married Dr. John Hunter Brooks, also a physician. The couple settled in Montclair, New Jersey, where they practiced medicine in adjoining offices. (*San Antonio Register*, January 17, 1964)

Cash, Christine Benton (1889–1988)

Texas native and pioneer teacher Christine Benton Cash taught students of all ages. She was born in Jefferson (Marion County) and attended public schools there. In 1906, she received her normal school diploma and a scientific diploma from Bishop College. She earned her B.A. from Bishop in 1926, an M.A. from Atlanta University in 1943, and in 1947 she was one of the first black Texas women to receive a Ph.D. (University of Wisconsin). In 1909, she married Larry Brown Cash, a teacher, minister, and later state treasurer of the National Association for the Advancement of Colored People. Initially, Christine Cash taught in a one-room school in Jefferson, but she soon moved to Pittsburg in Camp County, where she organized the Center Point High School, serving as its principal and later superintendent. She continually fought against discrimination and worked to improve conditions in black schools. Cash joined the Bishop College faculty in 1948, serving until 1956; she was also secretary of the Board of Trustees. She served in 1948 as a member of a Texas legislative committee which initiated public school reforms. She joined the faculty of Jarvis Christian College in Hawkins in 1958 and served as chair of the Department of Education and Certification and of Social Sciences until she was seventy-six. While there, she was named as one of the ten Piper Foundation Professors. She also received the Teachers State Association of Texas Award for Distinguished Career in Education. Dr. Cash belonged to Delta Sigma Theta and received recognition from Bishop College, *Who's Who in Colored America* (four times), and *Who's Who in American Education*. (Effie Adams, *Tall Black Texans* [Dubuque, Ia.: Kendall/Hunt Publishing Co., 1972], pp. 65–69; Dorothy Morrison and Rebecca Buard, *The Black Citizen in American Democracy: Black Culture in Harrison County—Past, Present, Future* [Marshall: Marshall Public Library, 1976], pp. 25–28; funeral program, December 17, 1988, courtesy Meredith Beal)

Chisum, Ethelyn Mildred Taylor (1895–1983)

Ethelyn Chisum's career in education is closely associated with Booker T. Washington High School in Dallas. She grew up in Dallas and attended Prairie View State Normal and Industrial College, from which she graduated in 1913. She began teaching in Smith County, but joined the Dallas public school system in 1916. At Booker T. Washington, she was attendance teacher, dean, and pupil personnel counselor for thirty-two years. Through her efforts, the first visiting nurse was hired for the school. During this time she also studied counseling at the University of Michigan. She organized the Dallas Counselors Club and was president of the Dallas Teachers Council, later the Classroom Teachers of Dallas. She worked with the Texas Education Agency and the National Education Association on special projects. After her retirement from the public schools, she joined the staff of the Upward Bound project at Southern Methodist University. She retired at age eighty-seven; her career had spanned sixty-six years. Her husband was Dr. John O. Chisum, an optometrist. Mrs. Chisum was a member of the Priscilla Art Club, Zeta Phi Beta sorority, and the Maria Morgan branch of the Young Women's Christian Association, which she helped to found. (Vivian Anderson Castleberry, *Daughters of Dallas* [Dallas: Odenwald Press, 1994], p. 130; John Oscar and Ethelyn M. Chisum Collection, Dallas Public Library)

Coleman, Bessie (1892–1926)

Bessie Coleman was one of the first licensed female pilots in the world and the first black aviator and barnstormer in the United States. She had a spectacular but brief career in air shows for circuses, carnivals, and fairs. She was born in Atlanta, Texas, the twelfth of thirteen children, and grew up in Waxahachie. Her mother, a former slave, was illiterate, but borrowed books from a traveling library so that young Bessie could learn to read. She also exempted Bessie from field work, instead assigning her the family's bookkeeping chores. Bessie took in laundry to earn money to attend Langston Industrial College in Oklahoma. When her funds ran out, she moved in with her brother in Chicago in 1915, working as a manicurist. Becoming interested in the air war in Europe during World War I, she decided to become a pilot. She was unable to find a flight school which would accept her, but obtained financial assistance and information from Robert Abbott, editor of the *Chicago Weekly Defender*. She enrolled in an aviation school in France, securing a pilot's license from the Fédération Aéronautique Internationale in 1921. When she returned to the United States, eager to open her own flying school, she began saving money earned through exhibition flights. Coleman performed widely to predominantly white crowds in the North and Midwest, but then switched to performing before largely black Southern audiences. She lectured to black audiences, encouraging them to become involved in aviation. She refused to perform in Waxahachie until the airport was desegregated for the occasion. In 1926, on the verge of opening her own flying school, Coleman met with a tragic end. At age thirty-four, she died during a dress rehearsal for the Negro Welfare League in Jacksonville, Florida. When her plane went out of control, she fell from the plane. She was not wearing a seatbelt or a parachute. A wrench left loose by a careless mechanic had jammed the control gears. Black aviators named their flying clubs and their magazine after Coleman. Today Bessie Coleman Drive is one of the main avenues leading to Chicago's O'Hare Airport. (Henry M. Holden, "Brave Bessie the Barnstormer," *Sisters* [Magazine of the National Council of Negro Women] [Spring 1989]: 6–8; Doris Rich, *Queen Bess: Daredevil Aviator* [Washington, D.C.: Smithsonian Institution Press, 1993]; Elizabeth Hadley Freydberg, "Bessie Coleman," in Darlene Clark Hine, ed., *Black Women in America, An Historical Encyclopedia* [Brooklyn: Carlson Pub., 1993], vol. 1, pp. 262–263)

Conner, Jeffie Obrea Allen (1895–1972)

Waco resident Jeffie Conner's accomplishments as a home demonstration agent, educator, and public servant stemmed from her earlier career as a teacher. She attended Mary Allen Seminary and graduated from Prairie View with a teaching certificate in 1914. She later returned to Prairie View and received her bachelor's and master's degrees in home economics in 1933 and 1944. After leaving Prairie View, she taught at two small schools near Waco. Beginning in 1922, she worked as a U.S. Department of Agriculture home demonstration agent, helping rural women improve their home management skills. She taught them poultry raising, meal preparation, canning, gardening, and sanitation. From 1932 to 1946, she supervised home demonstration agents in a seventeen-county district of East Texas. Conner was a member of the Negro Advisory Board of the Texas division of the National Youth Administration (beginning in 1935). Returning to public education, Conner was a supervisor for McLennan County schools between 1948 and 1957. Her club activities date from 1924 when she joined a Self Culture Club. She held positions in the Texas Association of Colored Women's Clubs (TACWC), as well as the National Association. In 1956, she began a two-year term as president of the TACWC. She was also active in the New Hope Baptist Church, the Blue Triangle Young Women's Christian Association, and Delta Sigma Theta. Governor John Connally appointed Conner to the Committee on Public School Education in 1967, and she pushed for public school integration in her last years. Her husband, Dr. George Sherman Conner, was a distinguished Waco physician, specializing in obstetrics and gynecology. Paul Quinn College awarded Jeffie Conner an honorary doctorate in 1954. (Virginia Lee Spurlin, "The Conners of Waco: Black Professionals in Twentieth Century Texas," Ph.D. diss., Texas Tech University, 1991; George and Jeffie Conner Papers, Texas Collection, Baylor University, Waco)

Covington, Jennie Belle Murphy (1881–1966)

Houston community leader Jennie Belle Covington made a career of service to others. She was a founder and first chair of Houston's Blue Triangle Branch of the Young Women's Christian Association in 1918. For a number of years Mrs. Covington was a member of the board of the Texas Commission on Inter-racial Cooperation, serving as state vice chairman, and she also chaired the Negro Women's Division. She helped found the Negro Child Center and the Houston Settlement Association and was active in the Missionary Society of Antioch Baptist Church. While a student at Guadalupe College in Seguin, she married physician Dr. B. J. Covington in 1902; a year later, the couple moved to Houston. In 1911, they made their home in a spacious two-story residence at Dowling and Hadley streets. By way of encouraging her daughter, Jessie Covington (later Dent), Mrs. Covington founded the Ladies Symphony Orchestra in about 1915. She and Jessie played the violin for the group, which performed at local concerts and social events. Jessie Covington Dent later became a concert pianist. In the days of segregation, the Covingtons often opened their home to celebrities like Marian Anderson, Booker T. Washington, and Paul Robeson. (*Houston Informer*, October 11, 1966; Jennie B. Covington Funeral Service Program, October 11, 1966, and other biographical items in Covington Manuscript Collection, Houston Metropolitan Research Center, Houston Public Library)

Craft, Juanita Jewel Shanks (1902–1985)

The granddaughter of slaves, Juanita Craft transformed the deep hurts of racial discrimination into a lifetime of courageous, nonviolent work for its elimination. She was born in Round Rock, of college-educated parents. One of the most salient events of her teenage years was her mother's death from tuberculosis after being refused hospital treatment in the days of segregation. Despite this devastating and potentially embittering experience, Craft graduated from Prairie View three years later, in 1921. After several years of teaching and clerking in Columbus and Galveston, she moved to Dallas in 1925. For nine years she was a maid at the Adolphus Hotel. When Craft joined the National Association for the Advancement of Colored People in 1935, her passion for civil rights found an organizational basis. She was named Dallas NAACP membership chair in 1942. In 1946, she became Texas field organizer, touring the state to organize dozens of local chapters. In the 1950s, her activities helped open the University of Texas and North Texas State University to blacks. Craft's work with children began in the mid-1940s when she headed the Dallas NAACP Youth Council. During that decade, she organized a dropout prevention campaign. Later, she escorted busloads of children on educational trips across the country and began an antilitter program with their help. In 1967, she and her young colleagues unlocked the State Fair of Texas to blacks, who previously were allowed to attend only on "Negro Day." She worked to integrate public facilities through sit-in demonstrations in the 1960s. Along with the Dallas Urban League, she aided efforts to establish open housing. Her campaign to end fraudulent recruiting by Dallas trade schools in the late 1960s won her the prestigious Linz Award. After serving as a Democratic party precinct chair for more than twenty years, Craft was the second black woman elected to the Dallas City Council in 1975 (at age seventy-three) and was reelected to a second two-year term. Craft was proud to have attended many White House conferences and met four presidents. A Dallas park was named for her in 1974, and she received many other awards, such as the Sojourner Truth Award, Woman of the Year, and Eleanor Roosevelt Award (1984). Her oral biography, edited by Chandler Vaughan, is *A child, the earth, and a tree of many seasons: The Voice of Juanita Craft*. (Dorothy Robinson, "Interview with Juanita Jewel Craft," January 20, 1977, in *The Black Women Oral History Project*, vol. 3, pp. 3–39, with permission of K. G. Saur Verlag, a Reed Reference Publishing Company, and the Schlesinger Library, Radcliffe College; David Strickin and Gail Tomlinson, interviewers, "Juanita Craft: Oral History Interviews," January 23, February 5, February 20, March 20, March 29, April 24, 1979 [Dallas: Dallas Public Library], 1984; *Dallas Morning News*, August 7, 1985; Juanita Craft Collection, Center for American History, University of Texas at Austin; Juanita Craft Collection, Dallas Public Library)

DeMent, Ada Bell (1888–1945)

A Mineral Wells resident and educator, Ada Bell DeMent was a clubwoman of the first rank. Her early posts with the National Association of Colored Women (NACW) included chair of the Peace and Function Committee and membership on the Board of Control. She served as senior state supervisor of girls before her election as president of the Texas Association of Colored Women's Clubs, serving from 1930 to 1934. Under her leadership, the TACWC doubled in size, activated a scholarship fund, promoted a training school for delinquent black girls, and cooperated with the (white) Texas Federation of Women's Clubs. DeMent was elected president of the NACW in 1941. Her term was cut short by her untimely death. In this post, she was instrumental in transferring the Frederick Douglass home in Washington, D.C., to the association. DeMent received an honorary doctorate from Bishop College in 1942. An active participant in the Women's Auxiliary to the National Baptist Convention, she became secretary of its Executive Committee. She was the wife of the Reverend C. DeMent. (Charles Harris Wesley, *The History of the National Association of Colored Women's Clubs: A Legacy of Service* [Washington, D.C.: NACWC, 1984], pp. 115–117)

DeWitty, Virgie Maye Carrington (1897–1980)

Musician Virgie DeWitty was a performer, teacher, director, and composer. Born in Wetumka, Oklahoma, she and her family moved to Austin when she was a young child. Her mother sang in the Ebenezer Baptist church choir for almost fifty years and played three instruments. Virgie DeWitty earned a diploma in education and music from Tillotson College and a B.S. degree in music from Prairie View A & M College. She furthered her musical training at the American Conservatory of Music (Chicago), earning a B.A. degree and a teaching certificate in light opera. She also studied at the Juilliard School of Music and the University of Texas at Austin. DeWitty's career began as a child soloist in the Ebenezer Baptist Church, where she later became music director. She also served as director of music for both the Missionary Baptist General Convention of Texas and the National Baptist Convention of America. DeWitty taught music both privately and in the Austin public schools. She was the first black to direct the commercially sponsored Bright and Early Broadcasting Choirs. At the time of her death she had composed over one hundred gospels, spirituals, and anthems, approximately sixty of which were published. She was active in Zeta Phi Beta sorority, the National Association for the Advancement of Colored People, and the Douglass Club. (Algerene Craig, "History of Ebenezer Third Baptist Church," typescript, Austin History Center, Austin Public Library; *Austin American-Statesman*, August 25, 1980, April 26, 1991; "Virgie!"—a musical tribute to Virgie Carrington DeWitty, June 27, 1992 [produced by Austin Together: A Celebration of Unity, Austin])

Dodd, Frederica J. Chase (1893?–1972)

Frederica Dodd was born in Dallas to accomplished parents. Her father, Frederick K. Chase, was an attorney, and her mother, Fannie Chase Harris, a former slave, was one of the first teachers in Dallas's first high school for blacks, Colored High School. Her mother remarried Dr. Charles A. Harris, a medical doctor and an AME minister, following the death of Frederica's father. Frederica Dodd started a teaching career, then became a social worker. After graduating in 1910 from what became Booker T. Washington High School, Dodd attended Howard University. With twenty-one other young women, she organized Delta Sigma Theta sorority in 1913. When she returned to Dallas after earning her degree in 1914, she taught for a year at her old high school. After marrying physician John H. Dodd in 1920, she had to give up the post because married women were not allowed to teach. She attended the Atlanta University School of Social

Work and began a second career with the Dallas Family Bureau, or United Charities. Dodd was a leader in founding the Maria Morgan branch of the Young Women's Christian Association for blacks in 1928. She helped to organize a Dallas Alumnae chapter of Delta Sigma Theta and belonged to the Priscilla Art Club. (Julia K. Gibson Jordan in collaboration with Charlie Mae Brown Smith, *Beauty and the Best: Frederica Chase Dodd, The Story of a Life of Love and Dedication* [Dallas: Dallas Alumnae Chapter of Delta Sigma Theta Sorority, 1985])

Dupree, Anna Johnson (1891–1977)

Beautician Anna Dupree's thrifty habits enabled her to invest in real estate and businesses and to give generously to charities she and her husband established. The granddaughter of slaves, she was born in Carthage and moved to Galveston as a teenager. She accepted employment in Houston as a domestic and learned beautician's skills on her own. In 1914, she married Clarence A. Dupree, who worked as a hotel porter. While her husband was overseas during World War I, Dupree saved nearly all she earned as a beautician. During the 1920s, she had her own shop and made house calls on white clients in River Oaks. By 1929, the couple had saved enough to invest in the Pastime Theater. Ten years later, they built the El Dorado Center, one of Houston's first black nightclubs. In 1940, Anna Dupree donated $20,000 for an orphanage, the Negro Child Center, which was built a few years later. The couple's second major philanthropic project was the Eliza Johnson Home for Aged Negroes, named for Dupree's mother, to which they donated both funds and their time. They gave a substantial gift toward construction of the first building on the campus of Houston College for Negroes (now Texas Southern University), as well as supporting the United Negro College Fund, a camp for black Girl Scouts, and Houston's first Little League teams for blacks. (*Handbook of Texas* [Austin: Texas State Historical Association, in press]; Yvette Jones, "Seeds of Compassion," *Texas Historian* 37, no. 2 [November 1976]: 16–21)

Durden, Mattie Ella Holman (1881–1972)

Educator Mattie Durden was born in Refugio and initially came to Austin in 1896 to attend Tillotson College. With her newly earned teaching certificate she returned to Refugio County to teach for several years. After her marriage to George Franklin Durden in 1902, the couple settled in Austin. Mrs. Durden reentered Tillotson, earning her high school diploma in 1909. She was the first married woman student in the college department and in 1915 was the first woman to graduate with an A.B.—as valedictorian. Further education was pursued at Tillotson and Samuel Huston colleges (1926–1927 and 1928–1929), Tuskegee Institute (1930), and the University of California at Los Angeles (1946). From 1911 to 1917, she served as matron and a teacher of high school subjects at Tillotson. She was the first person to head the Home Economics Department at Austin's Anderson High School, teaching and serving as department chair for over thirty years (1918–1951). As president of the Community Welfare Association, Durden helped organize the WPA (later Howson) Nursery School and the first well-child clinic for blacks in the city. She was active in the Young Women's Christian Association, the United Fund, and served on the board of Tillotson (later Huston-Tillotson) College from 1940 to 1952. The Davage-Durden Union Building is named for her. (*Handbook of Texas* [Austin: Texas State Historical Association, in press]; J. Mason Brewer, ed., *An Historical Outline of the Negro in Travis County* [Austin: Samuel Huston College, 1940], p. 56)

Fedford, Viola Cornelia Scull (1888–1974)

Galveston native and lifelong resident Viola Fedford was a prominent educator as well as a civic and club leader. Her grandparents, Horace and Emily Scull, and their children settled in Galveston at the conclusion of the Civil War in 1865. Viola Fedford graduated from the city's Central High School in 1906. She received a teaching certificate from Prairie View State Normal Institute and began her educational career in the Galveston public schools at age eighteen. She later received the B.S. degree from Prairie View and did graduate work at Roosevelt College in Chicago. In 1923, she married Bristol Marshall Fedford. Viola Fedford taught from 1912 to 1959 in all of the Galveston schools available to African-Americans during segregation—including West District School (now L. A. Morgan), East District School (renamed Booker T. Washington), and Central High. She held many offices at the local, regional, and state levels in the Texas Federation (later Association) of Colored Women's Clubs, completing her mother's term as state treasurer upon her mother's death, and in the 1940s served as state president for five years. Fedford organized three clubs in the Olivia Washington District, which included Galveston. She was a stalwart of the federation's local Hospital Aid Society, spending long hours collecting and distributing necessities and toys to black children who were patients in the segregated wards of John Sealy Hospital. Fedford was a member of Reedy Chapel AME Church, where she sang in the choir, directed youth choirs, taught in the Sunday School, was superintendent of the Sunday School and the Reedy Chapel Bible School, and was president of the Allen League of Christian Endeavor and of the Missionary Society. One of her daughters, Izola Ethel Fedford Collins, was elected to the Galveston School Board and served as its president in the 1990s. (Obituary, *Galveston Daily News*, May 21, 1974; unpublished biographical sketch by Izola Fedford Collins, May 1995, author's collection)

Fuller, Maud Anna Berry (1868–1972)

Maud A. B. Fuller was an educator and a national Baptist missionary leader. She was born in Lockhart and attended Guadalupe and Tillotson colleges. Her first career as public school teacher and principal gave way in the 1920s to increased work in the National Baptist Convention. When she moved to Austin, she joined Ebenezer Baptist Church. She established Young Women's Auxiliaries as well as local boys' and girls' groups under the auspices of the National Convention. Elected secretary of the Woman's Auxiliary National Baptist Convention of America in 1916, she was elevated to president in 1928, a position she filled with distinction for forty years. She wrote missionary literature, raised funds, and traveled extensively for the organization, including trips to Africa, where she secured land in Liberia for a mission. Fuller supported a home for the aged, helped educate a score of children (some from Africa), visited jails, and served as an advocate for the black community before the Austin City Council. Her husband, William Handy Fuller, operated the Fuller Funeral Parlor after 1932, in which she took an active interest. Union Baptist Theological Seminary in Houston granted her a doctor of humanities degree. (*Handbook of Texas* [Austin: Texas State Historical Association, in press]; M. A. B. Fuller, *Guide for Woman's Home and Foreign Missionary Societies and Circles* [Austin: n.p., ca. 1946]; M. A. B. Fuller, comp., *Historical Booklet of Religious, Business, Professional Men and Women* [Austin: n.p., 1948])

George, Zelma Watson (1903–1994)

Zelma George had varied careers as a sociologist, diplomat, musician, and lecturer. She was born in Hearne, but moved to Dallas as a child. The family left Texas in about 1920, when the Ku Klux Klan threatened her minister father for helping a black prisoner. She received her bachelor's degree from the University of Chicago in 1924, graduated from the American Conservatory of Music in 1927, and earned her Ph.D. in sociology in 1954 from New York University. She was a case worker and probation officer in Chicago in the 1920s before becoming dean of women at Tennessee State University in 1932. She moved to Cleveland in 1942 on a Rockefeller Foundation grant to study the origins and meanings of black songs. She starred in Gian-Carlo Menotti's *The Medium* and *The Consul* in New York in the early 1950s and is believed to be the first black woman to play a leading role in the American opera on Broadway. She also compiled a massive index of black music. Her attention turned international when, in 1959, she undertook a lecture tour to Europe, Africa, and Asia for the State Department and the next year served as a member of the U.S. delegation to the Fifteenth General Assembly of the United Nations. She won the Dag Hammerskjold Award for Contributions to International Understanding in 1961 and the Dahlberg Peace Award from American Baptists in 1969. In 1974, George retired from an eight-year stint as director of the Cleveland Job Corps Center; in 1982, she marched against nuclear armaments in her motorized wheelchair. She was included in the 1985 Radcliffe College exhibit *Women of Courage*. She was married to Clayborne George, a prominent lawyer and president of the Civil Service Commission of Cleveland. (*Who's Who in America: 1978*, p. 1180; *Cleveland Plain Dealer*, July 5, 1984, p. 1A, June 13, 1985, July 5, 1994, p. 1A; *Second Century Radcliffe News*, June 1985; *Austin American-Statesman*, June 15, 1986)

Gooden, Lauretta Holman (?–?)

A native of Sulphur Springs, poet Lauretta Holman Gooden attended school there as a child. Her family later moved to Texarkana. She began writing verse for her friends about the age of ten. Gooden's poems may have been published in local newspapers or in Dallas, where she and her husband, John, operated a successful grocery. Examples of her work, which show her ability to universalize her feelings, appeared in James Mason Brewer's anthology *Heralding Dawn*. Brewer called her verse "deeply emotional, intensely feminine, and vitally human." She addressed the topic of lynching in her poem "Question to a Mob." In "A Dream of Revenge," she describes feelings of rejection by a loved one. The Goodens raised their son, along with her sister's children. (J. Mason Brewer, ed., *Heralding Dawn: An Anthology of Verse* [Dallas: by the author, 1936], pp. 14–16; Lorraine Elena Roses and Ruth Elizabeth Randolph, *Harlem Renaissance and Beyond: Literary Biographies of 100 Black Women Writers* [Houston: G. K. Hall and Co., 1990], pp. 126–127)

Gunter, Alma Pennell (1909–1983)

Painter Alma Gunter spent her primary career as a nurse. During her youth in Palestine, she developed an early interest in art but had no teacher and little encouragement. After graduating from high school, she worked as a domestic, a seamstress, a hairdresser, and a dishwasher. With a higher-paying career in view, she enrolled in Prairie View School of Nursing in 1936. During her first year, she bought a set of paints and an instruction book from Sears, Roebuck. She won first prize for two years in an art and poetry contest sponsored by the Dilettante Literary Society, for both her art and poetry. After her graduation in 1939, she was employed as a registered nurse in Riverside and San Francisco, California, for more than twenty years. While a nursing student she began experimenting with painting and won several prizes in campus art competitions. Upon retirement as a nurse, she turned to art as a second career. Her paintings feature delightful scenes from childhood: washday, kitchen activities, and waiting for the ice man in summer. The religious works depict a baptism, a funeral, and a church dinner. She began receiving recognition in 1978 when her work was first exhibited in Palestine. Additional shows in Texas and elsewhere earned her national attention and a place in many private collections. Her canvases, brightly colored scenes of rural Palestine, have helped preserve a slice of that town's history. C. C. Gunter became her husband in 1941. (*Handbook of Texas* [Austin: Texas State Historical Association, in press]; Rose Sharp, "Alma Pennell Gunter," *Art Voices/South* 3, no. 6 [November/December 1980]: 32; *Remembrances of Two Artists: The Stitchery of Ruby Yount, The Paintings of Alma Gunter*, exhibit program [Lufkin: Lufkin Historical and Creative Arts Center, 1980]; *The Folk Art of Alma Gunter*, an exhibition presented by the Austin Public Library Carver Museum, May 6–June 5, 1982)

Hall, Josie Briggs (1869–1935)

Josie Briggs Hall was a teacher, moral educator, and writer. She was born in Waxahachie and was raised by an older sister after their parents died when Josie was eleven. She was active in the African Methodist Episcopal Church in Waxahachie, where she taught Sunday school at age twelve. By the time she was sixteen, she was teaching public school in Canaan, Texas. She attended Bishop College around 1886 but did not graduate and married Professor J. P. Hall, also an educator. For a time they lived in his home state of Mississippi, where he was a school administrator and both taught school. They moved to Mexia, Texas, where he was a principal and she taught at the Mexia Colored School for nine of the eleven years from 1893 to 1904. While living in Mexia, Mrs. Hall wrote "A Scroll of Facts and Advice" and a longer religious work, "Build Character, Build on the Foundation, Christ. . . ." *Hall's Moral and Mental Capsule for the Economic and Domestic Life of the Negro, as a Solution of the Race Problem* may have been the first book published by a black Texas woman. Its themes include educational psychology, womanhood, chastity, self-reliance, independence, and "the Negro Problem." Essays and poetry by Hall and others, including Booker T. Washington, are featured, as well as photographs of admirable blacks. Josie Hall founded a short-lived junior college at Doyle (Limestone County) and a school in Dallas for the domestic training of girls. (Josie B. Hall, *Hall's Moral and Mental Capsule for the Economic and Domestic Life of the Negro, as a Solution of the Race Problem* [Dallas: Rev. F. S. Jenkins, 1905], pp. v–vi; Doris Pemberton, *Juneteenth at Comanche Crossing* [Austin: Eakin Press, 1983], pp. 138–40; Willie McBay Benton, *History of the Mexia Public Schools, 1895–1968* [Mexia: n.p., 1968?])

Hare, Maud Cuney (1874–1936)

Maud Cuney Hare, born in Galveston, where she graduated from high school, is best known as a musician, music historian, and writer. She was the daughter of Norris Wright Cuney, a prominent Republican party politician and businessman, and Adelina Dowdie Cuney, who defied segregation and was active in civic work. In the 1890s, Maud studied piano at the New England Conservatory of Music in Boston and privately. While there, she refused to vacate the dormitory in the face of opposition by some white students and the administration. In 1897, she returned to Texas and took a one-year position as music director at the Deaf, Dumb, and Blind Institute for Colored Youth in Austin. She also taught at Prairie View State College (1903–1904). After 1906, she made Boston her home as the wife of William Hare. She collected songs from Mexico and the Caribbean, introduced the public to Creole music, and gave concert tours and lectures with baritone William Howard Richardson. She founded the Musical Arts Studio in Boston and promoted the Little Theatre movement there. The author of many articles on music, Cuney Hare also wrote a biography of her father, Norris Wright Cuney; edited a volume of poetry; and wrote a four-act romantic comedy, *Antar of Araby*, that she directed in 1929. The play features a black Arab warrior, the first foreign protagonist in a play by a black author. She was the editor of the music notes for *Crisis* and contributed to journals such as the *Christian Science Monitor*. One of her goals was to direct young blacks into the mainstream of art and music. Her most valuable contribution, *Negro Musicians and Their Music*, appeared in the year of her death. (*Handbook of Texas* [Austin: Texas State Historical Association, in press]; Ann Allen Schockley, *Afro-American Women Writers, 1746–1933: An Anthology and Critical Guide* [New York: Meridian, 1988], pp. 334–337; Maud Cuney Hare, *Norris Wright Cuney: A Tribune of the Black*

People [1913; reprint, Austin: Steck-Vaughn, 1968]; Lorraine Elena Roses, "Maud Cuney Hare," in Darlene Clark Hine, ed., *Black Women in America, An Historical Encyclopedia* [Brooklyn: Carlson Publishing, 1993], vol. 1, p. 529; Lorraine Elena Roses and Ruth Elizabeth Randolph, *Harlem Renaissance and Beyond: Literary Biographies of 100 Black Women Writers* [Boston: G. K. Hall and Co., 1990], pp. 148–151)

Hemmings, Myra Davis "Moms" (1887–1968)

Myra Hemmings of San Antonio not only had a remarkable career as an educator, but devoted countless hours to her church and civic groups and was widely known as a brilliant orator. Hemmings graduated from Riverside High School in San Antonio in 1909. At Howard University, from which she graduated with honors in 1913, she was the president of Alpha Kappa Alpha, was among the founders of the Delta Sigma Theta sorority, and served as its first president. She earned her master's degree in speech at Northwestern University. She was hired by the San Antonio Independent School District in 1913 to teach English and retired in 1964, teaching at Douglass High School and Phillis Wheatley. In 1922, she married John Wilbur Hemmings, an actor. In 1956, she served a term as president of the Alamo Teachers Council. Hemmings was an active member of the Second Baptist Church in San Antonio, where she was the first woman to serve on the board of trustees. With her husband, she established the Little Theatre Group at the church (later renamed in her honor). She was actively involved in the Order of the Eastern Star. Her death came only moments after she had delivered a speech at the Second Baptist Church's 89th anniversary celebration, entitled "Life Is a Prologue." (*San Antonio Register*, December 13, 1968; "Myra Lillian Davis Hemmings," Dallas Alumnae Chapter, Delta Sigma Theta, undated; Paula Giddings, *In Search of Sisterhood: Delta Sigma Theta and the Challenge of the Black Sorority Movement* [New York: William Morrow, 1988])

Hunter, Mary Evelyn V. Edwards (1885–1967)

Mary Hunter, the first black home demonstration agent in Texas, moved to LaPorte from her native Alabama after her marriage. She attended Prairie View Normal College in order to teach and earned her degree in 1926. She received a master's degree from Iowa State College in 1931. While at Prairie View in 1915, she was appointed a home demonstration agent in the infant United States Department of Agriculture's Extension Service. In the sixteen years during which she effectively headed the home demonstration program, it grew to over thirty thousand club members aided by twenty-three agents. Mrs. Hunter also appeared before county commissioners' courts to obtain funds for the local programs. One of her most successful campaigns encouraged families to purchase their homes and land, rather than remaining as tenants. Hunter was the first black to serve on the board of directors of St. Philip's Junior College in San Antonio. She wrote legislation establishing a state home for delinquent black girls and was secretary of the Texas Commission on Inter-racial Cooperation. In 1931, Hunter left Texas for Petersburg, Virginia, where she headed the home economics division at Virginia State College. Texas College in Tyler granted her an honorary degree. (*Handbook of Texas* [Austin: Texas State Historical Association, in press]; L. A. Potts, "Biography of Mrs. M. E. V. Hunter" [Petersburg, Va., 1958], typescript; Kate Adele Hill, *Home Demonstration Work in Texas* [San Antonio: Naylor Press, 1958], pp. 132–143, 156–157, 196–197)

Johnson, Amelia Elsenia Soders (1880?–1950s?)

Marlin was home to clubwoman Amelia Johnson. She was the holder of bachelor's and master's degrees from Prairie View College (later Prairie View A & M University), studied English and music at Howard University, and worked on a Ph.D. degree at the University of Southern California. Johnson was a public librarian and a teacher of English and music in Marlin schools. She was president of the Women's Missionary Union of the Marlin Baptist Church, on the Scholarship Committee of the Women's Auxiliary of the Texas Baptist Convention, and a board member of the Texas Commission on Inter-racial Cooperation. For four years, from 1926 to 1930, she served as president of the Texas Association of Colored Women's Clubs. Under her leadership, the group won passage of a state law establishing the Training School for Delinquent Negro Girls and worked to improve travel accommodations for blacks on segregated buses and trains. She also held several offices in the National Association of Colored Women, including the presidency of the Southwestern Region and the chair of its Young Women's Committee and of its Mother, Home and Child Department. She was instrumental in the creation of a public library in Marlin and was married to R. F. Johnson of Prairie View College. (*Women of Texas: A Brochure Honoring Miss Ellie Alma Walls, First Woman President of the Colored Teachers State Association of Texas*, 65th Annual Convention, November 24, 25, 26, 1949, Houston; A. W. Jackson, *A Sure Foundation: A Sketch of Negro Life in Texas* [Houston: Yates Publishing Co., 1940], pp. 294–295)

King, Silvia (ca. 1840?–1930s?)

Silvia King was born in Morocco, married, and had three children before she was abducted and taken to Bordeaux, France. She was drugged and placed in the hold of a slave ship which landed in New Orleans. There she was sold to a master named Jones and, along with other slaves, chained and marched to her new home near LaGrange. She had no choice in the matter of her next mate, Bob, who was forced upon her by her new owners. When the Joneses learned of her culinary skills, which she had acquired in France, she became their cook, but also helped in the vegetable garden and weaving room. She joined the Galilee Baptist Church near Rosebud in 1916. In addition to the medicines given out by the Joneses, King was familiar with various home remedies and folk medicine and provided interesting details of daily life in the "bottoms" to a Works Progress Administrator interviewer in the 1930s. Her interview, which has been reprinted several times, is one of the most interesting in the collection of Texas Slave Narratives. (Norman R. Yetman, ed., *Voices from Slavery* [New York: Holt, Rinehart and Winston, 1970], pp. 198–201; *Handbook of Texas* [Austin: Texas State Historical Association, in press]; George P. Rawick, ed., *The American Slave: A Composite Autobiography*, Series I, vol. 4, Series II, vol. 6 [Westport, Conn.: Greenwood Press, 1979], pp. 2224–2235)

Linton, Dolores Burton (1910–1980)

Dolores Linton devoted her career to improving the education of black children in the San Antonio area. Born in Seguin, she grew up in Central Texas, where her father taught school. After studying a year at Samuel Huston College, she began teaching at Pleasanton. There she learned of deplorable conditions in West San Antonio Heights, an isolated black community, which had no streets, electricity, sewers, churches, or schools. Students were assigned to a school five miles distant, but without transportation few attended regularly. In 1931, Linton won approval from the local school district to conduct classes in a nearby dance hall that was used only on evenings and weekends. With meager supplies and old textbooks, she taught all seven grades herself. Her salary was provided for only six months; the students' parents contributed funds for a seventh. Facilities were upgraded in 1934 and 1946, but the school still had no indoor plumbing or electricity. She married Walter Linton in 1937 and graduated from Samuel Huston College two years later. During World War II, she worked for the USO, then returned to teaching. She completed her master's degree at Our Lady of the Lake College in 1952, the same year in which the district replaced her old school with a modern four-room building to house 150 students and four teachers. The school closed under a desegregation court order in 1966. Linton continued to teach until her retirement in 1971. The Northside School District named the Dolores B. Linton Elementary School in her honor in 1980, and she was granted the Texas State Teachers Association's Human Relations Award posthumously in 1981. Our Lady of the Lake also named her one of their most distinguished graduates. She was active in Alpha Kappa Alpha sorority. (*Handbook of Texas* [Austin: Texas State Historical Association, in press]; Dolores Burton Linton, "The Growth and Development of the West San Antonio Heights School in District I," master's thesis, Our Lady of the Lake College, 1952)

Long, Kian (or Kiamatia) (180?–18??)

Kian Long was the slave and lifelong companion of Jane Wilkinson Long, the first Anglo woman known to have given birth in Texas. The two women first came to Texas from Mississippi in 1819 so that Mrs. Long could be with her husband, James, a filibusterer who was mounting a campaign to capture Texas from Spain. After a fundraising trip to the United States, the party again entered Texas and settled at Fort Bolivar, across from Galveston Island, this time accompanied by the Longs' five-year-old daughter, Ann. Dr. Long left the women and a number of soldiers at the fort when he left on his mission in September 1821. Gradually, the soldiers drifted away, while the women remained throughout the exceedingly bitter winter. Kian helped her mistress deliver her daughter Mary on December 21, 1821. The women and two children lived off the land and, with difficulty, survived the cold. One day, Kian warned Mrs. Long of approaching Karankawa Indians, and the two deceived them into thinking the fort was still occupied. After that, Kian usually wore a military outfit when she could be seen. Upon learning of James Long's death in March 1822, the women agreed to leave Bolivar Point. A local family escorted the group to San Antonio. Jane and her children and their household goods traveled on horseback while Kian walked. Existing primarily on the generosity of friends and trading possessions for necessities, Jane, Kian, and the two girls lived in San Antonio for about a year before returning to Mississippi. When they next entered Texas, it was as members of Stephen F. Austin's Old 300 Colony. They settled at San Felipe de Austin in December 1825. In 1828, Jane and Kian were living at Fort Bend (Richmond); in 1834, they opened an inn on a well-traveled route in Brazoria. On one occasion, an old creditor of James Long claimed title to Kian, who had been pledged as collateral. A friend paid the debt, and Kian was reclaimed.

The inn became the scene of many gatherings involving the leaders of the Texas War for Independence. The first gunpowder of the Revolution was stored behind the inn. In 1837, the women opened another inn on a Richmond land grant. They then moved to a nearby plantation, which prospered. By 1850, it was worth more than $10,000. Kian was allowed to marry, and her daughter Clarisa served Mrs. Long, a Confederate supporter, both in slavery and in freedom. Kian's granddaughter and namesake was employed by Mrs. Long at the time of the latter's death. (Martha Anne Turner, *The Life and Times of Jane Long* [Waco: Texian Press, 1969])

Madison, Mary (?–?)

Mary Madison, a free woman of color, came to Galveston in the early 1840s. In August 1846, she joined the predominantly white First Baptist Church. She petitioned the legislature to remain in Texas in about 1850. The eighty-two citizens who endorsed her petition agreed that she had always behaved with propriety and was a good citizen. Moreover, they valued her services as a nurse. Many of them had employed her and found her to be kind and attentive. Madison's petition, approved in December 1851, was one of only three to be granted. (First Baptist Church, Galveston, Membership Rolls, Rosenberg Library, Galveston; Petition 2-1/124, OFB 64-251, Archives Division, Texas State Library; H. P. N. Gammel, comp. and arr., *The Laws of Texas, 1822–1897* [10 vols.; Austin: Gammel Book Co., 1898], vol. 3, p. 1042)

Martin, Louise (1911–1995)

Photographer Louise Martin, a native of Brenham, developed an interest in photography at age eleven when her mother bought her a camera. By the time she was a high school junior, she edged out the company that usually took yearbook pictures and shot them herself. She later studied at the Art Institute and the American School of Photography in Chicago. She saved her money from a domestic job in Houston's River Oaks to pay her tuition at the University of Denver, where she received a degree in photography. At that time, no white southern schools were open to her. She opened a portrait studio in Houston in 1946 and was among the first African-American female photographers in the area. She earned a reputation as a society photographer at weddings and funerals, galas and graduations, with many notables, including Marian Anderson and Jesse Jackson, among her clients. In 1952, her exhibit at the Southwestern Photographers' Convention had to be hung in the hotel mezzanine because blacks were not permitted to ride the elevators. She was the first female member of the national Professional Photographers Association and won several top awards in that organization's juried competitions. She worked for years as a photographer for the Houston *Informer* and *Forward Times*. Her aerial shots of the crowds of mourners and her portraits of Coretta Scott King during the funeral of Martin Luther King earned her national acclaim. Martin was featured in Jeanne Moutoussamy-Ashe's *Viewfinders*, the first book to chronicle the lives of black women photographers. (Jeanne Moutoussamy-Ashe, *Viewfinders: Black Women Photographers* [New York: Dodd, Mead and Co., 1986], pp. 122–129; author's interview with Louise Martin, Houston, August 20, 1991; obituary, *Houston Chronicle*, July 14, 1995; "Acclaimed Photographer Martin Dies," *Houston Chronicle*, July 14, 1995)

McFarland, Fanny (ca. 1814–18??)

Fanny McFarland was brought to Texas by her owner, William McFarland, in 1827. He emancipated her in 1835, although her children were still slaves. In 1836, during the Texas War for Independence, she had to flee San Felipe de Austin, leaving all her property behind. By 1838, she had established herself in Houston. In 1840, she petitioned the Texas Congress to remain in Texas. Eighty-eight citizens, including Lorenzo de Zavala (Mexican supporter of Texas independence and interim vice president of the Republic of Texas), signed the petition. Although it was denied, she continued to reside in Houston until at least 1866 (perhaps with a stay in Brownsville, where she is listed in the 1850 census). One of Houston's first entrepreneurs, she engaged in real estate transfers and profited from her investments in land. (Andrew Muir, "The Free Negro in Harris County, Texas," *Southwestern Historical Quarterly* 46, no. 3 [January 1943]: 219; Fanny McFarland, Memorials and Petitions, October 30, 1840, Archives Division, Texas State Library, Austin)

Montgomery, Ellie Alma Walls (1890–1974)

Houston educator and social worker Ellie Walls Montgomery was born in San Antonio, attended Austin public schools, and graduated from high school in Houston. She earned the A.B. from Fisk University in 1911 and the A.M. from Columbia University. About 1913, she received a certificate from the New York School of Philanthropy (now the New York School of Social Work), and was one of the first two black fellows of the Urban League. During this time, she was a caseworker for the United Charities Organization. The data in her thesis were used by the Urban League to influence legislation for the improved care of delinquent girls in New York state. Her earliest teaching was as an assistant at Fisk University. She was girls' work secretary for the New York Urban League and a special investigator for them in Baltimore, Maryland. For forty-five years, beginning in 1915, she taught in Houston, both at Wheatley High School and at Houston Negro Junior College (later Texas Southern University). Mrs. Montgomery wrote a column for the *Houston Informer* between 1927 and 1934 and published studies of school drop-outs and juvenile delinquency in Houston in 1936. She was superintendent of Wesley Chapel AME Church for nine years. From 1926 to 1938, she served as secretary-treasurer of the Colored Teachers State Association of Texas and is author of its history, *The Sixty Year History of the Association*. In 1948, she became that group's first woman president. Her work with the CTSAT helped build a coalition of black organizations united to promote pay equalization of black and white Texas teachers and equalize educational opportunities. In 1949, the CTSAT dedicated their 65th Annual Convention and program brochure to her. She was a founder of Houston's Dorcas Home for Delinquent Girls and as president of the Houston Fisk Club raised funds for a scholarship fund. At age seventy-three, she finally fulfilled a sixty-year dream—to visit Africa. While there, she saw missions and schools supported by her church. (Ellie Walls Montgomery, *Report of a Survey of Negro Youths Not in School 1936* [Houston: Houston College for Negroes, 1936]; Ellie Walls Montgomery, *Juvenile Delinquency among Negroes in Houston, Texas*, Study Number 2 [Houston: Department of Sociology, Houston College for Negroes, 1936]; A. W. Jackson, *A Sure Foundation: A Sketch of Negro Life in Texas* [Houston: Yates Publishing Co., 1940], pp. 161–162; *Women of Texas: A Brochure Honoring Miss Ellie Alma Walls, First Woman President of the Colored Teachers State Association of Texas*, 65th Annual Convention, November 24, 25, 26, 1949, Houston; *Houston Post*, January 10, 1963; Vernon McDaniel, *History of the Teachers State Association of Texas* [Washington, D.C.: National Education Association, 1977], pp. 131–132; Dorothy Salem, *To Better Our World: Black Women in Organized Reform, 1890–1920* [Brooklyn: Carlson Publishing, 1990], pp. 195–196)

Morgan, Emily D. [West] (?–?)

A Texas-sized legend has grown up around Emily West, usually known as Emily Morgan, "the Yellow Rose of Texas." William Bollaert gave birth to the myth in an 1842 diary entry, noting that she "detained" General Santa Anna in his tent at the Battle of San Jacinto. This gave General Sam Houston and the Texas army a clear advantage on the battlefield, leading to their victory in eighteen minutes. The song "The Yellow Rose of Texas," first published in 1858, the tale goes, was based upon her heroism. The lyrics refer to the Yellow Rose as "the sweetest rose of color / This darky [songwriter] ever knew." The facts, however, indicate that Emily D. West was a New York–born free woman of color. She came to Texas in 1835, possibly as an indentured servant, with Mrs. Lorenzo de Zavala. She and Mrs. de Zavala were taken prisoner by General Santa Anna in April 1836 at the Morgan estate, where the de Zavalas were hiding. During the Battle of San Jacinto, Emily West escaped, losing her freedom papers in the process. She applied for a passport and most likely returned to New York shortly thereafter. (*San Antonio Sunday Express News*, March 2, 1986, p. 26-P; Eugene Holland and Ruth Lapham Butler, eds., *William Bollaert's Texas* [Norman: University of Oklahoma Press, 1956], p. 108; Martha Anne Turner, *The Yellow Rose of Texas: Her Saga and Her Song* [Austin: Shoal Creek Publishers, 1976]; Margaret S. Henson, "Emily D. West, a.k.a. Emily Morgan," unpublished biographical note, May 15, 1984; Margaret Henson, "She's the Real Thing," *Texas Highways* 33 [April 1986]: 60–61; Anita Bunkley, *Emily, The Yellow Rose—A Texas Legend* [Houston: Rinard Publishing, 1989])

Morgan, Tamar (?–?)

Tamar Morgan came to Texas in 1832 as a slave and lived near Brazoria. Two years later, she had earned money enough to purchase her freedom. She married Samuel Hardin, a free man, in 1838. The next year she and her husband petitioned the Texas Congress to be allowed to remain in the Republic. Sixty-five of their white neighbors supported them. Although the petition was not granted, Morgan and her husband remained in Texas. By 1840, she had acquired four lots in Brazoria, one hundred acres, and four slaves. She disappears from public records after 1844. ("Tamar Morgan," in *Handbook of Texas* [Austin: Texas State Historical Association, in press])

Osborne, Estelle Massey Riddle (1901–1981)

Born in Palestine, Estelle Osborne broke racial barriers in nursing, often under her first married name, Riddle. After graduation from Prairie View State College in 1920, she entered the nursing school at Homer G. Phillips Hospital in St. Louis, graduating in 1923. She passed the Missouri State Board Examination with a grade of 93.3 percent. She was the first black in nursing administration when she became head nurse of one of the largest wards in the hospital. In 1930, Osborne earned a bachelor of science degree in nursing education from Teachers College, Columbia University. One year later, she was the first black nurse to receive a master's degree in nursing. She accepted a position at the Harlem Hospital School of Nursing as the school's first black instructor. After several years as educational director of Freedmen's Hospital in Washington, D.C., Riddle took the post of superintendent of her St. Louis alma mater. From 1934 to 1939, she was president of the National Association of Colored Graduate Nurses (NACGN) and worked diligently to build up that group's membership. The newly founded National Council of Negro Women elected her a vice president in 1935. In 1946, upon receiving her master's degree, she became the first black on the nursing faculty at New York University in New York City. Osborne also negotiated over many years with the American Nurses Association (ANA) to win acceptance of black members in that organization. When the NACGN and the ANA merged in 1948, she was the first black board member appointed. Upon her retirement in 1967, she became associate general director of the National League for Nursing. (Darlene Clark Hine, *Black Women in White: Racial Conflict and Cooperation in the Nursing Profession, 1890–1950* [Bloomington: Indiana University Press, 1989]; Marie Mosley, "Estelle Massey Osborne," in Darlene Clark Hine, ed., *Black Women in America, An Historical Encyclopedia* [Brooklyn: Carlson Publishing, 1993], pp. 903–905)

Parsons, Lucy Eldine Gonzales (1853–1942)

Little is known of Lucy Parsons's early life, but her adult years as a labor organizer, radical speaker, and writer are well documented. She was the first black woman to achieve prominence in the American left. Her origins are disputed, as she claimed a mixed Spanish and Indian heritage, but contemporaries considered her black. In about 1871, Lucy became acquainted with Albert Parsons, a former Confederate army scout turned radical, in Waco. Shortly afterward, they began living as husband and wife and may have been married. They spent a year in Austin, where Albert was active among the Radical Republicans. Near the end of 1873, because of intolerance of interracial couples, they left the state permanently for Chicago, where they both joined the Workingmen's Party. Lucy championed the cause of the working class in articles for the *Alarm*, an anarchist journal which her husband edited, and contributed articles to the *Socialist*. In 1886, she organized sewing women into the Knights of Labor as part of the eight-hour day movement. The couple's involvement with the Workingmen's Party led to Albert's arrest after the Haymarket Riot in 1886 and his execution in 1887. Lucy campaigned impassionedly, but unsuccessfully, in his defense. Her early writings on lynchings and racist violence were published before those of Ida B. Wells. Her short-lived newspaper,

Freedom: A Revolutionary Anarchist-Communist Monthly, featured essays on rape, divorce, marriage, and the role of women's oppression under capitalism. The mother of two children, she was a strong believer in the nuclear family but believed that women would be emancipated only when wage slavery ended. She was among the founders of the Industrial Workers of the World in 1905. In 1927, she joined the International Labor Defense and, in 1939, the American Communist Party. In print and in speech, Parsons was a zealous champion of the economically oppressed during more than four decades of her activist life. (Carolyn Ashbaugh, *Lucy Parsons: American Revolutionary* [Chicago: Charles H. Kerr Publishing Company, 1976]; Robin D. G. Kelley, "Lucy Parsons," in Darlene Clark Hine, ed., *Black Women in America, An Historical Encyclopedia* [Brooklyn: Carlson Publishing, 1993], pp. 909–910)

Peterson, Eliza E. (18??–19??)

Although her personal life remains in the shadows, Mrs. Eliza Peterson made her mark publicly as a campaigner for prohibition among black women. Before beginning this crusade she was a music teacher in Texarkana. The Woman's Christian Temperance Union (WCTU) came to Texas in 1882 when national president Frances Willard toured the state and established the first two Texas chapters in Paris, one for whites and one for blacks. In 1897, Lucy Simpson Thurman, president of the Colored Division of the National WCTU and national superintendent of Colored Work, undertook organizing in the South (and Texas). The following year, after Peterson was elected state president of the Thurman Union (the black women's sector), membership grew rapidly. She traveled extensively, not only recruiting adults, but organizing children into Little Temperance Leagues and visiting seven of the state's thirteen black colleges in 1898. During the next year, her name appeared in newspapers as a speaker and organizer throughout the state. In 1909, she was elected national superintendent and began traveling throughout the South. She continued her work through 1918, when the Eighteenth Amendment to the U.S. Constitution (Prohibition) was ratified. An indefatigable speaker and traveler, she wrote many pamphlets and articles about temperance. (*Dallas Morning News*, February 6, March 6 and 20, 1905; January 21, February 11 and 18, March 4 and 25, 1907; January 25, February 22, March 22, 1909; Judith N. McArthur, "Motherhood and Reform in the New South, Texas Women during the Progressive Era," Ph.D. diss., University of Texas at Austin, 1992, pp. 14–15)

Pinkston, Viola Shaw (1892–1976)

Community worker Viola Pinkston was born in Terrell. She moved to Dallas with her husband, Dr. Lee Gresham Pinkston, and their three children in 1921. In 1935, she organized the Wednesday Morning Study Club. Later, she served as president of the Dallas City Federation of Colored Women's Clubs and chair of the committee on administration for the Maria Morgan Branch, Young Women's Christian Association (1946). Her other volunteer activities included work for the Lighthouse for the Blind and presiding over the Women's Auxiliary of the Lone Star Medical Association. Her husband was a well-respected physician. (Mamie L. McKnight, ed., *African American Families and Settlements of Dallas: On the Inside Looking Out* [Dallas: Black Dallas Remembered, 1990], vol. 2, pp. 109–110)

Pittman, Portia Washington (1883–1978)

Musician Portia Washington Pittman lived in Dallas from 1913 to 1928. As Booker T. Washington's oldest child and only daughter, Portia Pittman was among the southern black elite. Originally from Tuskegee, Alabama, she was educated at Framingham State Normal School and Bradford Academy (now Bradford Junior College), both in Massachusetts. Music was a large part of her curriculum. After graduating from Bradford in 1905, she traveled in Europe and studied piano for a year with Martin Krause, a former student of Franz Liszt. Her marriage to architect William Sidney Pittman in 1907 ended her musical training. The couple lived in Washington, D.C., where their three children were born, until her husband's career foundered. They then moved to Dallas, where Portia Pittman gave private music lessons and taught music at Booker T. Washington High School. She chaired the education department of the Texas Association of Negro Musicians in the 1920s. In 1927, her high school choir performed at the national convention of the National Education Association in Dallas to wide acclaim. Her husband's moodiness and temper, his lack of success in architecture, and an incident in which he struck their daughter resulted in Mrs. Pittman's leaving him and Dallas to return to Tuskegee in 1928. She continued to teach piano until 1944, then became involved in efforts to establish a national monument at her father's birthplace. In the 1950s, she moved to Washington, D.C., to live with her older son, Sidney, Jr., and later with her daughter Fannie. (Ruth Ann Stewart, *Portia: The Life of Portia Washington Pittman, the Daughter of Booker T. Washington* [New York: Doubleday and Company, 1977]; Stephanie J. Shaw, "Portia Marshall Washington Pittman," in Darlene Clark Hine, ed., *Black Women in America, An Historical Encyclopedia* [Brooklyn: Carlson Publishing, 1993], pp. 930–931)

Polk, Naomi (1892–1984)

The tenth and youngest child of former slaves, artist Naomi Howard Polk lived her entire life in Houston. As a child she often accompanied her mother to her job as a domestic. She started school before the turn of the century, but was forced to drop out early to care for her nieces and nephews. Twice widowed as an adult, she survived the Depression and supported her three children with the assistance of meager welfare checks supplemented by selling cosmetics for blacks and insecticides which she concocted. She rose early to write poetry and stayed up late to paint. All her work was lost when her home burned in 1961, and she spent the rest of her life replicating it. She mixed her own paints and painted on whatever surface was available—window shades, cardboard, and ceiling tiles. Because of the fragility of the materials, much of her work did not survive. Many of her works reflect a deep religious faith and a strong sense of her African-American heritage. Her art has been displayed in several exhibits in Houston as well as a traveling exhibit in 1989, *Black History/Black Vision*. Mark Smith, art critic for the *Austin American-Statesman*, said that, of the six artists featured in that exhibit, her work represented "the most affecting pieces in the show and the most sophisticated artistically, even though they are painted on cardboard or old window shades." Her self-portrait *Now where do I go from here?* was made into a poster and used as the symbol for the touring exhibition *Houston Women*, which opened in 1988. (Mark Smith, "That old-time religion is good enough for contemporary art," *Austin American-Statesman*, February 9, 1989; Lynne Adele, *Black Vision: The Visionary Image in Texas* [Austin: Archer M. Huntington Art Gallery (1989)]; Naomi Polk biographical panel, *Houston Women* exhibit, July–August 1988, at Innova, Houston)

Ransom, Ethel Blanche Wilson (1890s?–19??)

Ethel Ransom put aside a salaried career to devote her considerable talents to clubwork. She had been a teacher and a graduate nurse. She lived in Gainesville when she married Dr. Riley Andrew Ransom in 1915. The couple made their home in Fort Worth, where Dr. Ransom was owner of a hospital. In 1922, Mrs. Ransom was elected president of the Texas Association of Colored Women's Clubs. During her one term in office, the organization carried on a successful campaign to raise funds for the state home for delinquent black girls. She was also Texas state director for the national Anti-Lynching Crusaders. The Ethel Ransom Art and Literary Club in Houston, organized in 1927, is a tribute to her endeavors. After her death, Dr. Ransom renamed his facility the Ethel Ransom Memorial

Hospital. (Letterhead of the National Anti-Lynching Crusaders, Box 6, Mary Church Terrell Papers, Library of Congress; A. W. Jackson, *A Sure Foundation: A Sketch of Negro Life in Texas* [Houston: Yates Publishing Co., 1940], pp. 293, 567)

Routh, Sylvia (?–?)

Sylvia Routh, a slave owned by James Routh along with her six children, was the beneficiary of his will. He may have been the father of the children. At James Routh's death in July 1837, Sylvia Routh and her family inherited his 320 acres near Galveston Bay. She was to be freed and was to educate her children with three hundred dollars provided in the will, then bind them out until age twenty-one. The oldest two girls were to be hired out until they reached the age of twenty-one to Mrs. James (Ophelia) Morgan. Colonel James Morgan and Dr. George M. Patrick were executors of the will and guardians of the freed slaves. In April 1838, Colonel Morgan had Sylvia committed to the county jail, claiming that she had become "unruly," refusing to submit to his authority. The length of her stay in jail is not known. Five years later, in November 1843, she reappeared and petitioned the probate court for letters of guardianship of her six children. The title to the land on Clear Creek at last passed to her and her children. (Andrew Muir, "The Free Negro of Harris County, Texas," *Southwestern Historical Quarterly* 46, no. 3 [January 1943]: 225–226)

Simond, Ada DeBlanc (1903–1989)

Louisiana-born Ada Simond had major careers as a public health educator and as a historian, as well as being a secretary, teacher, author, and court bailiff. In 1914, the DeBlanc family moved to Austin, where Simond attended Samuel Huston College. She received her bachelor's degree from Tillotson College in 1934, then continued her education at Iowa State University, where she earned a master's degree in 1936. She taught high school subjects in Belton and home economics at Tillotson during the late 1930s. In 1942, she began a 24-year career with the Texas Tuberculosis Association, as a public health representative traveling to schools and communities in disadvantaged localities to teach about medical services, nutrition, and disease prevention. Simond's career in preserving local black history followed her first retirement in 1966. She wrote an award-winning semiautobiographical series of books for children telling the story of Mae Dee, the Let's Pretend Series. In conjunction with other Delta Sigma Theta members, she helped develop an exhibition on black history in Travis County. She contributed a newspaper column on black history for the

Austin American-Statesman and helped organize the W. H. Passon Historical Society. Recognized by many awards, Simond received an honorary doctorate from Huston-Tillotson College in 1982 and was inducted into the Texas Women's Hall of Fame in 1986. (Texas Women's Hall of Fame Nomination Form, 1985, Governor's Commission for Women Papers, Texas Woman's University, Denton; Ada DeBlanc Simond, "Notes and Documents—The Discovery of Being Black: A Recollection," *Southwestern Historical Quarterly* 76, no. 4 [April 1973]: 440–447; Ada DeBlanc Simond, Let's Pretend Series [Austin: Stevenson Press, 1970s])

Smith, Lucille Bishop (1892–1985)

Lucille Bishop Smith had a long career as an educator, businesswoman, and inventor of Lucille's All Purpose Hot Roll Mix, the first in the nation. She received her public school education in Crockett and attended Wiley, Samuel Huston, Prairie View, and Colorado State colleges. A home economist, Smith set up the first college-level Commercial Foods and Technology Department at Prairie View A & M University, published *Lucille's Treasure Chest of Fine Foods*, and established a family corporation, Lucille B. Smith's Fine Foods, Inc., at age eighty-two. In 1969, she was appointed to the Governor's Commission on the Status of Women. Smith received numerous awards, including Merit Mother of Texas (twice) and Prairie View A & M's Distinguished Partner in Progress award. In 1911, she married Ulysses S. Bishop. Their three children earned graduate degrees in their chosen fields. (Gladys Smith Hogan, "Lucille Bishop (Mrs. U. S.) Smith," *Worthy Mothers of Texas* [Belton: Mother's Committee, Stillhouse Publisher, 1976]; "Mrs. Lucille Bishop Smith" funeral program, January 17, 1985, St. Andrew's Methodist Church, Fort Worth, author's collection)

Teal, Elnora (?–19??)

Elnora Teal learned photography from her husband, Arthur Chester Teal, and came to be his equal in the studios they operated together. The couple met when he was working in Waco. After their marriage, they moved to Houston and opened the Teal Portrait Studio on Andrews Street in 1919. They later moved their location downtown to Milam Street. Business was so good, even during the Depression, that the couple opened a second studio on Dowling Street in Houston's Fourth Ward, the heart of the black community. Elnora ran the Milam Street studio while Arthur operated the new studio with a competent assistant, Lucille B. Moore. He toured the state photographing colleges such as Wiley, Bishop, and Prairie View. Elnora Teal photographed only at her studio, which was surrounded by black businesses. The famous tenor Roland Hayes was one of her treasured customers. During the 1940s, the couple ran Teal's School of Photography, which for several years was associated with Houston Junior College for Negroes. After her husband's death in 1955, Elnora Teal kept the studio functioning successfully for ten additional years. She was chair of the Arts and Crafts Committee for the Texas Association of Colored Women during the 1950s. Her sterling reputation was based upon her close attention to detail and the use of fine photographic paper. (Jeanne Moutoussamy-Ashe, *Viewfinders: Black Women Photographers* [New York: Dodd, Mead and Co., 1986], pp. 44–47; Carrie P. Hines, *The Surmounters* [Amarillo: Shepherd Printing Co., 1959], p. 135)

Tyler, Priscilla Laura (1882–1942)

Priscilla Tyler was one of Dallas's first college-educated black women schoolteachers. After graduating from high school in Dallas, she attended Howard University for two years and received a diploma in 1904 from its Teacher's College. She earned the B.A. degree from Colorado State Teacher's College. Her teaching career began in elementary school in 1906. She encouraged her students to attend operas at Fair Park. In 1924, she moved to Booker T. Washington High School, where she taught Spanish. There she organized the first scholastic group, the Pierian Club. She was also a founder of the Reading Circle and the G Clef Society and helped organize the Civic Music Guild to showcase touring black concert artists. She was active in the New Hope Baptist Church. (Sadye Gee, comp., and Darnell Williams, ed., *Black Presence in Dallas, Historic Black Dallasites* [Dallas: Museum of African-American Life and Culture, 1986], p. 110)

Wallace, Beulah Thomas "Sippie" (1898–1986)

Beulah "Sippie" Wallace was born in Houston. She had her first exposure to music in the Shiloh Baptist church, where her father was a deacon. By age seven she was the church organist. As a child she also heard blues and ragtime in touring tent shows. She began her career as maid and stage assistant to Madam Dante, a snakedancer. The two traveled around Texas, where Wallace gained a reputation as "the Texas Nightingale," singing at picnics, dances, tent shows, and holiday celebrations. In the 1920s, Wallace joined her brother George, a respected composer and music publisher in Chicago. Together the two developed a songwriting partnership and became famous as recording artists. Her first recordings, "Shorty George" and "Up the Country Blues" on the Okey label, were among the scores of hit records from this period. After the deaths of her brother and her husband, Matt, Wallace shifted to gospel music, a close cousin to the blues, and directed church choirs. In 1929, she recorded "I'm a Mighty Tight Woman" and "You Gonna Need My Help" for Victor Records. Her career floundered until 1966, when she returned to the blues scene with a successful concert tour of Europe. In 1977, at age eighty-eight, she appeared at Lincoln Center's Avery Fisher Hall. Shortly before her death, she sang "Women Be Wise, Don't Advertise Yo' Man" to a German audience. (Christopher Brooks, "Coming Home: An Interview with Sippie Wallace," *Texas Humanist* [July–August 1985]: 30–31; *New York Times*, November 1, 1986; Daphne Duval Harrison, "Sippie Wallace," in Darlene Clark Hine, ed., *Black Women in America: An Historical Encyclopedia* [Brooklyn: Carlson Publishing, 1993], pp. 1220–1223)

West, Emily D. Morgan. *See* Morgan, Emily D. [West]

White, Hattie Mae Whiting (1916–1993)

With her election to the Board of the Houston Independent School District in 1958, Hattie Mae White became the first black elected to public office in Texas in the twentieth century. White was born in Huntsville but moved to Houston as a child. She was valedictorian of her graduating class at Booker T. Washington High School. For two years, White attended Houston College for Negroes, and she graduated with highest distinction from Prairie View. She taught school for several years in Cameron and Jasper before returning to Houston. In 1941, White became the first black female board member of the YWCA of Houston and worked to integrate the Downtown branch. Her activities in local PTAs led to her involvement in the Parents Council, a group formed to promote integration in Houston schools. Her commonsense approach to the issue resulted in her election to the school board in 1958 with support by blacks and moderate whites, receiving 47 percent of all votes cast. Just days after her election, she became the target of a hate campaign by white supremacist groups. A cross was burned in White's yard and her car window was shot out. She won reelection to a second term in 1962, serving until 1967, but was defeated in a third bid. A trailblazer for civil rights during her turbulent two terms, she fought for peaceful desegregation and federal aid for programs such as free milk. Gertrude Barnstone, who served on the board with White, was a friend and ally on many of the controversial issues. After leaving the HISD board, Mrs. White held several teaching positions in public and private schools. Her husband, Dr. Charles E. White, was an optometrist. Mrs.

White was active in the League of Women Voters, Jack and Jill of America, Inc., the United Church of Christ, and Alpha Kappa Alpha sorority. In 1989, the Beach-White park was named for Mary Beach and Hattie Mae White. (Helen Hunter et al., eds., *Houston Women from Suffrage to City Hall* [Houston: League of Women Voters of Houston Education Fund, 1987], pp. 39–40; *Houston Chronicle*, September 17, 1989; *Houston Post*, August 8, 1993, p. A28)

White, Lulu Belle Madison (1907–1957)

Born in Elmo, in East Texas, political activist Lulu (or Lula) B. White attended Butler College for one year and graduated from Prairie View in 1928. After moving to Houston, she married businessman Julius White. She received a bachelor's degree in English from Prairie View College and embarked on a teaching career in a black community on the outskirts of Houston. Her husband's membership in the National Association for the Advancement of Colored People and her earlier activism while a student led her to abandon teaching to devote herself full time to NAACP activities, particularly its struggle to eliminate the state's white primary. In 1939, she became acting president of the Houston branch and then its full-time salaried executive secretary from 1943 until 1949, the first black woman in the South to hold such a position. Under her leadership the Houston branch grew to 5,679 members in 1943, then doubled to 12,000 members by 1945, the largest in the South. White chose the plaintiff, Heman Marion Sweatt, in *Sweatt v. Painter*, the case fought by the NAACP that resulted in the integration of the University of Texas. She tirelessly urged blacks to pay their poll taxes and vote, as well as to run for public office and to insist upon equal economic opportunity. In 1946, she was elected director of state NAACP branches. By 1949, Texas had almost 30,000 members. A dispute with Carter Wesley, editor of the *Houston Informer*, over the principle of "separate but equal" weakened her position. There were also repercussions from her support for Henry Wallace's presidential candidacy in 1948 and her appearance before the House Committee on Un-American Activities. In 1950, she became a national NAACP fieldworker. The NAACP established the Lulu White Freedom Fund in her honor. For many, Lulu B. White was the matriarch of the Texas civil rights movement. ("Lulu B. White," in *Handbook of Texas* [Austin: Texas State Historical Association, in press]; Merline Pitre, "Black Houstonians and the 'Separate But Equal' Doctrine: Carter W. Wesley versus Lulu B. White," *Houston Review* 12, no. 1 [1990]: 23–36)

White, Mattie B. Haywood (1867–1951)

Teacher and artist Mattie B. White was a native of Tennessee and graduated from Nashville's Walden University in 1884. She taught in Tennessee and Mississippi before accepting an offer to teach in Austin in 1888. The following year, she married Thomas J. White. In 1892, White opened Austin's first private school for black girls in her home; it was short-lived. She obtained her final employment in 1900, a job she held for over forty years without missing a single day's work. She taught art and handicrafts to students at the Deaf, Dumb, and Blind Institute for Colored Youth in Austin (later the Texas Blind, Deaf, and Orphans School). She used sign language, written instructions, and patterns to teach students to paint, draw, embroider, knit, and weave. White herself was a talented and versatile artist who painted bluebonnets and landscapes and did needlework. She was known for her collections of paintings and decorative arts. She was a state superintendent of the Mothers' Clubs and a member of the Woman's Christian Temperance Union. She was also active in the Ebenezer Baptist Church and helped her husband raise funds to purchase Emancipation Park, where Austin's Juneteenth celebrations took place. In 1909, she spoke at one such celebration; her subject was "The Opportunity and Responsibility of the Negro." (*Handbook of Texas* [Austin: Texas State Historical Association, in press])

Wiggins, Bernice Love (1897–19??)

Poet Bernice Love Wiggins was born in Austin; her father, J. Austin Love, was a laborer, a poet, and a state Sunday School director for the Holiness Church. When she was five, she was orphaned and went to live with an aunt in El Paso. Her first grade teacher encouraged her in her habit of inventing and reciting rhythmical lines. She began writing verses, many of which she recited in performance. She graduated from Douglass High School there. Her poems appeared in print in the *Chicago Defender*, the *El Paso Herald*, the *Houston Informer*, and *Half Century* magazine. She published a book of over one hundred of her poems, *Tuneful Tales*, in 1925. The subjects of her writing ranged widely—poverty, racism, the black church, love, women's rights, lynching, the role of black soldiers in World War I, and the injustice of laws against prostitution. James Mason Brewer, who compared her to the black poet Paul Laurence Dunbar, recited her poem "Church Folks," a satire in dialect, to open all his speeches for twenty years. Nothing is known of her after she moved to Los Angeles, California, in 1936. (Bernice Love Wiggins, *Tuneful Tales* [El Paso: by the author, 1925]; J. Mason Brewer, *Heralding Dawn: An Anthology of Verse*

[Dallas: by the author, 1936], pp. 41–42; Frieda Werden, "Bernice Love Wiggins," in Lina Mainiero, ed., *American Women Writers* [New York: Ungar Publishing Co., 1982], vol. 4, pp. 414–415; Lorraine Elena Roses and Ruth Elizabeth Randolph, *Harlem Renaissance and Beyond: Literary Biographies of 100 Black Women Writers: 1900–1945* [Boston: G. K. Hall and Co., 1990], pp. 347–348)

Yerwood, Connie (Connor) (ca. 1910–1991)

Connie Yerwood was one of the state's first black female physicians. She was born in Victoria but soon moved to Austin, where she attended public schools. Her father, Dr. Charles R. Yerwood, was a prominent physician; her mother, Melissa Brown Yerwood, a teacher. She was a graduate of Samuel Huston College (now Huston-Tillotson College). She received her doctorate of medicine degree from Meharry Medical College, Nashville, Tennessee, in 1933. She interned in pediatrics at Kansas City General Hospital, but gave her career its final direction by accepting a scholarship to the University of Michigan School of Public Health. In 1936, Yerwood returned to Austin and accepted a position with the Texas Department of Health, its first black physician. One of her long-term projects was to improve the health of mothers and infants in East Texas. As director of Maternal and Child Health Services, she trained midwives and set up immunization programs for children and prenatal and family planning clinics. She faced discrimination as a black woman repeatedly when Department of Health staff members with less experience were promoted above her until the Civil Rights Act of 1964. She was then named chief of the Bureau of Personal Health Services, the first woman to serve as a bureau chief in that department. She held that position until her retirement in 1977. Extensive civic activities included membership on the board of trustees of Huston College from 1937 to 1952 and then upon its merger with Tillotson (Huston-Tillotson) from 1952 to 1991—fifty-four years of service. She was the first black woman appointed to the national Field Committee of the Girl Scouts of America (1950s). She was president of the Lone Star State Medical Association. She was also active in the Rosewood Medical Clinic, Austin Mental Health and Mental Retardation Center, the Masonic Grand Chapter, OES, the Links, Inc., Alpha Kappa Alpha sorority, Douglass Club, and Wesley United Methodist Church. Huston-Tillotson and Bishop colleges awarded her honorary degrees. (*Austin American-Statesman*, June 16, 1991; Texas Women's Hall of Fame Nomination Form, Governor's Commission for Women Papers, Texas Woman's University, Denton)

Yerwood, Joyce (Carwin) (?–1987)

Joyce Yerwood, a native of Austin, practiced medicine for more than fifty years in New England. Like her sister, Connie Yerwood, after graduating from Samuel Huston College (now Huston-Tillotson), she earned a medical degree from Meharry Medical College in Nashville in 1933. She completed her internship in Kansas City, Missouri, and residency in Philadelphia. Following her marriage to Dr. Joseph L. Carwin, Joyce Yerwood moved to Stamford, Connecticut. From 1937 to 1955, she maintained an active medical practice in Port Chester, New York. In 1955, she moved her practice to Stamford, becoming the first black female family practitioner in Fairfield County. Dr. Yerwood devoted her practice to helping low-income women and children. She was instrumental in the establishment of a community center, which became known as Yerwood Center. Following her retirement in 1980, she was active in many organizations. She was chair of the board of trustees at Union Baptist Church in Greenwich, Connecticut. (*Austin American-Statesman*, December 1, 1987)

1777   The first census of Spanish Texas reports a population of 3,103; only 20 are classified as "Negroes."

1783   Manuel Patrón is fined for beating his wife, Juana Travieso, and calling her "mulata."

1792   The Spanish Census of Texas records 186 mulatto and Negro women as "free citizens."

1798   Rancher Doña Rosa María Hinojosa de Ballí of Reynosa, Mexico, and La Feria, Texas, owns a mulatto teenaged girl.

1807   Mexican Texas is a haven for runaway and freed slaves from the nearby United States South.

Felipe Elúa, a former slave from Louisiana, buys the freedom of his wife and their children and they move to San Antonio.

1818   Black women are being sold at Galveston's slave market.

1821   Mexico gains its independence from Spain and promises citizenship and equal rights for all Mexicans.

Moses Austin (like his son Stephen F. Austin) insists that Anglos coming to Mexico be allowed to bring their slaves *and* receive land for them.

1821–
1822   Jane Long and her slave Kian survive a bitter winter on Bolivar Island (across from Galveston).

1823   Mexico's Imperial Colonization Law provides that "there shall not be permitted . . . either purchase or sale of slaves that may be introduced into the empire. The children of such slaves, who are born within the empire, shall be free at fourteen years." This law is soon annulled with the overthrow of Mexican emperor Augustín de Iturbide.

Stephen F. Austin receives approval from the newly independent Mexican government to bring Anglo settlers and their slaves into Texas from the United States. Among these "Old 300" colonists are free people of color.

1824   A new constitutional congress in Mexico decrees that slave trade be prohibited "forever." Any slaves brought into Mexico in violation are to be freed. Mexican leaders seemingly disapprove of slavery but are ineffective in abolishing it.

1827   The Congress of Coahuila and Texas writes a constitution stating that slaves can be brought in for six months after adoption of the state's fundamental law. The slave population continues to increase.

1828   Stephen F. Austin, the "Father of Texas Independence," buys an old slave woman for $350.

1833   Free woman of color Celia Allen of San Felipe hires William B. Travis to defend her emancipation; she wins the case.

1834   Tamar Morgan buys her freedom with the proceeds of her own labor and becomes an independent landowner in Brazoria County.

1835   One hundred slaves on the Brazos River plot to revolt, divide the cotton farms, and make the whites work for them. They are arrested, many whipped, and a few executed.

1836   Emily West [Morgan], later known as the Yellow Rose of Texas, allegedly helps Sam Houston's army win the Battle of San Jacinto (and Texas independence).

Texas wins its independence from Mexico. The Provisional Government recognizes as citizens all free people of color living in Texas as of January 1836. By March, the new constitution forbids them from staying "without the consent of Congress." Those who remain live in fear of banishment.

The slave population of Texas is 5,000; the free people of color number about 150.

1837   A joint resolution of the Texas Congress permits free people of color resident in Texas at the date of the Declaration of Independence to remain in the Republic.

Sylvia Routh and her six children are emancipated by James Routh, who leaves them 320 acres of land and money.

1838   Sally Vince, Harris County, is freed by her master in his will. His brother tries to claim her but she petitions the court and wins her freedom.

1839   A $100 reward is offered in Austin for the apprehension of Jim, his wife, Paggy, and two servants.

Free woman of color Charity Bird, Jefferson County, is a successful baker.

1840   The Texas Congress prohibits immigration of free people of color and requires free blacks in Texas to remove themselves within two years on penalty of sale into slavery, provides for exemptions by act of Congress, and also forbids manumission of slaves except by permission of Congress.

Fanny McFarland, a Houston laundress and free woman of color who had been emancipated earlier, petitions the Texas Congress for permission to remain free. Her petition is refused, but she remains anyway and profits from real estate investments. The petitions of two other Houston laundresses, Zelia (Zylpha) Husk and Diana Leonard, are also turned down, but they too remain.

1841   In Sabine County, Nancy and her daughter Isabella are jailed for the alleged murder of their master. After their escape, a $200 reward is offered for their capture.

1845   Texas joins the Union. The legislature makes it illegal for any free black to remain in the state without its consent.

The *Houston Telegraph and Texas Register* advertises a $20 reward for a runaway "little negro girl," eight or nine years old.

Caroline, a slave on the Groce Plantation in Hempstead, is the champion cotton-picker for several days.

1846   The legislature legalizes punishment for anyone selling a free person into slavery.

Eleven of the nineteen members of the Colored Church in Galveston (part of the First Baptist Church) are women.

1847   Emeline, a free woman of color who has been enslaved, hires a law firm and sues her enslaver. A Harris County jury frees her and awards her damages of one dollar.

1850s   Silvia King, a Moroccan-born slave, recalls in later life that LaGrange slaves had all-night religious ceremonies, including ring dances, shouting, and praying.

1850   Two men, a pregnant woman, and five children flee Smith County, presumably headed for Indian Territory.

        The U.S. Census counts 186 free colored women in Texas and 29,461 female slaves.

        Mary Madison, a free woman of color, "valuable citizen," and respected Galveston nurse, petitions the legislature for permis sion to remain; it is granted in 1851.

1851   Dr. John and Puss (Silvia) Webber, an interracial couple with eight children, are forced from their Webberville home near Austin by racists.

        Sojourner Truth makes her famous "And a'n't I a woman?" speech at a women's rights convention in Akron, Ohio.

1853   Jane Elkins, a Dallas slave hired to care for a Mr. Wisdom's children, pleads "not guilty" to having murdered him. She is hanged, possibly the first woman in Texas to be so punished.

1854   An Austin overseer whips a slave woman to death with a leather strap. He flees the area.

        German immigrants in San Antonio pass a resolution declaring slavery to be "a monstrous social wrong that should be abolished."

1855   Three men and one woman, armed with guns, are captured near Willbarger's Creek near Austin, on their way West.

        J. D. Nix of Harris County is convicted of assault and battery for cutting a slave woman with a knife; he is fined $25 and ten days in jail.

        "Mrs. Ewing's negro woman" drowns herself in Houston.

1856   Two hundred Colorado County slaves organize a revolt, but are discovered. Women may have been among them.

        David Webster of Galveston emancipates his slave Betsy and leaves her his entire estate, including horses, household goods, and twenty-one town lots. Her petition to the legislature to remain is signed by several dozen whites.

1858   The Texas legislature passes a law permitting free blacks the right to enslave themselves voluntarily in order to escape liens and judgments and to avoid expulsion from the state. Rachel Grumbles of Travis County chooses Aaron Burleson as her owner.

Margaret is arrested for allegedly killing her Liberty County master, Solomon Barrow, by lacing his bread with arsenic. After being released by a hung jury, she is sold to an unsuspecting new master.

Lucy Dougherty murders her Galveston mistress with a hatchet following an argument. On the eve of her execution, she says, "Yes, and I would do it again."

1860s   Melinda Rankin, a white Presbyterian missionary, is fired from her job as director of the Rio Grande Female Seminary in Brownsville for Unionist sympathies.

1860   Elizabeth Ramsey, a Matagorda County slave, is freed as the result of a fund-raising campaign conducted by her now-free daughter, Louisa Picquet, of Cincinnati, Ohio, from whom she had been sold some twenty years previously in Georgia.

There are 355 free blacks and some 180,000 slaves in Texas.

Betty and Sam escape on horseback from their Robertson County owner.

In Bastrop County, a free black woman and her six children go into voluntary enslavement to avoid being sold for debt and being expelled from the state.

A free woman of color, the Widow Ashworth of Jefferson County, owns $11,444 in land; and Harriet McCullough Reynolds, Jackson County, has six thousand cattle which were valued at $3,300.

In Fannin County, Emma, a slave, and two male slaves are hanged for killing their master.

Mrs. M. L. Capshaw, a white woman, runs a Houston school for blacks in the African Methodist Church.

1861–   During the Civil War, slave women stay up late at night weaving
1865   cloth and sewing clothing for the soldiers.

1862   Fannie Perry, a slave of the Perry family in Harrison County, writes to her husband, Norfleet Perry, who has accompanied his master to the Civil War battlefront.

1865   With the end of the Civil War, General Gordon Granger lands at Galveston on June 19 and declares Texas slaves to be free under

Abraham Lincoln's Emancipation Proclamation of January 1, 1863.

The Thirteenth Amendment to the U.S. Constitution abolishes slavery.

The U.S. Congress creates the Bureau of Refugees, Freedmen, and Abandoned Lands to help the freed slaves, including the establishment of schools.

Former slave women withdraw from fieldwork to be full-time wives and homemakers. Economic necessity soon forces them back.

1865– About 20,000 black adults and children achieve some degree of
1870 literacy.

1866 Lucy Grimes is beaten to death for refusing to punish her child for a minor offense against her employer.

Mary E. Warren is listed as a photograph printer in the Houston City Directory, perhaps the first black in photography in the U.S.

Matilda Boozie Randon and her husband, the Reverend Eli Randon, receive 1,500 acres in Washington County from her former owners because of an illegitimate child she had borne by the owners' son.

1867 Freedwoman Louisa Nash signs a domestic service contract with her Liberty County employer. She obligates herself to cook, iron, and milk, and not to leave the premises without his permission. He agrees to furnish her and her child with housing, food, and medicines.

Dallasite Frank Waller "knocked down & whipt Rachel," a free woman, because the bread she made does not suit him.

A white Galveston teacher praises the quickness of her black students in a report to the American Missionary Association. A white teacher in a Freedmen's Bureau school in Hempstead praises the enthusiasm of her black pupils. Galveston has several flourishing schools, some controlled by blacks. Matagorda blacks hire a freedwoman as a teacher.

Black women are committed to the state prison in Huntsville for minor offenses. A laundress is sentenced to two years for allegedly stealing a nightgown.

Celia Miller owns a nondiscriminatory "disorderly house" in Galveston.

Stephen and Adaline Curtis receive a marriage license in Brazos County.

Most of the work of the Union League in Millican "is done among Negro women."

1868   The state constitutional convention appoints a special committee to collect evidence on widespread violence. The report indicates 183 major crimes against black women by whites.

Mrs. M. L. Capell, a white widow, opens a school for black children in Dallas, but insufficient funds cause its closing.

The Fourteenth Amendment to the U.S. Constitution is ratified, extending citizenship to blacks.

The Ku Klux Klan is active statewide. In Waco, they beat twenty black women, mass rape a freedwoman, and attempt to rape a 7-year-old.

The first woman suffrage resolution is introduced into the Texas Constitutional Convention but is rejected.

Black women in Harris County form two clubs (a Grant and Colfax Club and a Thaddeus Stevens Republican Club) and attend political gatherings in large numbers.

White and black Freedmen's Bureau teachers are harassed and threatened. In Circleville near Austin, a female black teacher's school is burned and she is forced to return to the North.

After the death of her former white owner and lover, Phyllis Oldham petitions for and wins homestead rights to their house and farm in Burleson County.

1868–   Sharecropping largely replaces the gang labor system used un-
1869   der slavery. Some women work as domestics for wages, at an average salary of five dollars a month.

1869   Six of the ten black delegates to the Texas Constitutional Convention support woman suffrage.

The state's new constitution provides for a system of free public schools, but subsequent legislatures never appropriate adequate funds and money is not equitably distributed between black and white schools.

In Houston, "80 negro women and 150 negro men" attend a meeting of Radical Republicans in July.

Caroline Poe, an ex-slave, teaches in a Freedmen's Bureau school in Marshall. In 1871, she becomes a public school teacher and later a leader of the Woman's Christian Temperance Union (WCTU).

1870s   Black women help establish churches throughout the state. Delilah Harris gives land for the Smith Chapel AME Church in Limestone County. The New Hope Baptist Church in Dallas numbers five women among its six founders. Eight women and five men found the Metropolitan AME Church in Austin. Houston women found an orphanage.

Black women flood the Freedmen's Bureau with marital problems—beatings, infidelity, lack of child support, and breaches of promise. They also file complaints against white men.

1870   The Fifteenth Amendment to the U.S. Constitution gives black males the vote but excludes women.

There are 10,603 domestic workers in Texas, including 1,017 laundresses, mostly black women. The *Dallas Herald* reports that "the washerwomen of Dallas" are plotting to strike.

The black family structure mirrors that of white families; most are two-parent families headed by males.

1871   Five black East Texas public schools are burned.

Sarah Barnes, a white missionary, founds the first normal school or teacher institute for blacks in Texas, the Barnes Institute in Galveston.

1873   White Democrats regain control of state government. Authority over education is ceded to the counties.

Lucy and Albert Parsons of Waco, a mixed couple, flee racism for Chicago.

1874   Hannah Perryman, a freed slave, homesteads on eight acres in Polk County. Other black women around the state own property.

1875   The U.S. Civil Rights Act of 1875 provides for equal access to public accommodations without regard to race.

1876   Mary Miller sues in federal court after being denied a seat in a Galveston theater. The court finds the owner guilty, fines him $500, then reduces it to one dollar.

The Texas Constitution mandates a system of free public, but segregated, schools.

1877   The U.S. District Court, Western District Texas, rules that the action of Houston and Texas Central Railroad Company officials in denying admission of Milly Anderson to the first-class "ladies' car" in 1876 is unlawful under the U.S. Civil Rights Act of 1875.

Black women try to integrate the ladies' circle of the Sherman opera house. The manager refunds their money rather than granting them entrance.

Paul Quinn College opens in Waco as a vocational training school. The American Missionary Association founds Tillotson College in Austin.

Galveston laundresses strike for $1.50 a day.

More than three-quarters of black children are enrolled in school—more than in any other southern state.

1878   Prairie View State Normal School opens as a coeducational school; Miss E. V. Ewing is hired as "Preceptress, matron." Women are among its first teachers.

1879   In response to violence and harsh economic conditions, hundreds of blacks from Texas and other southern states leave for Kansas. They are known as the Exodusters. Madam Walker travels in Texas discussing "the political destiny of the colored race" and the Exoduster movement.

Josie Briggs Hall, age 10, encourages older adults to attend Sunday School in Waxahachie.

ca.
1880   Emily Brown donates land for the St. Emily United Methodist Church in Chambers County.

Dallas laundress Hope Thompson invests $50 in a downtown lot and sells it twenty years later for $25,000.

Some black women settle in West Texas—as laundresses in the towns and at army forts and as domestics to ranch families.

1880   The Texas census counts 4,643 laundresses (quadruple the number in 1870), still mainly black.

In Dallas, black girls as young as seven help their mothers take in washing or work as servants in private homes.

1881   Matilda Lewis founds the Macedonia Baptist Church in Georgetown in her backyard.

Two public schools for blacks, with a number of black female teachers, open in Galveston.

Former slaves found Bishop College in Marshall. Tillotson College opens in Austin.

Women are among the early workers of the Grand Order of Odd Fellows, organized in Houston in 1881.

1882   Mrs. Walter Burton, the wife of a state senator from Fort Bend County, is thrown from a moving train for refusing to leave the white coach.

Frances Willard, national president of the WCTU, organizes two chapters in Paris, one for whites and one for blacks. The "colored pastor's wife" presides over the black chapter.

Texas voters authorize a state university at Austin for blacks, but the legislature never establishes one.

1882–   Black female teachers earn $35 a month; white females, $47.80;
1884   black males, $42; and white males, $72.

1883   The U.S. Supreme Court declares the Civil Rights Act of 1875 unconstitutional.

The Texas State Convention of Negroes denounces a miscegenation law, unequal public schools, treatment of convicts, and segregated public accommodations. The men condemn the "practice of yoking or chaining male and female convicts together."

The University of Texas opens for whites only in Austin.

1884   The Colored Teachers State Association of Texas is organized. Two public schools for blacks open in Dallas.

1885   Galveston's Central High School opens—the first in the state for blacks.

Two black women are forcibly ejected from the "dress circle" for white ladies of a Waco theater and arrested for creating a disturbance.

1886   The Colored Farmers' Alliance is founded throughout the state, with many Texas women and men as members.

Mrs. Norris Wright Cuney (Adelina Dowdie Cuney) tricks a railroad conductor on a train from Galveston to Houston who denies her admittance to the first class coach by climbing in through the window and taking a seat.

Mary Allen Seminary for girls, named after a white Presbyterian woman, opens in Crockett.

1887   Albert Parsons (Lucy Parsons's husband) of Waco is hanged in Chicago, along with other anarchists, for their alleged role in the Haymarket demonstrations for an eight-hour work day.

          Mrs. Caroline Poe is elected state organizer of "colored work" for the WCTU.

          The state's Deaf, Dumb, and Blind Institute for Colored Youth opens in Austin.

1889   Robert L. Smith and his wife, Isabelle, organize the Farmers Improvement Society and a Ladies' Auxiliary.

          Former slave Dolly Lang, Falls County, signs a sharecropping agreement with Mrs. V. C. Billingsley for the use of 48 acres, agreeing to pay her the first three bales of cotton as rent.

          The Reverend and Mrs. W. L. Dickson organize an orphanage in Gilmer; she is the matron.

          Prairie View becomes Prairie View State Normal and Industrial College.

1890s   Laundresses in Madisonville work for 30–50 cents a day.

          There are black seamstresses and dressmakers in many cities.

1890   Miss L. A. Bowers, a graduate of Fisk University, teaches in the Galveston high school for blacks.

1891   Maud Cuney Hare of Galveston refuses to vacate the integrated dormitory at the New England Conservatory of Music in Boston where she is a student.

          The legislature passes a separate coach law, the first of a series of Jim Crow laws.

          The Masonic Grand Chapter, Order of the Eastern Star, is founded in Texas.

          Lucy Parsons begins publishing her newspaper *Freedom: A Revolutionary Anarchist-Communist Monthly* in Chicago.

          Mary Hankins Jones is president of the Women's Home Mission Society in Harrison County.

1892   Eight Dallas teachers organize the Ladies Reading Circle.

          Mrs. Mattie B. White, a graduate of Walden University in Nashville, Tennessee, organizes a short-lived private school for girls in Austin.

Dallas Colored High School opens. Houston's first Colored High School begins construction.

Black female teachers earn $205 annually as compared with $292 for white males, $260 for white females, and $252 for black males.

1893　　Maud Cuney Hare, studying in Boston, suggests to her father, Norris Wright Cuney, that night schools be founded in Galveston. He acts on her suggestion.

There are two black nurses in Marshall.

White women found the Texas Equal Rights Association in Dallas to work for suffrage.

Ida B. Wells (Barnett), who launched a national antilynching crusade in 1892, condemns the lynching of Henry Smith in Paris, Texas.

1894　　Austin women organize the Heart's Ease Circle of King's Daughters and later found a home for the aged.

1895–　These are the peak years of lynching in Texas.
1897

1896　　The U.S. Supreme Court in *Plessy v. Ferguson* rules that "separate but equal" public facilities are constitutional.

The National Association of Colored Women is organized, with Mary Church Terrell as first president.

ca.　　A trained nurse founds the Feagan Hospital to serve Houston
1897　　blacks.

1897　　Lucy Thurman, president of the Colored Division, National WCTU, and national superintendent of Colored Work, organizes fifteen chapters in Texas.

Maud Cuney Hare teaches at the Deaf, Dumb, and Blind Institute for Colored Youth in Austin. She refuses to perform before a segregated audience in the city's opera house.

The Grand Court, Order of Calanthe, the richest black women's fraternal organization in the U.S., is founded in Houston.

1898　　Isabella E. Mabson of Galveston files suit in district court against the Missouri, Kansas and Texas Railway Company for being ejected from the palace car.

Mrs. Eliza E. Peterson, Texarkana, is elected president of the state's Thurman WCTU Union (for black women) and begins organizing "colored" chapters around the state.

The Sisters of the Holy Family, a black Catholic order, sends four sisters to Galveston to run a school.

Black women are members of Texas lodges of the Invincible Sons and Daughters of Commerce, a national society of black merchants and consumers.

1899– The Phillis Wheatley Club in Fort Worth becomes the first
1901 Texas club to affiliate with the National Association of Colored Women.

ca. Elsie Osby Nelms helps build the Mount Zion CME Church in
1900 Shelby County and is president of the Women's Missionary Society.

Julia Smith Green is principal of a school in Schulenburg.

Josie Briggs Hall opens a college for black women in Doyle, Limestone County.

Priscilla Tyler promotes opera attendance by black students in Dallas.

Mr. and Mrs. A. W. Rysinger open Rysinger's Central Millinery Emporium in downtown Austin.

Nancy Scott founds the Nancy Scott Home for Decrepit Old Ladies in Austin.

1900s Austin women give "chair socials," "pillow case entertainments," and "laundry equipment fairs" to help furnish Samuel Huston College.

Mrs. R. S. Lovinggood, wife of the president of Huston College, attends the UT School of Library Science. Because she is light-skinned, UT admits her without knowing she is black.

1900 Black illiteracy rate drops statewide from 75.4 percent in 1880 to 38.2 percent in 1900. Texas leads the South in the number of black high schools.

Isabelle Smith, president of the Farmers Improvement Society Ladies' Auxiliary, addresses 500 FIS delegates, men and women.

1900– Texas ranks third in the number of lynchings as mobs kill over
1910 100 blacks during this period.

1901   Mary (Mrs. Melvin) Wade prints the *Dallas Express*.

Mrs. G. M. Turley is chief of the women's department heads for the Colored Fair in Dallas.

Sarah Ellis, San Antonio, enters Northwestern University to study music but is segregated alone in a dormitory room on the first floor.

Thirty-two chapters send representatives to Austin for the tenth annual meeting of the Masonic Grand Chapter, Order of the Eastern Star.

1902   Mrs. Eliza Jane Lethridge, age 18, is president of the Women's Missionary Society of the Palestine Baptist Church in Victoria.

A state law requires the payment of a poll tax to vote.

The Married Ladies Social, Art and Charity Club is organized in Houston.

Prairie View is upgraded with a "four year course of classical and scientific studies."

1903   Alice Dunn Logan, a Texas club leader, is on the Executive Committee of the National Afro-American Council.

1904   Mrs. J. A. Jones organizes children of the Wesley Chapel AME Church in Georgetown into a "Nail Club" to collect pennies and buy nails for a new building.

Several women give papers at a parade sponsored by the Women's Nineteenth of June Committee in Galveston.

Pauline Atkinson and her mother open a restaurant in Galveston.

Mrs. Mary Alphins, state organizer for the Negro Disciples of Christ, begins working with the Christian Woman's Board of Missions to plan a school for black youth. It eventually opens (1913) as Jarvis Christian Institute in Hawkins.

1905   Lucy Parsons is a founding member of the Industrial Workers of the World.

The Texas Association of Colored Women's Clubs is organized by Mrs. M. E. Y. Moore in Gainesville.

Josie Hall's book *Hall's Moral and Mental Capsule for the Economic and Domestic Life of the Negro* is published.

The Colored Branch of the Rosenberg Library in Galveston opens, the first of its kind in the U.S.

Galveston women give a benefit supper for the Avenue L Baptist Church.

Austin's first black principal is a woman—Mrs. L. E. Morton, Brackenridge School.

The *Galveston Evening Tribune* hires black women to sell subscriptions.

1906   Dr. Ollie L. Bryan, the first black female graduate from Meharry Dental College, opens a practice in Dallas.

The Austin City Council passes an ordinance requiring streetcar segregation. Black domestics join other workers in a boycott.

Teacher Laura Pierce organizes the Douglass Club of Austin to study literature and do philanthropic work.

The Colored Institute of Houston, composed primarily of women, stresses the importance of kindergarten, manual training, and good health.

Mrs. Charles Etta Jones is a clerk for the Excelsior Life Insurance Company in Dallas, eventually becoming secretary-treasurer.

1907   Graduating seniors Ellie A. Walls (Montgomery) and Mable L. Cook give commencement speeches at Houston's Colored High School.

Mrs. Mary Keys Gibson of Fort Worth, age 53, a former slave, is the first black in the South to receive a nursing certificate from an accredited school—the Chautauqua School of Nursing in Jamestown, New York.

Texas passes a law abolishing the practice of midwifery without a license, but the law is largely ignored.

Mrs. J. C. Scott and her husband run a real estate business in Fort Worth.

1908   Teacher Christine Cash wins a dispute with the Camp County superintendent of schools for a longer school year. Later, as administrator of the Center Point School, she develops a major physical plant, organizes a PTA, and expands academic and vocational curricula.

Alpha Kappa Alpha Sorority is founded at Howard University.

The National Association of Colored Graduate Nurses is founded.

Mrs. Booker T. Washington speaks in Houston to the 1908 Art Club Dinner.

Mrs. Fannie Forrest Faulkner Dogan, wife of Wiley University's president, earns her B.S. degree there.

ca. 1908– 1909   The Colored Women's Hospital Aid Society of Galveston provides patients with clothing, holiday extras, and entertainment.

Houston PTA women furnish schools with pianos, sewing machines, playground equipment, and bookcases.

1909   The National Association for the Advancement of Colored People is founded.

Dr. Mary Smith Moore advertises her services as a physician and surgeon at Hubbard Sanitarium in Galveston.

Eliza E. Peterson is elected national superintendent of Colored Work for the WCTU.

Houston women organize Mothers' Clubs.

Mattie B. White speaks at Austin's Juneteenth celebration on "Opportunities and Responsibilities of the Negro."

Christia Daniels Adair, age 16, is superintendent of a Methodist Sunday School in Edna.

ca. 1910   The Women's Progressive Club is founded in San Antonio.

1910   Over half of black women in Texas age 10 or over are in the paid labor force; of these, over half work in agriculture, and one-third in domestic service. Black women constitute 42.4 percent of all employed Texas women.

Nationally, black female teachers outnumber their male colleagues 3–1. Black girls in Texas surpass boys in literacy rates.

Mrs. Pearl Augusta Light organizes Houston's first kindergarten for black children at the Antioch Baptist Church.

Black women own businesses throughout the state, including grocery stores, millinery shops, and restaurants. There are also black professional women who are doctors, nurses, and midwives.

There are 173 Courts of the Heroines of Jericho (a Masonic Order) with over 3,400 members.

A Dallas vigilante mob lynches a black man accused of having assaulted a white girl in Sherman.

Wiley College, Marshall, has a YWCA branch, possibly the first in the state for blacks.

1911   Mrs. J. A. (Lillie Bell Price) Pendleton and her minister husband found and co-edit the *Church of God Review* in Houston.

The Priscilla Art Club, Dallas's oldest black women's club, is organized.

Teacher Christine Cash wins an increase for herself and her assistant from Pittsburg school officials.

Baptist teacher Eliza Davis, Taylor, helps found a mission school in Liberia.

1912   Texas has six hospitals serving blacks.

Delta Sigma Theta Sorority is founded at Howard University. Myra Davis Hemmings of San Antonio is elected president. At the time she is also president of Alpha Kappa Alpha.

1913   Delta Sigma Theta members march in a suffrage parade in Washington, D.C.

Ellie A. Walls (Montgomery) of Houston is the first black woman in the U.S. to get a degree in social work, from the New York School of Philanthropy (later New York School of Social Work).

Mrs. Bessie A. Johnson, the wife of a physician, organizes the Progressive Club in Wichita County. The Colored Women's Progressive Club is organized in Galveston.

One-half of Prairie View's graduates are women.

The *Crisis* publishes Maud Cuney Hare's biography of her father, *Norris Wright Cuney: A Tribune of the Black People*.

Dr. Sarah Howland Shelton, a "good, gentle" dentist, opens a practice in Austin.

1914   Mrs. Dagmar Ferrell is the first black visiting nurse in the Houston public schools.

Mrs. David Abner, Jr., is treasurer of the Women's National Baptist Auxiliary Convention meeting in Harrison County.

Pianist Maud Cuney Hare, a Boston resident, gives a concert in her hometown of Galveston as part of a national tour.

Women are founding members of the Houston Branch, NAACP.

1915 Mary Evelyn V. Hunter is appointed the first extension agent in Texas to work with black women.

Mrs. B. J. Covington organizes the Ladies Symphony Orchestra in Houston in which she and her daughter, Jessie Covington Dent, play the violin.

The Married Ladies Social Club of Houston requires that members be "respectably living with husbands."

A black club leader makes a fund-raising appeal for a Negro Orphan's Home at a regional meeting in Abilene of the all-white Texas Federation of Women's Clubs.

The 10th annual convention of the Texas Association of Colored Women's Clubs meets in Houston.

The Royal Society Art Club is organized in Galveston at the home of Mrs. John Carr.

Houston business women include boarding house operators, a cement block manufacturer, a clothes cleaner, manicurists, a midwife, nurses, and restaurant owners. Estella B. Jackson is executive manager of A. G. Perkins and Co., a law, land and loan business, and first black female notary public in Houston.

Mattie E. Durden is the first married woman to receive a B.A. from Tillotson College and is class valedictorian.

Mrs. Annie Hagen organizes a nurses' training club in Houston.

1916 Mrs. Carrie E. Adams operates a day nursery in Beaumont. She is elected president of the Texas Association of Colored Women's Clubs.

Mrs. C. H. Graves founds the Graves Hospital for blacks in Temple; it operates until the 1950s.

A mob of 10,000 turns out in a holiday-like atmosphere to watch Jesse Washington being burned and mutilated in Waco.

Bishop College grants eight bachelor's degrees and twenty-two diplomas, probably for teachers.

ca.
1917 Mrs. Julia Caldwell Frazier is Dallas's first female school principal (Dallas Colored High).

1917   The Texas Federation of Colored Women's Clubs endorses woman suffrage. Galveston women organize the Negro Women Voters' League.

Black Texans support the war effort by buying Liberty Bonds, planting victory gardens, practicing food conservation, and working for the Red Cross.

Albertine Hall Yeager and her husband, Charlie, provide day care in their home for mothers working in war industries.

Mrs. Mabel Wesley is principal of the Crawford Elementary School in Houston (until 1939), the largest public school in Texas headed by a woman.

Mrs. L. A. Pinkney appeals to the Galveston Relief Association regarding the need for an old age home. She and other women prepare comfort bags for soldiers.

The pistol whipping by a Houston policeman of a black woman and racial harassment of black soldiers stationed at Camp Logan lead to a riot. Four whites are killed, and a number of black soldiers are court-martialed and executed.

1918   Christia Adair organizes an interracial mothers' club in Kingsville to fight gambling houses frequented by teenaged boys.

Mrs. B. J. Covington organizes the Blue Triangle Branch YWCA in Houston.

Women are one-third of the founding members of the Dallas Branch NAACP.

Sarah Harris, nursing graduate of Freedmen's Hospital of Washington, D.C., works for San Antonio Health Dept.

Fannie A. Robinson is secretary-treasurer of the Teachers State Association of Texas and of the Grand Court, Order of Calanthe.

Carrie E. Adams represents Texas at the National Association of Colored Women convention in Denver.

Mrs. S. G. Kay is chair of the Harris County Colored Teachers Institute.

Mrs. E. P. Sampson, on behalf of the El Paso Colored Woman's Club, applies for membership to the Texas Equal Suffrage Association. The matter is referred to the National American Woman Suffrage Association, which refers it back to the state. The final decision is not known.

Christia Adair and other black women work with white women in Kingsville collecting signatures on petitions demanding the vote in primary elections.

After Texas women win the right to vote in Democratic Party primaries, black women try to register. Over 1,500 register in Harris County; they are refused in Tarrant County. They go to court in Beaumont, but the case is dismissed. Christia Adair and her friends in Kingsville are not allowed to vote in the primary.

1919   Black teachers receive 60 percent of white teachers' pay in Houston.

Elnora Teal and her husband, Arthur, open a photographic studio in Houston.

A mass meeting of black men in LaGrange endorses women's suffrage.

Antisuffragists campaign on the platform that votes for women will mean socialism and black domination of the South.

1920s   The Ku Klux Klan is active in Texas.

Major blues and jazz performers of the day appear at Ella B. Moore's Park Theatre and Hattie Burleson's dance hall in Dallas.

Richard Grovey organizes the Third Ward Civic Club in Houston; members include the "washerwoman, the maid, . . . the cook, . . . the teacher."

Black women enter undergraduate schools in larger numbers, mainly in black southern colleges.

Beulah "Sippie" Wallace of Houston, the "Texas Nightingale," records many blues hits. Arizona J. Dranes is among the earliest Texas female gospel artists to earn wide recognition, recording with Okey records in Chicago.

1920   The Nineteenth Amendment gives women the vote.

For the first time, black women vote in Texas. Three Houston women run for office on the "Black and Tan" ticket of the Republican Party (state representative, Harris County clerk, and school superintendent). Mrs. F. L. Long places third with 4,000 votes in the county clerk's race.

The number of black Texas female beauticians, barbers, and manicurists increases fourfold from 1910. Some sell Madam C. J. Walker's beauty products.

The first class of registered nurses graduates from Prairie View.

The Texas Commission on Inter-racial Cooperation is founded, with an equal number of black and white women and men.

Christia Adair becomes a Democrat after Republican presidential candidate Warren G. Harding refuses to shake hands with black schoolchildren.

Zeta Phi Beta Sorority is founded at Howard University.

The Ladies Reading Circle of Dallas establishes a home for young working girls.

Texas leads all states with eleven lynchings.

1921   Bessie Coleman, of Atlanta, Waxahachie, and Chicago, earns a pilot's license from the Fédération Aéronautique Internationale in France, becoming the first black female pilot in the U.S. She gives her first exhibition flight in 1922 on Long Island.

Madam L. E. Coleman founds the Coleman College of Beauty Culture in Dallas.

Over 500 Ku Klux Klansmen march down Congress Avenue in Austin, carrying signs reading "Good Negroes Need Have No Fear" and "White Supremacy."

Mrs. G. B. M. Turner is president of the San Felipe Jitney Association in Houston.

Black women graduate as nurses from the "colored hospital" in Galveston, part of the UT Medical Branch.

1922   Prairie View awards baccalaureate degrees for the first time; most of the female recipients are nursing majors.

Elderess O. A. Laws holds a revival meeting at the Church of God in Galveston.

Mrs. Georgia Blakemore Williams of Tyler earns a pharmacy degree from Meharry Medical School and later opens her own pharmacy in Tyler.

Mrs. M. R. McKinney, a Corsicana nurse, writes national club leader Mary Church Terrell about the deplorable health conditions and the inadequate hospital for blacks and her plan to build a modern hospital.

Annie Maie Mathis, Austin, is hired as the first black maternity and infancy nurse for the Texas Bureau of Child Hygiene.

ca.
1923
The Texas Association of Colored Women's Clubs publishes its first *Annual Review*.

1923
The State Fair of Texas designates October 24 as Ku Klux Klan Day.

After winning the governorship on an anti-Klan platform, Miriam A. "Ma" Ferguson drives an antimask bill through the legislature.

Black residents of Quakertown in Denton are forced from their homes by city leaders who wish to build a park near Texas State College for Women (now Texas Woman's University).

Dr. Thelma Patten-Law opens a medical practice in Houston.

Mrs. Ethel Ransom, a Texas clubwoman, is state director for Texas of the National Anti-Lynching Crusaders, organized in 1922.

The legislature passes the White Primary Act.

1924
Olive Durden Brown of Austin organizes the first Alpha Kappa Alpha chapter west of the Mississippi—at Wiley College in Marshall.

Monette Moore, a Gainesville pianist, records with the Choo Choo Jazzers in New York, launching a fifty-year career.

Jeffie O. A. Conner, a McClennan County home demonstration agent, teaches children how to make cups from tin cans to replace the common dipper.

1920s
and
1930s
Jessie Covington Dent, Houston, wins acclaim as a touring concert pianist, particularly on the campuses of traditionally black colleges.

1925
Wichita Falls women organize the City Federation of Colored Women's Clubs.

The Dallas Inter-racial Committee under the auspices of the Texas Commission on Inter-racial Cooperation organizes a kindergarten, a mothers' club, a room registry, and an employment bureau.

Texas has its first lynchless year.

Mrs. L. A. Pinkney is publicity chair for the National Legislative Council of Colored Women, which supports a national anti-lynching bill and a child labor amendment.

There are 150 high schools for blacks.

Nanette Harrison Fowler edits the *Negro Musician* for the Texas Association of Negro Musicians.

Bernice Love Wiggins, Austin and El Paso, publishes a book of her poetry, *Tuneful Tales*.

Mrs. Isabell H. Williams opens the Hampton Williams School of Embalming in Dallas—the first for blacks in Texas.

1926 The national YWCA adopts an interracial charter, committing itself to involving more black women.

The National Association for the Study of Negro Life and History launches Negro History Week.

Jessie Daniel Ames, a white leader of the Texas Commission on Inter-racial Cooperation, lobbies legislators on behalf of a school for delinquent black girls.

Gwendolyn Bennett of Giddings is a key figure in the Harlem Renaissance; she is an assistant to the editor of *Opportunity* magazine and publishes short stories in *Ebony* and *Topaz* and drawings in the *Crisis* and *Messenger*.

Prairie View obtains accreditation.

1927 Artemisia Bowden becomes president of St. Philip's College in San Antonio and thus Texas's first female college president.

Responding to pressure by the Texas Association of Colored Women's Clubs and a few white allies, the legislature authorizes a state training school for delinquent black girls.

Mrs. Carrie E. Adams of Beaumont is chair of Ways and Means for the National Association of Colored Women.

The Ethel Ransom Art and Literary Club is founded in Houston and commits to providing a children's playground.

Black Austin women found the Community Welfare Association and later organize a neighborhood playground and a nursery school and help found the Carver Branch Library.

1928 The Maria Morgan YWCA opens in Dallas through the joint efforts of black and white women.

Mrs. Maud A. B. Fuller of Austin is elected president of the Woman's Baptist Convention of America and holds the office for forty years. She founds women's and youth groups.

1929 Mrs. Mattie B. Glover is elected superintendent of nurses at the Fort Worth Negro Hospital and School of Nursing.

Ruby and Leon Richardson found the *Houston Defender*.

Maud Cuney Hare, Galveston, directs her play *Antar of Araby* in Boston.

1930s   Black Presbyterian women in Houston organize scouting for black girls, the first in the south.

Christia Adair is the first black woman elected to the general board of the Methodist Episcopal Church.

Virginia (Virgie) Carrington DeWitty directs the Bright and Early Broadcasting Choir on Austin's KVET radio station.

The Shelton sisters, a singing group, perform on their own radio station in Hillsboro.

Blacks benefit from better-paying jobs in the wake of the oil boom in West Texas.

Black women and youth are underrepresented in New Deal programs, such as the NYA and WPA. Black women appeal to President and Mrs. Franklin D. Roosevelt.

Annie Webb Buchanan West is a spiritual leader and fortune-teller in Corsicana.

Because public school teachers are not allowed to be married, Frederica Chase Dodd switches to social work in Dallas.

Marzelle Cooper-Hill is Dallas County's first black probation officer.

With increased urbanization, 77 percent of black women state-wide hold nonfarm jobs, in comparison to 49 percent of black males.

1930   The vast majority (77 percent) of black women work as domestics, personal servants, seamstresses, and in other nonfarm employment, as compared to 69 percent in 1910.

Mary Elizabeth Branch becomes president of Austin's Tillotson College. She later wins accreditation for the institution, thus becoming the only black female president of a senior college accredited by the Southern Association of Colleges and Secondary Schools.

Alpha Tau Omega Chapter, Alpha Kappa Alpha, is the first black woman's Greek organization in San Antonio.

Olive Durden Brown, Austin, graduates with a degree in library science from Hampton Institute in Virginia.

Eddie Mae Dupree, Marshall, leaves the Baptist Church and establishes a preaching ministry in the Mount Zion Spiritual Churches.

Former Texas suffrage leader Jesse Daniel Ames founds the Association of Southern Women [white] for the Prevention of Lynching in Atlanta, Georgia.

1931   Estelle Massey Riddle Osborne of Palestine is the first black nurse to earn a master's degree in nursing at Columbia University and later is the first black nurse elected to the board of the American Nurses Association.

Dolores Burton Linton founds a school for poor San Antonio children in an abandoned dancehall.

San Antonio women open the Ella Austin Orphanage.

Marian Anderson performs in Waco, where she stays with Dr. George and Jeffie Conner. Because of segregation, Anderson stays with host families when she visits Texas cities.

Josephine and Valmo C. Bellinger publish the *San Antonio Register*.

Women help found urban libraries; the Dunbar Branch Library for blacks opens in Dallas.

Myra and J. W. Hemmings launch community theater productions at the Second Baptist Church in San Antonio. The Houston Negro Little Theatre begins.

1932   Black women number 8 percent of the state's industrial workers. Most of these work in laundries.

Doris and Carter Wesley begin running the *Informer and Texas Freeman* in Houston.

Women organize black Galveston voters on behalf of the Quinn-for-Sheriff Club.

Miss Annie Maie Mathis, state public health nurse, addresses the Texas Commission on Inter-racial Cooperation and, in 1934, conducts a survey of health conditions among Houston County blacks.

Erma Jewell Hughes founds the Hughes Business College in Houston.

The San Antonio School Board votes to dismiss all married teachers with husbands earning more than $2,000.

1933   Connie and Joyce Yerwood of Austin earn medical degrees from Meharry Medical College in Nashville.

Mrs. Alice Taylor King and her husband, Charles B. King, establish the King Funeral Home in Austin.

The Grand Court, Order of Calanthe, helps thousands of its members during the Depression by lending them money.

Inez Prosser from Yoakum and Austin is one of the first black women to earn a Ph.D. from the University of Cincinnati.

The Houston Civic Opera presents the opera *Aïda* with a large number of blacks in the cast before a segregated audience.

The City Council of Colored Mothers PTA of Austin sponsors a summer roundup of health activities for children.

Houston's Colored Carnegie Library opens.

Eloise Lundy is one of Dallas's first black WPA parks and recreation workers.

Representatives of black Texas colleges refuse to use a freight elevator to attend a convention of home economics instructors at Dallas's Adolphus Hotel.

1934   Estelle Massey Riddle Osborne as president of the National Association of Colored Graduate Nurses appeals to the American Nurses Association to integrate.

All seven gubernatorial candidates pledge to end lynching.

Nell Gray Washington represents the San Antonio NAACP at the national NAACP convention in Oklahoma City.

1935   Drusilla Tandy Nixon, wife of Dr. Lawrence Nixon, plaintiff in an early white primary case, organizes the black Girl Reserves of the YWCA in El Paso. Juliette Ross Johnson establishes a Girl Scout troop for blacks in Austin.

Rezolia Cleopatra Grissom Thrash is the only black represented in the Annual Dallas Allied Arts Exhibition.

Houston's Black Women for Social Change protest injustices against citizens.

East Texas teacher Dorothy Robinson is responsible for sixty-three children ages 7–17, grades 1–7, in a one-room school in Anderson County.

Mary McLeod Bethune founds the National Council of Negro Women. She is also appointed by President Roosevelt to the Advisory Board of the NYA.

Wiley and Prairie View colleges have over 700 students; Wiley awards 42 A.B. or B.S. degrees; Prairie View, 64.

Edna Kincheon, Waco, is national secretary of Delta Sigma Theta sorority.

Midwives still deliver over half of the black babies born in the U.S.

1936 Dr. Connie Yerwood is employed as the first black physician by the Texas Department of Health.

The Texas Centennial celebration at the State Fair of Texas includes a Hall of Negro Life, with work by women among the exhibits. Black leaders organize the Texas State Conference of Branches of the NAACP and the Texas State Negro Chamber of Commerce.

Dr. Mary Elizabeth Branch and Jeffie O. A. Conner serve on the Black Advisory Board to the Texas National Youth Administration.

The Works Progress Administration employs 4,500 black women in sewing projects, food canning, recreation, home demonstration, music education, and library work.

Maud Cuney Hare's *Negro Musicians and Their Work* is published.

Black women are active in the Black Chamber of Commerce in Dallas.

1937 Minnie Flanagan and Marzel Hill lead a voter registration campaign for the Progressive Voters League of Dallas.

The Texas NAACP is revived in Dallas and elects Mrs. P. R. Lubin treasurer.

The Blue Triangle YWCA is organized in Waco by Mrs. Corine Bolin.

The National Association of Colored Women meets in Fort Worth. Mrs. I. W. Rowan is chair of the Mother, Home & Child Department.

Barbara Goodall, a Chicago attorney originally from Corsicana, may have been the first black woman from Texas to be admitted to a bar association. She is honored by the Dallas chapter of Zeta Phi Beta.

Ollie Lee McMillan Mason is the first black nurse at Dallas's Parkland Hospital.

1938   Black women's organizations work for the passage of a federal antilynching bill.

The Houston public schools sponsor a program to train "perfect" domestic servants.

Anna and Clarence Dupree open the El Dorado Ballroom in Houston.

1939   Lulu B. White becomes acting president of the Houston Branch, NAACP. Later, as an NAACP fieldworker and membership director, she is the first full-time salaried executive secretary of NAACP and builds the Houston branch to the largest in the South. In the 1930s and 1940s, White and her co-worker, Juanita Craft of Dallas, organize dozens of branches throughout the state.

Singer Etta Moten of Weimar wins the Town Hall Endowment Series in New York City. Singer/dancer Daisy Richardson launches a stage career in Houston.

1940s   Anna Dupree, a Houston beautician and philanthropist, provides seed money for a home for the aged.

Lullelia Harrison of Houston is elected national president, Zeta Phi Beta Sorority.

Edna Carter, a charter member of the San Antonio NAACP, leads a campaign of selective buying to gain more and better jobs for blacks.

1940   The Maria Morgan branch, Dallas YWCA, opens a new debt-free building.

Anna Dupree donates $20,000 to establish an orphanage in Houston, the Negro Child Center, built ca. 1944.

The nation experiences its first lynchless year.

1940–   White Dallasites commit nineteen acts of violence against blacks
1941   to keep them from moving into South Dallas.

Forty-six black women receive aid to obtain professional training at out-of-state schools.

1941   Governor W. Lee "Pappy" O'Daniel signs an appropriations bill for $60,000 to erect a home for "delinquent colored" girls, authorized by the legislature in 1927.

1941–   During World War II, black women serve in the Women's Army
1945   Auxiliary Corps (later renamed the Women's Army Corps, WAC).

Black women benefit from higher wages. By the end of the war, wages of some Dallas maids increase from $1.50 to $5 a day.

Black women get new industrial jobs. Olivia Rawlston is president of the Dallas International Ladies Garment Workers Union "B" (segregated) local at Nardis, which makes garments for the armed forces. Black women in Kingsville work for the Missouri Pacific Railroad shop carrying mail, cleaning boxcars, handling freight, and steaming engines. They earn good pay in Fort Worth packinghouses. Black women at the Dickson Gun Plant in Houston earn 72½ cents an hour, compared with 85 cents for black men, $1.29 for white females, and $1.57 for white males.

Black women support the war effort on the home front.

Elizabeth "Tex" Williams, Houston, is a photographer and photo lab technician for the U.S. Air Force. In 1949, she is the first black woman to graduate from the Fort Monmouth, New Jersey, Photo Division School—first in her class.

The Grand Court, Order of Calanthe, purchases $100,000 in War Bonds.

Ruby Wyatt Mitchell of Houston and Ella Ruth White of Dallas work for the War Department in Washington, D.C.

Drusilla Tandy Nixon opens her home in El Paso to black servicemen, leading to the establishment of a USO.

Mrs. Ada Bell DeMent of Mineral Wells is president of the National Association of Colored Women.

1942–   Etta Moten, Weimar, sings the role of Bess on Broadway in
1945   Gershwin's *Porgy and Bess*.

Albertine Hall Yeager and her husband run a day care center in Galveston for children of mothers in war industries.

1943   Dallas black women raise $5,000 for the War Chest.

Dallas Metropolitan Council Branch, National Council of Negro Women, is organized.

Mary Yerwood Thompson, Austin, earns a master's degree in social work from Atlanta University.

Black Texas women are sworn in as part of the first inductees of the Women's Army Auxiliary Corps to train at Fort Des Moines, Iowa, in 1943. The oldest WAAC is Mary Bingham August Anderson, Houston, who joins at age 41. Black women also join the Army and Navy Nurses Corps.

Lulu B. White is the full-time salaried executive secretary of the Houston branch, NAACP.

Thelma Paige Richardson wins a judgment in the case *Paige v. Board of Education, City of Dallas*, resulting in pay raises to black teachers to achieve pay equalization.

1943–
1951
Lillie Portley, president of Houston's Fifth Ward Civic Club, leads a drive to gain suffrage in primary elections. She also trains and registers voters.

1944
The U.S. Supreme Court in *Smith v. Allright* outlaws Texas "white primaries," leading to a large increase in the number of black voters. Zenobia Trimble casts the first vote by a black in Wichita County.

Prairie View College's Co-Eds, an all-women's band, sweeps to national acclaim.

Traveling by train from San Francisco to her home in Palestine, Dorothy Robinson is excluded from the dining car, while German prisoners-of-war are allowed to eat there.

1945
World War II ends.

Maud Fuller of Austin secures land for a mission in Liberia.

Black and white women charter a YWCA in Corpus Christi.

Prairie View is upgraded to become Prairie View A & M University.

Under the leadership of Lulu B. White, the Houston branch of the NAACP doubles its membership to 12,000, the largest in the South.

1946
The Links, Inc., is founded in Philadelphia.

Dr. Connie Yerwood establishes a prenatal clinic and well child conference in Madisonville.

Juanita Craft speaks in Austin and other Texas cities for the NAACP. Her slogan is "The Fight Is On!"

Lulu B. White is elected state director of branches for the NAACP.

Louise Martin opens a photography studio in Houston.

YWCAs are integrated.

Black women picket the White House, protesting lynchings.

1946–
1950s
The National Council of Negro Women and Jack and Jill of America, Inc., an organization serving children, form Texas chapters.

Protestant women achieve greater acceptance as ordained ministers in the Methodist, United Church of Christ, and Disciples of Christ denominations.

Black women hold publishing positions with *Sepia* magazine in Fort Worth.

1947
Mrs. Eddie Hayes McDonald of Houston is elected president of the Adult Commission of the National Conference on Christian Education, the first woman and first black.

Houston College in Houston is reorganized as Texas State University for Negroes (later Texas Southern University)—the legislature's response to the demand by blacks for admission to the University of Texas.

1948
President Harry Truman issues an executive order requiring fair employment in the federal service.

Lucille Bishop Smith, a home economics teacher at Prairie View, creates Lucille's All Purpose Hot Roll Mix, the first in the U.S.

Edith Irby Jones is the first black admitted to the University of Arkansas College of Medicine. She later opens a practice in Houston.

Estelle Massey Osborne is elected to the board of the American Nurses Association, the same year it admits black nurses.

NAACP leader Lulu B. White is called before the House Un-American Activities Committee. She is also labeled a Communist for supporting the presidential candidacy of Henry Wallace.

Erma LeRoy of Houston runs unsuccessfully as an independent for the state legislature.

Ellie Walls Montgomery is the first female president of the Colored Teachers State Association of Texas.

1949   Esther Phillips, Houston, tours the South with Johnny Otis's rhythm and blues show.

         Christia Adair becomes secretary of the NAACP in Houston.

         Mrs. Nannie B. Aycox is president of Paul Quinn College.

         The Harris County Council of Organizations is founded to protect the benefits of the victory over the white primary.

1950s   Virginia Carrington DeWitty, Austin, conducts choirs for the National Baptist Convention of America.

         Zelma Watson George, a Hearne native, stars in two Gian-Carlo Menotti operas in New York—*The Medium* and *The Consul*.

1950   The U.S. Supreme Court rules in *Sweatt v. Painter* that segregation in higher education is unconstitutional. Heman Marion Sweatt becomes the first black to enroll in UT-Austin's Law School.

         Christia Adair leads the Houston NAACP in integrating department store dressing rooms, the airport, and the library, joining hundreds of other black women and men throughout the state who are fighting for equal accommodations.

         Elzira Marie Shelton and her husband are the first black couple to buy a house in South Dallas. Although a bomb is thrown, the Sheltons refuse to move.

         Pianist Viola Dixon becomes the first black Texan to play with the Dallas Symphony Orchestra. A female gospel group, the Chariottes, begins its career in Austin and later records for Houston's Duke Records. Evelyn Johnson begins managing the Buffalo Booking Agency, specializing in blues, soul, and rhythm and blues.

         Willie Lee Glass is the first black consultant for home economics with the Texas Education Agency.

1951   Domestic workers receive coverage under social security.

         Dr. Thelma Patten-Law organizes a Houston chapter of the Links, Inc.

1952   Anna Dupree funds the Eliza Johnson Home for Aged Negroes in Houston.

         The Blue Triangle YWCA in Houston dedicates a new facility.

         Mrs. C. L. Gilbert is the first black Democratic precinct chair in Dallas County.

Florence "Bu" Pleasant launches a piano career in San Antonio.

1953   Mrs. Annie Harris, president of the Houston branch, National Council of Negro Women, condemns police brutality against a pregnant black mother before the City Council.

Margie A. Duty is the first black female Houston policewoman.

Del Mar College in Corpus Christi is one of the first in the South to integrate.

1954   Charlye O. Farris of Wichita Falls, a 1953 graduate of the Howard University Law School, becomes the first black woman admitted to the State Bar of Texas.

Texas women win the right to serve on juries through a state constitutional amendment.

White Citizens Councils fight integration.

The U.S. Supreme Court rules "separate but equal" public schools unconstitutional (*Brown v. Board of Education*).

1955   The Interstate Commerce Commission bans segregation on buses involving interstate travel. Rosa Parks refuses to vacate her seat on a bus in Montgomery, Alabama.

Lincoln High School students led by NAACP youth director Juanita Craft protest racial segregation at the State Fair of Texas in Dallas.

Dr. Connie Yerwood is president of the Lone Star State Medical Association (for blacks).

Pearl Anderson donates her Dallas home valued at $350,000 to the Community Chest Trust Fund.

The American Friends Service Committee in Dallas tries to place black women in secretarial jobs.

1956   The state attorney general vows to outlaw the Texas NAACP on charges of barratry. He puts Christia Adair, executive secretary of the Houston branch NAACP, on the stand for seventeen days in Tyler, but she divulges no names.

Lillie Marie Alonzo, Nina McGowan, two attorneys, and a *Houston Informer* reporter are arrested for attempting to eat in the Harris County Courthouse cafeteria.

A lawsuit is filed in federal court asking that Beneva Williams and Delores Ross be admitted to white public schools nearest their Houston homes.

Barbara Jordan graduates magna cum laude from Texas Southern University in Houston.

Although UT-Austin integrates its classes for undergraduates, blacks are barred from varsity athletics and dormitories.

Hattie Briscoe receives her law degree from St. Mary's University (Catholic) in San Antonio, probably the first black woman to receive a law degree from a Texas university.

1957   Frances Blake Wallace and Jeffie Conner become supervisors of black schools for Harris and McLennan counties, respectively.

Juanita Craft is elected director of branches for the Texas State Conference NAACP.

The Reverend Perry Joy Jackson, Galveston, is the first black woman appointed as an itinerant minister among the Texas United Methodist Church conferences.

Barbara Conrad, Pittsburg, is forced from her operatic role opposite a white male at UT by racists. She goes on to an international operatic career.

1958   Mrs. Charles E. (Hattie Mae) White is elected to the Houston School Board, the first black Texan to hold office in the twentieth century.

1959   Blanche Mae Preston McSmith, a native of Marshall, is appointed to the Alaska legislature to fill an unexpired term.

1960s   Florence Phelps and Mable Chandler organize "Interested Women" to integrate Dallas department store dressing rooms.

Lucille Crawford is founding president of the Black Austin Democrats. Lenora Rolla, Fort Worth, helps organize chapters of the NAACP and the Southern Christian Leadership Conference.

Ruth Jefferson of Dallas organizes a sit-in by welfare rights mothers when the state welfare department reduces the monthly payment for her and her five children from $135 to $123.

The Black Pride movement renews interest in Juneteenth celebrations.

1960   After buying a home in a white neighborhood, Sally R. Fagan, a Dallas teacher, is not rehired.

The sit-in movement, which begins in Greensboro, North Carolina, spreads to Texas, with demonstrations in several cities.

Lillian K. Bradley receives a Ph.D. in mathematics from UT-Austin, the first black woman to earn the doctorate there.

Camellia Hudson-Franklin desegregates ice skating classes at Dallas's Fair Park Ice Arena.

1961 Black women are admitted to Texas Woman's University.

Dr. Zelma George of Hearne receives the Dag Hammerskjold Award for her work as a U.S. delegate to the United Nations.

1962 Ada Anderson organizes the Mothers Action Committee to integrate Austin's Ice Palace.

1963 Mary Ann Goode from Galveston and Zona Perrett from San Antonio become the first black secretaries at the Texas legislature.

Black Texans join thousands of citizens in the March on Washington for Jobs and Freedom, highlighted by Martin Luther King's speech, "I have a dream."

Black women register at Texas A & M for the first time.

1964 The 24th Amendment to the U.S. Constitution outlaws the poll tax as a requirement for voting.

The U.S. Civil Rights Act outlaws racial discrimination in public accommodations and employment.

Dr. Connie Yerwood is finally promoted to director of Maternal and Child Health Services, the Texas Department of Health.

The Texas Association of Colored Women's Clubs changes its name to the Texas Association of Women's Clubs.

Carolyn White becomes the first black employee at Houston's City Hall.

The Houston public schools participate in the federal lunch program after holding out for almost twenty years.

1965 With the passage of the Voting Rights Act of 1965, black women begin voting in larger percentages than black men or white women.

1966 Barbara Jordan from Houston is elected to the Texas Senate, the first black to serve in the legislature since 1899.

After earlier being denied admission to Baylor University, Vivienne Malone-Mayes returns with a Ph.D. in mathematics from UT-Austin as Baylor's first black professor.

Rita Moore of Austin goes to work for the Texas Employment Commission. Blacks begin working for state government in larger numbers.

Virginia Stull becomes the first black woman to graduate with a degree in medicine from the University of Texas Medical Branch, Galveston.

The U.S. Supreme Court upholds the ban on the poll tax.

The black Teachers State Association of Texas merges with the formerly white Texas State Teachers' Association.

1967   John Connally appoints Jeffie O. A. Conner to the Governor's Committee on Public School Education and Ada Anderson to the Governor's Committee on the Status of Women.

Julia Scott Reed writes a column, "Open Line," in the *Dallas Morning News*, probably the first by a black woman for a major southwestern daily.

1968   Joan Winn graduates from the Law School of Southern Methodist University and is later a judge in Dallas.

Wilhelmina Delco is the first black to win election to the Austin School Board.

Juanita Craft is the first black recipient of Dallas's Linz Award for citizenship.

Velma Roberts is founding president of an Austin chapter of the National Welfare Rights Organization.

1969   Dorothy Robinson is appointed to the Advisory Council for Technical-Vocational Education of the Texas Education Agency. She also becomes principal of an integrated school in Palestine.

Le Oneita Holland files the first lawsuit in the Dallas area under the Fair Housing Act of 1968.

Shirley Marks of Tyler is admitted to Harvard Medical School and becomes the second black female student to graduate there. She later practices psychiatry at the VA Hospital in Houston.

Bertha Knox Collins is appointed as the mayor's assistant for youth affairs in Fort Worth, the first high-ranking black woman in city government.

Alpha Tau Omega Chapter, Alpha Kappa Alpha, San Antonio, receives a federal grant from HUD to build an apartment complex for the elderly.

Singer Eloise Laws of Houston makes a national television debut on the *Merv Griffin Show*.

1970s   Ada Simond writes the semiautobiographical series Mae Dee—Let's Pretend about an Austin girl growing up around 1900.

Louise Lewis runs for mayor of Houston.

Some urban blacks mark Ramadan, an annual Islamic devotional period, and Kwanzaa, ceremonies to celebrate pan-African heritage and unity.

1970   Joan Snell is elected to the Lubbock City Council.

Joan Winn begins work as a trial attorney for the U.S. Labor Department in Dallas.

There are at least 90,000 domestic workers in Texas, 64 percent of them black. The median income for full-time domestics is $2,300. Median earnings of black women in the South in clerical and sales jobs are approximately 95 percent of white women's.

1971   The National Women's Political Caucus is founded.

1972   Barbara Jordan is elected to the U.S. Congress, the first black ever to represent Texas; she serves until 1978.

The Black Performing Arts Theatre in Houston sponsors a benefit performance featuring Ossie Davis and his wife, Ruby Dee, national chair of the Black Women's Unity Drive for the National Council of Negro Women.

Title IX of the Federal Educational Amendments prohibits sex discrimination in institutions receiving federal funds.

Following the death of Carter Wesley, his wife, Doris Wesley, continues publishing the *Houston Informer*.

Texas voters approve an equal rights amendment to the state constitution by a 4–1 majority.

Flutist Bobbie Humphrey, Dallas, is the first female instrumentalist to record for the Blue Note jazz label.

Houston native J. e Franklin has her play *Black Girl* adapted for a feature film. She is a director at the New Federal Theatre in New York City.

Augustine Williams is the first black female director of examinations for the Texas Cosmetology Commission.

Dallas nurse Eddie Bernice Johnson is elected to the Texas House.

Senfronia Thompson, Houston, is elected to the Texas House.

Ada C. Anderson is elected a trustee of Austin Community College.

1973   In *Roe v. Wade*, the U.S. Supreme Court establishes a woman's constitutional right to an abortion.

Lucy Patterson is the first black woman elected to the Dallas City Council.

Iola Johnson is one of the first television anchorwomen in Texas, appearing on WFAA-TV, Chapter 8, an ABC affiliate in Dallas.

Barbara James becomes the first black woman to chair Dallas's Central YWCA.

1974   Judith Craven is the first black woman to graduate from Baylor College of Medicine, Houston.

Maudrie M. Walton is elected to the Fort Worth school board.

The minimum wage is extended to cover domestic workers.

Former Prairie View home economics professor Lucille Bishop Smith founds a family corporation, Lucille B. Smith's Fine Foods, at age 82 to market the hot roll mix and other products she has developed.

During the Watergate hearings considering the impeachment of President Nixon, Congresswoman Barbara Jordan as a member of the House Judiciary Committee makes a stirring speech about the U.S. Constitution.

Sarah Jordan Powell, Houston, becomes a Christian music minister and gospel recording artist.

Kathlyn Gilliam is elected to the Dallas School Board.

Wilhelmina Delco is elected to the Texas House from Austin.

1975   Dorothy Robinson wins the National Association of Negro Business & Professional Women's National Achievement Award.

The Maria Morgan Branch, Dallas YWCA, opens a new building in South Oak Cliff.

Juanita Craft is elected to the Dallas City Council, winning 2–1.

Eddie Bernice Johnson of Dallas chairs the Texas House Committee on Labor, the first woman to chair a major House committee.

Gloria Scott of Houston is elected national president of the Girl Scouts, the first black woman to hold this position.

Selma Wells is the first black and first woman appointed to the Texas State Board of Pardons and Paroles.

1976   Barbara Jordan addresses the Democratic National Convention—the first black to keynote a major party's national convention.

Betty Lockhart founds the Dallas Committee on Household Employment to increase benefits for domestic workers.

Dallasite Yvonne Ewell is the first black female assistant superintendent of schools in Texas.

Clara J. McLaughlin of Houston publishes the *Black Parents' Handbook: A Guide to Healthy Pregnancy, Birth and Child Care.*

A National Women of Achievement chapter is founded in Houston by Judge Alice Bonner.

Austin leaders of Delta Sigma Theta receive a grant from the national American Revolution Bicentennial Administration to mount a black heritage exhibit.

Beverly Porter founds the first Texas chapter of the Lupus Erythematosus Society.

Jo Long of Lubbock becomes director of San Antonio's Carver Community Cultural Center.

Lou Nelle Sutton, San Antonio, serves as a legislator to fill her husband's unexpired term and is elected to a full term in 1977.

Lanell Cofer is elected to the Texas House from Dallas.

Eddie Bernice Johnson is appointed by President Carter as regional director for the Health, Education and Welfare Department.

1977   Jewel Prestage, the first black woman to receive a Ph.D. degree in political science in the U.S. (1954, University of Iowa), becomes a member of the Judicial Council of the national Democratic Party and dean of the Benjamin Banneker Honors College at Prairie View A & M University.

A Houston park is named for civic and civil rights leader Christia Adair.

Azie Taylor Morton of Austin is named U.S. Treasurer by President Jimmy Carter.

Gloria Scott presides over the plenary session of the International Women's Year conference in Houston.

Debra Stamps is the first female agricultural major at Prairie View A & M University.

Vicki Miles is the first black woman hired as a law clerk for a federal district judge in Houston.

1977–
1978
Barbara Hayes Foreman is the first black female deputy sheriff in Travis County.

1978
Dr. Yvonne Ewell is appointed associate superintendent, Dallas Independent School District, the first black woman in Texas to hold such a position.

Unemployment compensation becomes effective for household workers.

After retiring as a nurse, Alma Gunter, Palestine, becomes a painter.

1979
Stella Youngblood of Houston becomes the first black woman from Texas to graduate from the U.S. Naval Academy at Annapolis.

Josephine Bellinger, publisher of the *San Antonio Register*, represents the Black Press of America at the 9th Annual Afro-American Conference in the Sudan.

Gabrielle McDonald is appointed a federal district judge in Houston.

Late
1970s
Joan Winn is appointed judge of a district court in Dallas. Harriet Murphy becomes an Austin municipal judge and, in 1988, the presiding judge. Alice Bonner of Houston becomes judge of the 80th State District Court.

1980s
Delia Matthison, Dallas, is appointed to the United Methodist Church's national board of "global ministries."

Houston native Debbie Allen wins Emmys for her role in the television series *Fame*. Phylicia Rashad, her sister, is widely known for her role as Clair Huxtable on *The Cosby Show*.

A new generation of black writers and poets such as Harryette Mullen and Hermine Pinson achieve recognition and publication.

Aaronetta Pierce is a San Antonio Art Museum docent and major patron of the arts.

1980   Ada DeBlanc Simond wins Austin's Distinguished Service Award.

Kathlyn Gilliam is the first woman and first black elected president of the Dallas Independent School District.

Juneteenth becomes a state holiday.

Ruby Williams co-founds Austin's Black Arts Alliance.

The number of black Texas women in service jobs drops to 36 percent in 1980 from 74 percent in 1950.

1981   Black women provide information and expertise to develop the touring exhibit *Texas Women—A Celebration of History*, now permanently housed at Texas Woman's University, Denton.

Zina Garrison, Houston, at age 17, is the first black player to win the junior singles tennis championship at Wimbledon in England.

1982   The U.S. Congress passes an extension of the Voting Rights Act.

Annette and Bill Hamilton found Annette 2 Cosmetiques in Dallas.

State Treasurer Ann Richards appoints Winsome Jean as investments director for the Texas Treasury.

1983   Lavonne Mason of Austin is appointed to the Board of Regents for Texas Woman's University.

Anne Lundy is music director and founder of the Scott Joplin Chamber Orchestra in Houston, specializing in the work of black composers.

1984   Juanita Craft receives the Eleanor Roosevelt Pioneer Award from Texas Woman's University.

Helen Cloud Austin, San Antonio, is named Social Worker of the Year by the National Association of Social Workers.

Dr. Mary Evans Sias becomes executive director of the Metropolitan YWCA in Dallas.

The National Political Congress of Black Women is founded because Democratic presidential candidate Walter Mondale fails to interview even one black woman as a vice-presidential running mate.

Myra McDaniel, an Austin attorney, is appointed Texas secretary of state by Governor Mark White.

After her death, the paintings of Naomi Polk, Houston, become known.

Clara J. McLaughlin is the first black woman in the U.S. to own a national TV network affiliate, the East Texas Television Network in Longview.

1985   Women and World Issues, an Austin interracial group, sponsors a binational conference, "Women and Food Production: A Texas-Mexico Dialogue."

Bishop College in Dallas honors Thirty Texas Women of Courage in conjunction with a *Woman of Courage Exhibition* sponsored by the Schlesinger Library of Radcliffe College.

Kathlyn Gilliam organizes the Political Congress of African-American Women in Dallas with 300 members.

Dr. Edith Irby Jones is the first female president of the National Medical Association (of black physicians).

1986   The U.S. Supreme Court rules that sexual harassment constitutes illegal job discrimination.

The Museum of African American Life and Culture in Dallas sponsors a touring exhibition, *Black Texas Women—They Showed the Way*.

Carolyn Wright is elected as a district countywide judge (256th state district court) in Dallas.

Eddie Bernice Johnson is elected to the Texas Senate.

1987   Gloria Randle Scott becomes president of Bennett College in Greensboro, North Carolina.

Naomi Carrier, Houston, collaborates with Ruthe Winegarten in adapting the oral history *I Am Annie Mae* as a musical. It premiers at St. Edward's University in Austin, produced by Women and Their Work.

Some 3,000 demonstrators join food workers at Stephen F. Austin University in Nacogdoches, mainly black female members of the Texas State Employees' Union, demanding back pay and a union contract for them. The university finally accedes to their demands.

Dr. Yvonne Ewell is elected president of the Dallas School Board.

Brenda P. Kennedy is judge of the Travis County Court-at-Law #7.

1988 Dionne Bagsby wins election as a Tarrant County commissioner, the first black woman in Texas to hold such a position.

Karyne Conley is elected to the Texas House from San Antonio.

Sheila Jackson Lee is elected to the Houston City Council.

1990 Carlette Guidry-White, a sprinter at UT-Austin, is named South-west Conference Athlete of the Year.

Barbara Taft coordinates the Austin Peace Project and a peace festival.

The African American Women's Hall of Fame, coordinated by the Austin chapter of National Women of Achievement, inducts twenty-four nominees.

Marguerite Ross Barnett becomes president of the University of Houston, the first African-American and eighth president of the university's central campus.

Colonel Marcelite Harris of Houston is the first black woman to become a brigadier general in the U.S. Air Force.

Iris Jones is appointed Austin city attorney.

Bernice Hart is elected president of the Austin School Board.

Toni Luckett is elected president of the Student Assembly, UT-Austin.

Dr. Theresa Hearn-Haynes runs unsuccessfully for governor in the Democratic primary.

Willie Marie Iles is elected mayor of Goodlow.

1990– Algenita Scott Davis of Houston serves as president of the Na-
1991 tional Bar Association.

Barbara Hayes Foreman is chair of the Austin Commission for Women.

Staff Sergeant Debra Mobley-Sadler of Fort Hood runs a cam-ouflaged field kitchen in Saudi Arabia during the Gulf War.

Governor Ann Richards appoints a record number of blacks and women to her staff and to state boards and commissions.

1991   The Dallas Rainbow chapter of NOW, consisting mainly of women of color, is organized.

Barbara Conrad sings the "Star Spangled Banner" at the inauguration of Texas governor Ann Richards.

Winsome Jean organizes Sojourner's Trust in Austin, an organization of black women, to raise funds for political candidates and to identify potential black female candidates for appointments to governmental boards and commissions.

Governor Ann Richards appoints Willie Lee Gay, Houston, as the first black on the Texas Historical Commission and Allison Leland, Houston, to the Texas A & M Board of Regents.

Hazel Obey is director of planning and program development for the Texas General Land Office.

Wilhelmina Delco is appointed speaker pro tempore of the Texas House of Representatives, the first woman to hold this position. Senfronia Thompson of Houston is appointed chair of the Judicial Affairs Committee.

Charles Wilson and Rebecca Lee are on the Marshall City Council.

Dr. Sebetha Jenkins is appointed president of Jarvis Christian College in Hawkins.

Prairie View A & M graduate Francine Frazier Floyd is named national Black Engineer of the Year and joins Motorola Corporation in Austin in 1992.

Izola Collins and Ann Simmons are on the Galveston School Board.

1992   Dr. Judith Craven is president of United Way, Gulf Coast, and co-chair, Texas Summit on Adolescent Pregnancy Prevention.

Cassandra Thomas of Houston is president of the National Coalition against Sexual Harassment and director of the Houston Area Women's Center Rape Crisis program.

Barbara Burton chairs Austin Capital Metro.

Gaynelle Griffin Jones of Spring is appointed to the First Court of Appeals in Houston.

Black enrollment at U.S. colleges is at an all-time high—747,000 women and 476,000 men.

Six black women now serve in the legislature.

Helen Giddings and Yvonne Davis of Dallas are elected to the Texas House of Representatives.

State Representative Eddie Bernice Johnson of Dallas is elected to the U.S. Congress.

The state's historically black colleges include Huston-Tillotson College, Jarvis Christian College, Paul Quinn College, Texas College, and Wiley College.

Dr. Mae C. Jemison of Houston is the first black woman in space, as science mission specialist on NASA's space shuttle *Endeavor*.

Clarissa Davis, an All-American basketball player at UT-Austin, is a member of the U.S. Olympic bronze medal women's basketball team.

Barbara Jean Jacket, Prairie View, is head coach of the U.S. women's track and field team at the Olympic Games in Barcelona, Spain.

National Coalition of 100 Black Women sponsors a Black Women's Health Care Conference in Houston.

1993   Dr. Dorcas Bowles is appointed dean of the University of Texas at Arlington School of Social Work.

Dr. Barbara White is appointed dean of the University of Texas at Austin School of Social Work.

1994   Izola Collins is elected president of the Galveston School Board.

Sheila Jackson Lee of Houston is elected to the U.S. Congress.

Dawnna Dukes is elected to the Texas House from Austin.

Dr. Carol Surles assumes the presidency of Texas Woman's University.

1995   Dr. Ruth Simmons of Houston becomes president of Smith College.

Dallas District Judge Carolyn Wright is confirmed by the Texas Senate and is sworn in as a justice on the state's 5th Court of Civil Appeals. She is the first African-American female justice on the appellate court in this seven-county district.